Antipodean George El

C000047975

In *Middlemarch*, George Eliot famously warns readers not to see themselves as the centre of their own world, which produces a 'flattering illusion of concentric arrangement'. The scholarly contributors to *Antipodean George Eliot* resist this form of centrism. Hailing from four continents and six countries, they consider Eliot from a variety of de-centred vantage points, exploring how the obscure and marginal in Eliot's life and work sheds surprising light on the central and familiar. With essays that span the full range of Eliot's career—from her early journalism, to her major novels, to eccentric late works such as *Impressions of Theophrastus Such*—*Antipodean George Eliot* is committed to challenging orthodoxies about Eliot's development as a writer, overturning received ideas about her moral and political thought, and unveiling new contexts for appreciating her unparalleled significance in nineteenth-century letters.

Margaret Harris is Challis Professor of English Literature Emerita, The University of Sydney. She edited *The Journals of George Eliot* (with Judith Johnston, 1998) and *George Eliot in Context* (2013). Her other publications include studies of Victorian fiction, especially that of George Meredith.

Matthew Sussman is Senior Lecturer in English at The University of Sydney. He is the author of *Stylistic Virtue and Victorian Fiction: Form, Ethics, and the Novel* (2021), as well as articles on Anthony Trollope, Henry James, Elizabeth Gaskell, and Matthew Arnold.

The Nineteenth Century Series
Series editors: Joanne Shattock and Julian North

The series focuses primarily upon major authors and subjects within Romantic and Victorian literature. It also includes studies of other nineteenth-century British writers and issues, where these are matters of current debate: for example, biography and autobiography; journalism; periodical literature; travel writing; book production; gender; non-canonical writing.

Recent in this series:

Dickens and the Bible
'What Providence Meant'
Jennifer Gribble

Gender, Writing, Spectatorships
Evenings at the Theatre, Opera, and Silent Screen in Late Nineteenth-Century Italy and Beyond
Katharine Mitchell

Women's Writing and Mission in the Nineteenth Century
Jane Eyre's Missionary Sisters
Angharad Eyre

Writing for Social Change in Temperance Periodicals
Conviction and Career
Annemarie McAllister

Antipodean George Eliot
Edited by Margaret Harris and Matthew Sussman

G.W.M. Reynolds Reimagined
Studies in Authorship, Radicalism, and Genre, 1830–1870
Edited by Jennifer Conary and Mary L. Shannon

For more information about this series, please visit:
https://www.routledge.com/The-Nineteenth-Century-Series/book-series/ASHSER2017

Antipodean George Eliot

Edited by
Margaret Harris and
Matthew Sussman

Routledge
Taylor & Francis Group

NEW YORK AND LONDON

First published 2023
by Routledge
605 Third Avenue, New York, NY 10158

and by Routledge
4 Park Square, Milton Park, Abingdon, Oxon, OX14 4RN

Routledge is an imprint of the Taylor & Francis Group, an informa business

© 2023 selection and editorial matter, Margaret Harris and Matthew Sussman; individual chapters, the contributors

The right of Margaret Harris and Matthew Sussman to be identified as the authors of the editorial material, and of the authors for their individual chapters, has been asserted in accordance with sections 77 and 78 of the Copyright, Designs and Patents Act 1988.

All rights reserved. No part of this book may be reprinted or reproduced or utilised in any form or by any electronic, mechanical, or other means, now known or hereafter invented, including photocopying and recording, or in any information storage or retrieval system, without permission in writing from the publishers.

Trademark notice: Product or corporate names may be trademarks or registered trademarks, and are used only for identification and explanation without intent to infringe.

ISBN: 978-1-032-26714-2 (hbk)
ISBN: 978-1-032-42451-4 (pbk)
ISBN: 978-1-003-36282-1 (ebk)

DOI: 10.4324/9781003362821

Typeset in Sabon
by Newgen Publishing UK

Contents

About the Contributors

Thomas Albrecht is Professor of English at Tulane University in New Orleans. He has written about George Eliot and ethics in his book *The Medusa Effect: Representation and Epistemology in Victorian Aesthetics* (2009) and in *The Ethical Vision of George Eliot* (2020), as well as in several journal articles and book chapters.

Sneha Kar Chaudhuri is Associate Professor at the West Bengal State University. Her principal research interests are in Neo-Victorian Studies and Victorian literature and also include postmodern and postcolonial fiction, adaptation studies, gender studies, popular culture, and films.

Debashree Dattaray is Associate Professor in Comparative Literature and Deputy Coordinator, Centre for Canadian Studies at Jadavpur University, Kolkata. Her areas of research and publication are environmental studies, indigenous studies, and comparative Indian literature methodology. She is the author of *Oral Traditions of the North East: A Case Study of Karbi Oral Traditions* (2015) and has co-edited *Ecocriticism and Environment: Rethinking Literature and Culture* (2017).

Fionnuala Dillane is Professor in Nineteenth-Century Literature and Culture, School of English, Drama, Film and Creative Writing, University College Dublin. Her research and teaching interests include Victorian print cultures, memory studies, gender, and George Eliot. She is the author of *Before George Eliot: Marian Evans and the Periodical Press* (2013), joint winner of the Robert and Vineta Colby Prize for 2014.

Robert Dingley, until his retirement, taught English Literature at the University of New England, Armidale, NSW. He has published extensively on nineteenth-century British writing in *Victorian Review*, *Nineteenth-Century Feminisms*, *Victorian Literature and Culture*, *Cahiers Victoriens et Edouardiens*, and elsewhere.

Tim Dolin is Emeritus Professor, Curtin University, Western Australia, where he taught literary studies. He is the author of *George Eliot* (2005), and General Editor (with Christine Alexander) of the Cambridge Edition of the works of the Brontës, and a member of the editorial board of the Cambridge Edition of Thomas Hardy.

Moira Gatens is Challis Professor of Philosophy Emerita, The University of Sydney. Her research interests include Spinoza, social and political philosophy, feminist philosophy, and philosophy and literature. A recent publication is *Institutional Transformations: Imagination, Embodiment, and Affect* (2020), ed. Danielle Celermajer, Millicent Churcher, and Moira Gatens.

Helen Groth is Professor of English in the School of Arts and Media at The University of New South Wales. She is the sole author of *Victorian Photography and Literary Nostalgia* (2004) and *Moving Images: Nineteenth-Century Reading and Screen Practices* (2013), as well as the co-author of *Dreams and Modernity: A Cultural History* (2013). She is currently working on a book on rioting and the literary archive.

Margaret Harris is Challis Professor of English Literature Emerita, The University of Sydney. She edited *The Journals of George Eliot* (with Judith Johnston, 1998) and *George Eliot in Context* (2013). Her other publications include studies of Victorian fiction, especially that of George Meredith.

Penny Horsley works as a senior secondary English teacher. Her research interests are in Victorian studies and George Eliot's writing in particular.

Julia Kuehn is Professor of English at The University of Hong Kong. Her research lies in nineteenth-century English literature and culture, with a particular focus on the realist novel, women's writing, popular writing, and travel writing. She is currently completing a comparative study of selected English and German realist novels.

Matthew Sussman is Senior Lecturer in English at The University of Sydney. He is the author of *Stylistic Virtue and Victorian Fiction: Form, Ethics, and the Novel* (2021), as well as articles on Anthony Trollope, Henry James, Elizabeth Gaskell, and Matthew Arnold.

Joanne Wilkes is Professor Emerita of English at The University of Auckland. Her interest in George Eliot is of long standing, and she has worked extensively on nineteenth-century literary criticism by women, notably in her *Women Reviewing Women in Nineteenth-Century Britain: The Critical Reception of Jane Austen, Charlotte Brontë, and George Eliot* (2010). Other interests include Margaret Oliphant, Jane Austen, and Lord Byron.

Acknowledgements

Antipodean George Eliot started life as a conference in February 2020, just ahead of the pandemic restrictions that did in fact preclude one presenter from travelling to Sydney. We acknowledge the support of the (then) School of Literature, Art and Media at The University of Sydney, both in the form of funds from the SLAM Mobility and Engagement Fund (applied to travel costs of key speakers) and in the ready and cheerful day-to-day assistance of professional staff Charlie Tapper, Lynn Cook, and the team from Finance. The presence of Joy Redfern of the George Eliot Fellowship made a welcome connection with George Eliot's country.

Participants in the conference generated searching discussion that encouraged production of this volume. In the preparation of *Antipodean George Eliot* for publication, the restructured School of Art, Communication and English provided funding for indexing. We are particularly grateful to the contributors who responded enthusiastically to editorial requests, even amidst ongoing disruption.

Texts and Abbreviations

All references to George Eliot's novels and stories, except where specifically indicated otherwise, are to the Oxford World's Classics editions which reproduce the text of Oxford's Clarendon, acknowledged as the standard edition of the fiction. Chapter references, rather than page references, are provided. Titles are abbreviated as follows:

AB	*Adam Bede*
'BJ'	'Brother Jacob'
DD	*Daniel Deronda*
FH	*Felix Holt, the Radical*
'LV'	'The Lifted Veil'
M	*Middlemarch*
MF	*The Mill on the Floss*
R	*Romola*
SC	*Scenes of Clerical Life*—the individual stories abbreviated as 'Amos', 'Gilfil', 'Janet'
SM	*Silas Marner*

Other titles are abbreviated as follows:

Essays	*Essays of George Eliot,* ed. Thomas Pinney (London: Routledge and Kegan Paul, 1963)
GEL	*The George Eliot Letters*, 9 vols, ed. Gordon S. Haight (New Haven and London: Yale University Press, 1954–78)
TS	*Impressions of Theophrastus Such*, ed. Nancy Henry (Iowa: University of Iowa Press, 1994)

Introduction

Margaret Harris and Matthew Sussman

Though widely celebrated during her lifetime, by the 1940s, George Eliot was in a state of academic despond. 'Dickens, yes; Hardy, yes; Trollope, maybe; George Eliot? Who? She was not even an also-ran', recalls Thomas Pinney.[1] Yet this scholarly nadir was followed by the 'rediscovery' of Eliot's works in the 1950s and 60s, and their critical elevation in the 1970s and 80s. No longer forced to occupy a defensive position, critics of Eliot have, in the past 30 years, surveyed the outer reaches of the author's extraordinary output, encompassing her journalism, poetry, scientific expeditions, reading habits, foreign travels, compositional strategies, and more. In 2001, George Levine maintained that 'the case may now reasonably be made … that George Eliot was indeed the greatest of Victorian novelists'.[2] Two decades on, in a postscript to that declaration, Levine and Nancy Henry acknowledge Eliot's historical significance ('The intellectualism of her work makes it a repository of the ideas, values, and self-conscious critiques of the period'[3]), while Isobel Armstrong and Carolyn Burdett affirm 'the immediacy of Eliot's writing … despite the distance of history'.[4]

One of George Eliot's most famous metaphors is that of the pier-glass and its properties, developed in the rich passage of rumination that opens chapter 27 of *Middlemarch*:

> Your pier-glass or extensive surface of polished steel made to be rubbed by a housemaid, will be minutely and multitudinously scratched in all directions; but place now against it a lighted candle as a centre of illumination, and lo! the scratches will seem to arrange themselves in a fine series of concentric circles round that little sun. It is demonstrable that the scratches are going everywhere impartially, and it is only your candle which produces the flattering illusion of a concentric arrangement, its light falling with an exclusive optical selection.[5]

An implication of the metaphor is that exalted reputations can produce halo effects that risk distorting our perception of their charismatic subject. In this collection, we do not dispute the claim that 'no writer seems more central to the institution of the British novel than does Eliot'[6] nor do we gainsay

DOI: 10.4324/9781003362821-1

the impact of Eliot's 'polymathic status'.[7] The past 50 years have more than confirmed this author's greatness as novelist and intellectual. However, the consolidation of a reputation tends to solidify other aspects of a writer as well, hardening areas of erstwhile neglect or contestation into well-worn certainties, even orthodoxies of the sort that the Eliot scholar might well resist. What does it mean now to look at Eliot askance—to resist seeing her as the centre of a flattering arrangement and instead to consider the scratches on her pier-glass as irregular, disordered, and stochastic? What new insights are revealed by approaching Eliot and her works from a self-consciously de-centring vantage point?

The title *Antipodean George Eliot* arises from the editors' own geographical position in the literal Antipodes. Along with many of the contributors to this volume, both are residents of Australia, a land with which Eliot had few ostensible connections (especially compared to Dickens and Trollope, who sent some of their sons to be settlers there—a migration that Eliot herself contemplated but on which she never embarked, leaving her nephew Edward Clarke to make the journey). Still, as Paul Giles has shown, the idea of the 'Antipodean' encompasses more than geographical displacement. In *American Literature and the Antipodean Imaginary*, Giles defines 'antipodality' as 'a heightened version of comparative consciousness, within which the phenomenological selfhood of any given culture is refracted through alternative perspectives'.[8] Such a heightened consciousness may lead to new understandings of 'transnational engagement', insofar as the 'topsy-turvy' essence of the Antipodes casts a 'ludic' light on the hegemony of Anglocentric customs.[9] However, an antipodean sensibility may also be mobilised to 'illuminate areas that have been repressed or overlooked in traditional accounts'[10] of a given literature or culture because it resists the complacency of established truths. Eliot's critics have long been alert to tensions within her own life and career, noting, for example, that her works seem to provide no place for the type of woman that Mary Anne Evans was to become,[11] or that (speaking of *Felix Holt, the Radical*) 'her philosophical vision is ultimately irreconcilable with a political perspective'.[12] Such debates are inevitable for an author so capacious and intellectually engaged. Yet even the irony of tensions can reify into dogmas that obscure the light cast by alternative perspectives.

The contributors to this collection share the antipodean spirit of thinking sceptically about the various 'centres' of Eliot's work, though their essays are not wilfully iconoclastic. Instead, they approach the full breadth of Eliot's career with an emphasis on uncharted peripheries, asymmetrical arrangements, and evidence hiding in plain sight, discerning new lines of connection against the background of well-known constellations. For example, in the first chapter of this volume, 'George Eliot Elsewhere', Fionnuala Dillane swerves away from the tendency to dwell on Eliot as an artist of familiar landscapes such as the Midlands of her childhood and the early novels. In contrast, she considers 'the places she avoided writing about, places outside of her known geographies of Western Europe', which generate but also threaten the certitude and here-ness of 'home'. With attention to some of the under-travelled byways of Eliot's own *oeuvre*, such as the long poem 'A Minor Prophet' and the verse drama *The Spanish Gypsy*, Dillane tests the limits of Eliot's cosmopolitanism, for which 'elsewhere is entirely and always contextual and contradictory'. In this pursuit, Dillane's chapter reaches to Eliot's untitled, unfinished, and unpublished last novel.

Julia Kuehn, in 'Before *Scenes of Clerical Life*: Eliot's 1854-57 Travelogues as Poetic Practice', echoes the title of Dillane's *Before George Eliot: Marian Evans and the Periodical Press* (2013), while challenging Dillane's demonstration of the importance and significance of Marian Evans' career as editor in her evolution into George Eliot. Kuehn argues for the author's little-analysed German travelogues as 'apprentice work' for *Scenes of Clerical Life*. Her discussion takes her 'elsewhere', both generically and geographically, drawing especially on Eliot's journals, and including 'her rare aesthetic asides, like chapter 17 of *Adam Bede*', which invokes Dutch painting to maintain that art requires 'the faithful representing of commonplace things' to tap into 'the secret of deep human sympathy'.[13]

The value of sympathy has always lain at the heart (both literal and figurative) of Eliot's narrative ethics, and unsurprisingly a number of chapters tackle the issue in some degree: in particular, those by Moira Gatens and Thomas Albrecht. For these authors, Eliot's understanding of sympathy relies less upon feeling with or for others than in recognising their fundamental difference from oneself. In 'A Roar of Sound: Eliot on Sympathy and the Problem of Other Minds', Gatens, herself a philosopher, reads 'The Lifted Veil' as a cautionary tale about the limits of sympathy and its 'potential abuses in the moral arena' with reference to Adam Smith, Ludwig Feuerbach, and Benedict Spinoza. Treating sympathy as a scientific fact as well as a moral concept, Gatens calls 'The Lifted Veil' a 'philosophical thought experiment' that reveals 'what mere knowledge of the other's mind might entail: not sympathy and concern but antipathy and repulsion'. If the narrator of 'The Lifted Veil' suffers from an excess of mind-reading, Thomas Albrecht shows how Romola (like Esther Lyon, Dorothea Brooke, Daniel Deronda, and other of Eliot's protagonists) must learn to widen her circle of concern. However, he locates the inspiration for her mature ethics in the unexpected figure of Savonarola, the Dominican friar sometimes seen as an obstacle to her development. According to Albrecht, Romola's 'inner and outer responses to Savonarola … take sublime forms', characterised by awe, mental expansiveness, and an 'openness to uncertainty and otherness'. The discourse of the sublime thus offers an 'antipode' to the more familiar language of commonality and fellow-feeling, asserting *Romola*'s importance to Eliot's moral imagination.

The reverberations of alterity take curious forms in Robert Dingley's chapter on 'George Eliot and "the Case of Wagner"'. Dingley recounts a meeting in 1877 between Eliot and Richard and Cosima Wagner, during which Eliot (provocatively) claimed that her partner, G.H. Lewes, was Jewish. Noting that Wagner is one of the major German composers not mentioned directly in *Daniel Deronda*, Dingley reveals how Wagner constitutes a 'shadowy presence' behind both that novel and also Eliot's thinking on race and national identity. While Eliot could hardly be accused of anti-Semitism, her '*later*' thought' shares Wagner's commitment to 'the reassertion of distinctive national identities', suggesting that Eliot and Wagner are less 'hateful contraries' than 'inverted mirror reflections'. Conversely, Sneha Kar Chaudhuri and Debashree Dattaray reveal how George Eliot herself is the 'shadowy presence' behind the work of two celebrated novelists of the Bengal Renaissance, Saratchandra Chattopadhyay and Bibhutibhushan Bandyopadhyay. Drawing on Homi Bhabha's notion of 'colonial mimicry', Chaudhuri and Dattaray show how George Eliot's provincial realism was adapted 'to imagine the agrarian rustic world as an idyllic utopian space flawed by problems of economic decline, social prejudices, and moral backwardness'. Despite significant environmental differences between nineteenth-century England and Bengal—and the relative lack of interest in India as an 'elsewhere' in Eliot's works—her novels (especially *The Mill on the Floss*) prove a resonant transnational influence.

The relation of parts to wholes—including that of fiction to reality—animates three chapters on Eliot's political footprint. In her chapter on *Felix Holt, the Radical*, Helen Groth examines how the riot unleashes chaotic energies that ironically reaffirm 'the value of the peaceful many'. Providing a detailed account of Eliot's engagement with the legislation of Reform between 1832 and 1867, as well as the Riot Act of 1714, Groth shows how moments of social confusion juxtapose self-interest with communal enrichment, highlighting the group's need for clear-thinking and selfless individuals. Her discussion adds fresh dimensions to critical approaches based on 'literature and the law'.

The prospects of Reform also interest Joanne Wilkes, particularly as they seem foreclosed by the deflationary 'Finale' to *Middlemarch*. But where Groth focuses on fictional characters, Wilkes examines the writings of Christian Isobel Johnstone, a 'real-life female political journalist of the 1830s' of the sort that eludes Eliot's narrative representations. Wilkes' detailed account of the political background to *Middlemarch* generates disconcerting questions about the ways events can play out, canvassed in concentration on the Lydgate–Bulstrode plot. Had Eliot known of such a person as Christian Isobel Johnstone, would this have influenced her vision for how 'meaningful and beneficial change can eventuate'? An adequate understanding of Eliot's politics beckons comparison with real-life exemplars.

Tim Dolin invokes explicitly Australian contexts as he turns to the life and career of Charles Henry Pearson, a British-Australian politician known for his combination of socialist economic policies with racially motivated restrictions on immigration. In *National Life and Character: A Forecast* (1893), Pearson laments the cosmopolitanism of *Daniel Deronda*, which dramatises the risk 'when a relatively civilised lower race is freely admitted to a liberal polity'. According to Dolin, the increasingly globalised world that put British novelists in conversation with Australian politicians reveals the potential, but also the limits, of liberal sympathy, where egalitarianism and xenophobia make distinctly antipodean bedfellows.

Finally, two chapters are dedicated to Eliot's last-published work, *Impressions of Theophrastus Such*, which still remains an object of critical vexation. Matthew Sussman rejects the temptation to examine *Impressions* in light of Eliot's novels, redescribing it as a 'confessional anatomy' that blends first-person autobiography with social satire. He further contextualises the text within nineteenth-century debates about wit and the sense of humour, placing *Impressions* in implicit dialogue with related comedic works (none of them novels) by Thackeray, Arnold, and Meredith. Inspired by the proliferation of ethical approaches to Eliot's fiction, which usually emphasise Feuerbach and Spinoza, Penny Horsley shifts the ground by reading *Impressions* as a disquisition on Aristotle's nineteenth-century legacy, especially the value that both he and Victorian culture placed on habit. Although *Impressions* questions the relation of habit to character, and critiques 'gender performance' as 'a product of time-worn cultural habit', Horsley ultimately finds 'hope' in the power of altering one's habits, and with them, one's identity, that is attested by the text.

To revert to the candle and the pier-glass. When the 'exclusive optical selection' is deranged by moving the candle, other connections and conversations among and between the chapters in *Antipodean George Eliot* declare themselves. Thus, Robert Dingley's discussion of Wagner calls for a recalibration of *Daniel Deronda*'s philo-Semitism, as does Tim Dolin's account of a little-known Australian-British academic, historian, and politician for whom the novel represented the inexorability of liberal decline. Reference to *Impressions of Theophrastus Such* recurs: Moira Gatens leads off her discussion of 'The Lifted Veil' and *Middlemarch* by quoting a reflection on 'wise judgment' from Eliot's final work, while Penny Horsley and Matthew Sussman reorient Eliot's *Impressions* towards new philosophical and generic horizons. Julia Kuehn and Fionnuala Dillane look at some of the very earliest and latest of Eliot's writings, suggesting commonalities, but also differences, in Eliot's lifelong obsession with place, even as Sneha Kar Chaudhuri and Debashree Dattaray show how Eliot's most pastorally nostalgic novel found new life on colonial frontiers. Helen Groth, Thomas Albrecht, and Joanne Wilkes reveal how Eliot's less appreciated works, or even her most celebrated, retain the power to disappoint, provoke, and surprise, challenging orthodoxies in how we understand George Eliot's development as a novelist, her ethical and philosophical ideas, and her relationship to real-world contingencies.

The contributors to this volume, in short, attend to lesser-known pathways in Eliot's life and career in order to see how the obscure, the marginal, the counter-intuitive, and the overlooked can recalibrate our sense of what is dominant, foregrounded, or central in her work. In doing so, they join the 'ludic' spirit of antipodean unsettling to the appreciation that Eliot's 'little sun' inevitably elicits. This is, in fact, the very spirit of good-natured exploration enunciated in *Middlemarch,* when, at the end of chapter 17, Farebrother says to Lydgate: 'You are a sort of circumnavigator come to settle among us, and will keep up my belief in the antipodes. Now tell me all about them in Paris.'

Notes

1 Jean Arnold, Lila Marz Harper, and Thomas Pinney, 'Introduction', in *George Eliot: Interdisciplinary Essays*, ed. Jean Arnold and Lila Marz Harper (London: Palgrave, 2019), 5.
2 George Levine, 'Introduction: George Eliot and the Art of Realism', in *The Cambridge Companion to George Eliot*, ed. George Levine (Cambridge: Cambridge University Press, 2001), 1.
3 Nancy Henry and George Levine, 'Introduction: George Eliot and the Art of Realism', in *The Cambridge Companion to George Eliot*, 2nd edn, ed. Nancy Henry and George Levine (Cambridge: Cambridge University Press, 2019), 16.
4 Isobel Armstrong and Carolyn Burdett, 'Introduction', *19: Interdisciplinary Studies in the Long Nineteenth Century*, 29 (2020), 1–2.
5 George Eliot, *Middlemarch*, ed. David Carroll (Oxford: Oxford University Press, 1986), ch. 27.
6 Amanda Anderson and Harry E. Shaw, 'Introduction', in *A Companion to George Eliot*, ed. Amanda Anderson and Harry E. Shaw (Chichester: Wiley-Blackwell, 2013), 2.
7 Armstrong and Burdett, 'Introduction', 1.
8 Paul Giles, *American Literature and the Antipodean Imaginary: Imperialism, Transnationalism, Surrealism* (Oxford: Oxford University Press, 2014), 24.
9 Giles, *American Literature*, 25.
10 Giles, *American Literature*, 26.
11 At the height of debates about Eliot's position on the 'Woman Question', Zelda Austen memorably titled an essay, 'Why Feminist Critics Are Angry with George Eliot', *College English*, 37.6 (1976), 549–61.
12 Juliette Atkinson, 'Critical Responses: 1970-Present', in *George Eliot in Context*, ed. Margaret Harris (Cambridge: Cambridge University Press, 2013), 86.
13 George Eliot, *Adam Bede*, ed. Carol A. Martin (Oxford: Oxford World's Classics, 2008), ch. 17.

1   George Eliot Elsewhere

Fionnuala Dillane

> What *is* remarkable, extraordinary—and the process remains inscrutable
> and mysterious—is that this quiet, anxious, sedentary, serious, invalidical
> English lady, without animal spirits, without adventures, without extrava-
> gance, assumption, or bravado, should have made us believe that nothing in
> the world was alien to her; should have produced such rich, deep, masterly
> pictures of the multifold life of man.[1]

At the time of her death, George Eliot was primarily celebrated for being an
exceptional recorder of the rural English midlands through her character-
full, dialogue-rich early novels. More recent readings of her work have
probed the ways she was drawn to types of cosmopolitanism that eschewed
any narrow sense of the regional: her narrative voices, it has been argued,
promote an ethical detachment constitutive of a critically reflective, wider
world-belonging. In part, such openness made her work portable property across the English-speaking world in the nineteenth century. Much
as we understand her wandering English in Europe (Gwendolen Harleth,
Henleigh Grandcourt, Daniel Deronda, Will Ladislaw, Dorothea Brooke) as
dangerously untethered, either morally or emotionally, 'at the same time',
as Amanda Anderson argues, Eliot 'valorizes cosmopolitan artistic culture
and a reflective relation to tradition, both of which she saw as enabled by
cultivated detachment as well as instructive forms of exile'.[2]

This chapter sets out to add another, less assured dimension to George
Eliot's not-England by considering the places she avoided writing about,
places outside of her known geographies of Western Europe. These antipodes
of not-taken exiles, unknown inhabited realities, and other-world imaginaries
operate beyond the spatial and chronotopic cartographies through which
she shapes, frames, and anchors her canonical realist novels. George Eliot's
less-discussed discomfort with otherness that fails to resolve into meaningful relation is woven into the unstable textures of these elsewheres-for-
her. Her partial turn to more direct engagement with transimperialism and
planetary consciousness in her later writings is suggestive of this recognition
of failed relationality. It is indicative of a pronounced disjuncture between
her celebrated cultural and political cosmopolitanism that rejects racial

DOI: 10.4324/9781003362821-2

othering and the structurally racist realities of an imperial expansionism through which she lived and from which she profited.[3]

In contrast to the commanding perspective Henry James with no small irony suggests pervades John Walter Cross' *George Eliot's Life*, George Eliot's knowledge of the world has its limits, and not because of the 'sedentary' state, 'invalidical' nature, or deficiencies of 'animal spirits', 'bravado', or 'adventures' that permeated Cross' editorialised version of his wife's letters. Eliot and Lewes were inveterate and robust travellers, embarking on a 40-day tour of Spain in the late 1860s, for instance, that involved all modes of available transport from trains to mules. Rather, her urbanely and deliberately navigated accommodations of otherness reached their edge in the confronting elsewheres that this well-travelled woman never visited, including the Americas, Ireland, Africa, and Australia, all places implicated in and structured by their relation to the British Empire.

As Lauren Goodlad reminds us, it cannot be claimed that 'Victorian culture was built around a coherent idea of Britain as an imperial nation-state', much less George Eliot's work. 'To the contrary', Goodlad maintains, 'the appealing notion of England as the archetypal *non*-empire—a maritime and commercial power diffusing progress without resort to political oppression—was the ideological heart of the early-Victorian era's "free trade imperialism." '[4] But as George Eliot demonstrates, increasing interest in the imbrications of questions of race and nationalism in her work from the mid-1860s, from *The Spanish Gypsy* (1868), to *Daniel Deronda* (1876) and *Impressions of Theophrastus Such* (1879), such non-historical attitudes to the material reality of imperial formations are not sustainable for her. She struggles with the ethical difficulties of contending with the problematic of empire. In her 1865 poem, 'A Minor Prophet', she diverts her critique of totalising expansionist ideology onto America via the target of her satire, the American of Puritan English descent, Elias Baptist Butterworth; in *Impressions*, she ups the scale to the planetary, in the speculative dystopian and totalitarian machine worlds of the future imagined through the eyes of Theophrastus Such. It seems that poetry and the form of the pseudo-biographical essay permit experiments with world imaginaries not otherwise available to the realist novelist who eschews the scientific romances, sensation fiction, and adventure romances that more typically accommodated explorations of empire in the nineteenth century (and in terms that so regularly displayed overtly racist politics). For George Eliot, 'elsewhere' is imagined in non-realist forms. We are left unmoored in these less familiar genres for Eliot, unmoored by the inevitably partial geographies of the distant past and near future they attempt to suggest. This felt disorientation gives some sense of George Eliot's personal panic about the oblivion of an afterlife because of the analogical relation of 'elsewhere' with 'unknown', and—in terms of the afterlife—the unknowable. But more broadly, the confrontation of an unknown but potentially encounterable elsewhere signals an anxiety or unease about the consequences of imperial exploitation in which she was implicated, most materially as a shareholder in the railways that provided the vital infrastructure for imperial expansion and resource extraction, and more personally, for instance, through the jingoistic and naïve accounts of South African colonialism in letters from her (failed) settler stepsons in the late 1860s.[5]

George Eliot's ethical claims for compassion, the widely registered appreciation of her championing of cultural difference, marginalised others, and the value of enlarged sympathy, cannot accommodate the violence that shores up both the British Empire and, via the market for her work in settler colonies and those railway stocks, her bank account. These antipodal tensions, refracting what Nathan Hensley has identified in another context as the 'conceptual antimonies of liberal imperialism', underpin her 'empire' poem, *The Spanish Gypsy*.[6] It is a stagey, uneven mixed-genre intervention in debates about national, personal, religious, and racial claims that in the end pursues the grimly charted logic of its opening observations about palimpsestic waves of imperial war on peoples and landscapes. Imperial aggression, so often folded into religious wars, is as inevitable and cyclical as faith systems and economic systems, 'Since God works by armies'.[7] The verse drama abandons any sense of the possibility of lived identifications with national or racial belonging without violence or oppression. Its tragic end is one of irresolution and failure: the lovers part in despair; the king of the gypsies is dead; his heir, Fedalma, knows that her mission to 'settle' with her gypsy community in Africa, to build a new nation elsewhere, is a doomed enterprise. In this poem, George Eliot takes us to Moor-influenced Southern Spain but not to Africa, bringing together the trace concerns about the place of 'elsewhere' in George Eliot's work up to that point.[8] It marks a shift towards her more fractured, more formally experimental works of the 1870s, including serial fiction, *Middlemarch* (1871–72) and *Daniel Deronda*, poetry, *The Legend of Jubal and Other Poems, Old and New* (1878), and *Impressions of Theophrastus Such*. This shift perhaps explains her turn towards the matter of Ireland, finally, in her barely sketched out, unfinished novel.

As *Antipodean George Eliot* demonstrates, places, movement, the foreign, the transnational, and the transposed in George Eliot's writing provoke a variety of different approaches to the work of this English novelist: Australia and India feature, as do less familiar generic territories such as George Eliot's travel journals and *Impressions*. That final volume of interconnected essays or chapters (the debate is ongoing) is richly resonant with unsettled textual geographies. There we find the representation of various loci and a global imaginary promulgated by her irascible and contradictory narrator. Theophrastus extols the sensitivity of the Cherokee readers of his only published work, and digresses on Australian botany, African deserts, the English midlands, and the question of Irish Home Rule as he traverses not just space but time too, from his childhood to late middle-age, from Ancient Greece to a fantasy future. That 'elsewhere' is always already somebody else's 'local'

or home or 'here' is a feature of this territorial text as well as a given definitional parameter of both 'local' and 'elsewhere'. We see as much in George
Eliot's travel journals and in more recent readings of the networked and
mobile representation of place that feature in her midlands novels.[9] This
emphasis counters early responses to her work that celebrated her mapping
of the place and people of Warwickshire as close to documentary in nature,
fixed and knowable in content, reassuring in its affects.

Village Life: Circumscribing George Eliot, the Novelist of Middle England

Arjun Appadurai has written of the production of the local not as physical
space but as a structure of feeling.[10] We are familiar with the latter concept from the work of Raymond Williams (for instance, in *Marxism and
Literature*, 1977), which shows how the realist novel creates the feeling
reader entrained to respond to the pathos, sentiment, or tragedy of plot
as a sensate human body (rather than as part of a potentially more dangerous social body). That affective capacity of George Eliot's grounding
realism was much celebrated by her first English readers in an exponentially
dislocating nineteenth century. The obituary pieces that followed George
Eliot's death in December 1880 emphasised that the happy legacy of the
works she had left behind to secure her place in literary history was over-
whelmingly based on her early stories that captured an England fading from
view. The representation of ordinary life in the Warwickshire countryside
of her birth was established as the source of her genius and the reason for
her widespread appeal. A quotation from *Daniel Deronda* appears early in
Alexander Allardyce's long obituary in *Blackwood's Magazine* to suggest the
core of the writer's vision:

> A human life, I think, should be well rooted in some spot of a native
> land, where it may get the love of tender kinship for the face of earth,
> for the labours men go forth to, for the sounds and accents that haunt
> it, for whatever will give that early home a familiar unmistakable diffe-
> rence amidst the future widening of knowledge; a spot where the defin-
> iteness of early memories may be inwrought with affection, and kindly
> acquaintance with all neighbours, even to the dogs and donkeys, may
> spread not by sentimental effort and reflection but as a sweet habit of
> the blood.[11]

Eliot's work, Allardyce asserts in what became an influential argument, is
heavily invested in the idea of local rootedness as the foundation not only
for the creative life but for the well-developed life.

Most obituary and memorial pieces reinforced Allardyce's line without
drawing out the implications figured in that mixed-register claim for 'a sweet
habit of blood': is this the realm of hereditary morality, which underscored

British claims for its civilising imperial missions, or a loosely tagged expression for feelings that run deep, becoming reflexive because so generationally habitual? T.E. Kebbel's commemorative piece in *Fraser's* is entitled, tellingly, 'Village Life of George Eliot'.[12] Leslie Stephen is enthusiastic in his praise of her exceptional genius in his *Cornhill* obituary, emphasising the early work up to *Silas Marner*. 'The sphere which she has made especially her own', he insists, 'is that quiet English country life which she knew in early youth.'[13]

The need to root George Eliot in her county, and by implication, in her country (decidedly England, not Great Britain and definitely not Great Britain and Ireland as it was during her lifetime), gained momentum after her death as her champions continued to seek the 'origins' of her fictional creations. Pastoral scenes are dominant in commemorative books, newspaper articles, and periodical pieces that followed, though most of her works from 1865 onwards are set in towns, cities, or manor houses. So ubiquitous was this ruralisation that even those works set entirely outside England were 'made' part of the English countryside. In *George Eliot: Her Early Home*, for instance, verses from *The Spanish Gypsy* are reprinted and illustrated with sketches of native English foliage.[14] The jarring and discordant form and rhythms of this fractured verse-drama are corralled into a mappable biographical coherence by this partial and very selective translation—or perhaps, more accurately, transplantation.

Allardyce's account of George Eliot's core worth is coloured by a squarely gendered view of what constitutes the writer's achievement, that strain in critical appraisal that needs to keep the writer, and especially the woman writer, in her local place:

> Not the depth of her self-acquired culture—not even her subsequent association with persons of the highest intellect and experience of the world—did for her what her country nurture in the Midlands had done … When she leaves the English Midlands and its folk, we may still be impressed by her genius; but we are conscious of an admixture of art, which we never detect so long as she is within her own special province.[15]

In contrast, more recent debates about that provincial dimension to George Eliot's work have stressed the portability of the sense of place constructed in her writings. Her representations of provincial life, Ian Duncan has proposed, gain identity by differentiating themselves from the metropolis, unlike regional fiction, which 'specifies its setting by invoking a combination of geographical, natural-historical, antiquarian, ethnographic and/or sociological features *that differentiate itself from any other region*'.[16] This generalised 'provincial' is one reason why George Eliot has local, national, and global appeal, as Nancy Henry points out: 'Eliot's novels preserved a distinctive Englishness and provided a touchstone of national identity for colonial emigrants and readers throughout Great Britain.'[17] Henry, however, rightly observes a different dynamic in her later works, which registers that 'she perceived this Englishness to be in a state of transformation under the pressures of colonial dispersion and cosmopolitanism at home'.[18]

Scholars have continued to deepen readings that tease out the dynamics of the provincial, regional, and global in George Eliot's work, readings that stress how her so-called 'rooted' locale is structured by its mobile relation to elsewhere via multidirectional currents of global trade that shaped all of England, not just the larger metropolitan centres or ports. Lauren Goodlad, drawing out the ways Victorian literature more generally is 'the product of palpably transnational forces and global perspectives', sees this 'worlded quality' in Eliot's late fiction.[19] For John Plotz, Eliot's provincial novels are a medium of a particular type of cosmopolitan modernity: the draw of provincial life is based on its 'capacity to locate its inhabitants at once in a trivial (but chartable) Nowheresville and in a universal (but strangely ephemeral) everywhere'.[20] As Margaret Harris observed in 2019: '[t]he image of Eliot as simply the eulogist of a pastoral world and (in the terms proposed by the subtitle of *Middlemarch*) as a student of provincial life, always specious, is now anachronistic.'[21]

Local *and* the Global: George Eliot, the Critical Cosmopolitan

We can agree that the determined reading of George Eliot as a 'eulogist' of a pastoral world that is specific to her corner of England does little to reflect the range of her wider view as a novelist of towns and cities as well as of country life. Kathleen McCormack's tenacious archival work in *George Eliot's English Travels: Composite Characters and Coded Communications* (2005) importantly expands George Eliot's England and charts the incessant mobility of her life that produced transversal palimpsestic layerings of place. The resulting fictions can be indexed to the actual landscapes of her travels but move well beyond the boundaries of the Warwickshire of her youth, and her settings are registered as amalgams, not singularly distinctive. Of course by the time George Eliot started writing fiction, that Warwickshire was already an 'elsewhere' for Marian Evans. As far as we know, she never returned to her childhood home after her elopement with George Henry Lewes. She never returned to the home of her beloved sister Chrissey once their brother Isaac cut ties with the scandalous Marian Evans. She never returned to her elsewhere within Warwickshire, 'Rosehill', the home of the free-thinking Brays in Coventry, her place of sanctuary and release during her tumultuous early adulthood. And despite being based in and around London for most of the rest of her life from 1850 to her death in 1880, she spent more than a quarter of that remaining time travelling, on the move. In *George Eliot in Society: Travels Abroad and Sundays at The Priory* (2013), McCormack follows her from Malaga to Budapest, from Berlin to the Scilly Isles. 'Home' and elsewhere thus become affects, 'interaction[s] in the making', to borrow a phrase from Brian Massumi, or constantly renegotiated structures of feeling rather than fixed or fixing locations.[22]

Even in that apparently most detailed of emotional and affecting imagined returns to the once-home, the 'Brother and Sister' sonnet sequence of the 1870s, 'home', as a prescribed place and felt state, is ephemeral, passed, past, divorced from the self through long years of living away and separation from the family whose politics Eliot did not share, and, as many have argued, that stifled her to the point at which enforced exile was inevitable.

In her reading of the micro-mobilities at play in Eliot's representation of provincial life, Ruth Livesey challenges accounts of George Eliot's realist novels as reinforcing status quo, fixity, or what is presented, contrarily, as positive rootedness or provincial stasis. The multidirectional propulsive patterns in Eliot's local fiction, as Livesey puts it, 'unravel the idea that mobilities and moorings are oppositional'.[23] 'Home' thus becomes a permanently renegotiated concept in her work. And by implication, so does 'elsewhere'. Livesey's examples include *Felix Holt* and *Silas Marner*. These works, she suggests 'problematize nostalgic ideas of home and return by highlighting the patterns of movement, rest, and encounter'.[24] As such, they test fixed notions of 'elsewhere-here', and scramble our sense of the antipodal so we don't quite know where we stand.

Moving further outward, accounts of the writer's cosmopolitanism, the cosmopolitan mobility of her characters, and the more heterogeneous, globalised forms of her later work extend this dynamic relationality. John Rignall, among others, has long argued for the need to read George Eliot as a decidedly European novelist and associates the travel sequences in her later novels with the overlapping conditions of modern life: rootlessness, dislocation, cosmopolitanism, and 'mobile capital'.[25] Amanda Anderson stresses the philosophical and ethical dimensions to that mobility which manifests a 'cultivated partiality, a reflective return to the cultural origins that one can no longer inhabit in any unthinking manner'.[26] Everywhere thus becomes partially othered through this distancing, partially elsewhere. As Bruce Robbins reminds us more generally, though, we must be mindful of 'the salient ambiguities of the term cosmopolitanism: the scale at which it should be taken to apply'.[27] Robbins considers the waning of cosmopolitan perspectives through the nineteenth century, following Charlotte Sussman's reading of the fall-off in global boycotts after successful campaigns that contributed to the abolition of slavery in Britain and its colonies (though the exploitation of labour in the colonies continued). Robbins concludes that a narrowing global consciousness apparently coinciding with claims for a more expansive cosmopolitanism suggests that 'there … existed a nineteenth-century cosmopolitanism that can be disengaged from imperialism'.[28]

Discomfort with this uneven proposition might explain why George Eliot cannot write about current and former British colonies as anything other than the most marginal elsewhere in her otherwise richly detailed realist novels. To do so would demand the frank and ethical negotiation of an imposed otherness that defines the relation of the peripheral to the central in George Eliot's writings, which her levelling humanism otherwise strives to retune as a dynamic of equal exchange or coevality. There can be no solidarity or sympathy in the power dynamics of imperialist politics, so it seems that Empire must remain an elsewhere if George Eliot is going to stay ethical. Yet, as Nancy Henry, Oliver Lovesey, and Alicia Carroll (for instance) make clear, the pressure of racial otherness and Britain's implication in aggressive imperialism press on themes and figurative language in her novels and longer poems. Gillian Beer observes that Eliot's writings are full of orphans, migrants, the displaced: think Hetty, Maggie, Romola, Mirah, and Gwendolen all taking off or being taken off elsewhere by water. Such representations, Beer implies, indicate some of the quandaries that George Eliot is trying to process:

> How to inhabit an inland community with little sense of the sea that surrounds our islands and of the global ties beyond? How to descry the effects of empire in novels that are located in an England that does not yet much reflect on its own colonial privilege?[29]

Empire as Elsewhere for Others

The disavowal of empire and lack of direct engagement with colonial privilege, it has been argued of mid-nineteenth-century novelists more broadly, surfaces in how writers constitute 'the colonies' not in dynamic relation with England but as blurry elsewhere. They are peripheral plot devices that ultimately draw the text (and reader) back to the centre, home, England. Jason Rudy, among others, has traced this displacement of the 'English' other to the 'other' of the colonies as a trope of mid-Victorian fiction. 'The failure of middle-class Britons to imagine the colonies with any significant detail',[30] Rudy suggests, is amply demonstrated in the marginal and incomplete registering of the elsewhere of colonial Britain as anything other than an off-stage for unnarrated action that provides momentum for the main action of the novels (Magwitch's return from Australia in *Great Expectations*), palatable resolution (Hetty's deportation in *Adam Bede* to Botany Bay, from where she is returning when she dies), and the space for lower middle-class, working-class, and aimless sons of the more educated and privileged (such as those of Dickens, Trollope, George Henry Lewes) to find their way in the world. Rudy cites Elleke Boehmer's summary account of this phenomenon in *Great Expectations* and *Adam Bede*: 'Australia acts to relieve social and sexual embarrassment'.[31] Australia surfaces as a solution to the poverty problem for George Eliot too, namely, the financial and social insecurity of her sister Chrissey and her six children. But, as Rudy says of Dickens' predominantly middle-class readers, Australia was an 'abstraction, not a realistic destination'.[32]

The resettlement plan did not go ahead for Chrissey. George Eliot never went down under, another of many 'antipodean narratives not taken'.[33] But her investments in railways in the informal Empire increased and her family connection to South Africa intensified in the late 1860s as it became the destination for Lewes' younger, directionless sons Thornton and Bertie.[34] With these circumstances, there was no avoiding Empire for George Eliot, though, as Nancy Henry explains in *George Eliot and the British Empire*, her domestic life from the late 1860s routinely trafficked with parts of the Empire, in the letters home from her stepsons and also in Lewes' regular correspondence with Robert Bulwer-Lytton, writer, diplomat, and Viceroy of India from 1876 to 1880. The overt racism in letters from the Lewes brothers is a matter of record. Henry traces how George Eliot redacted the casual and expressed violence of their experience when communicating news about her stepsons to other correspondents.[35] She did not take on Empire as a subject nor did she visit any of the countries where English was now commonly spoken because of colonisation. Henry's argument that George Eliot did not write about Empire because she did not go to these countries is reasonable but provokes a question: why did this restless traveller not go beyond continental Europe? Ireland, for instance, was on her doorstep: a place that featured in the work of so many of her contemporaries, including Trollope, Thackeray, Harriet Martineau, and her closest friend, Barbara Bodichon.

Henry has recorded the ways in which throughout her writing life George Eliot's work registers knowingness about the problematically blurred elsewhere of empire. She draws out Eliot's critique of English provincial ignorance of the West Indies in 'Brother Jacob' (1864), including the sham cosmopolitanism and extractive aggression of the unsubtly named David Faux. The negative associations that gather around Harold Transome, including his presumed exploitation of his slave wife (and the mother of his child), bought, it is suggested, from the profits of 15 years of trade in what was the Ottoman Empire, offer another implicit critique of such practices. Noting that Eliot never visited any of the colonies (unless you count the internal colonies of Scotland and Wales), Oliver Lovesey argues that, in the mid-Victorian period, the setting of *The Spanish Gypsy* in southern Spain would have been considered a marginal space between Europe and North Africa.[36] He also suggests that Harold Transome's nameless wife 'is not given a story' because her story is already 'too well known', citing a range of popular nineteenth-century texts and artworks by Lord Byron, Eugène Delacroix, and others that featured Greek slaves. 'In this sense, there was no need for an extended account of Mrs. Harold Transome because she was a symbol of Greek oppression by the Ottoman empire in the figure of a Greek maiden subject to colonialism's sexual violence'.[37] It is worth adding, though, that Eliot's writings are celebrated for the ways they move beyond symbol or metaphor to individualised lives and powerfully resonating metonymical narratives. So why not here? Alicia Carroll and Lovesey in different but suggestive ways parse George Eliot's aesthetic engagement with the subaltern other in terms that resist structuring George Eliot's relation with imperial elsewheres as simply cultural annexation or cultural absorption. But George Eliot does not attempt to narrate or picture for us a Smyrna,

Jamaica, Botany Bay, Palestine, or Bengal. Empire remains 'trace', liminal, implicated but not fleshed out in the ways that scenes in a German gambling house are figured in *Daniel Deronda,* or Rome as a substantial place and powerful metaphor resonates through *Middlemarch*. She 'kept to the cosmos of her own experience', as Lovesey puts it.[38]

However, there is a distinct turn from the mid-1860s in her non-fiction work: she represents America, if very briefly in 'A Minor Prophet', a poem that offers a satirical take on the mocked prophet's vision of future global domination as an annihilating perversion of coeval cosmopolitanism. The entangled geographies of Spanish (Catholic) and Al-Andalus (Islam) empires in southern Spain feature in the landscapes described in *The Spanish Gypsy* at the point of Spanish imperial expansion to the Americas and the expulsion of gypsy and Jewish populations. Her last published work contains her most overt critique of British colonialism including its role in the annihilation of indigenous people in America, 'historic rapacity' against the Hindoos [sic], and the violent oppression of the Irish (*TS*, ch. 18). Her last planned novel, intriguingly, includes a plot that involves an Irish claimant to an English estate.

My final section of this chapter will consider some of the ways these imaginings of elsewhere were inflected in George Eliot's more peripheral works, writings that disruptively think through her navigation of centre and periphery models, and that fail; works that end inconclusively in minor and negative keys; works that were never popular in her time. The kinds of kinship networks that provide structural coherence and emotional pay-off in George Eliot's fictions such as *Adam Bede, Silas Marner, Romola,* and *Felix Holt*, both familial and imitative of familial structures, are not possible in the uneven and violent relations that frame the dynamics of centre-periphery models. As Pablo Mukherjee has written more broadly, 'the material reality of the mode' in which such relational models were established, 'that of conquest and exploitation' meant 'that this kinship could not in any sense be admitted as being equal. A hierarchic category of difference had to be established: one that could justify the extent of global inequality and suffering.'[39] Nancy Henry concludes '[W]ith the British Empire, Eliot seems to have run up against the limits of her realism, or at least the limits of what she was willing to represent'.[40]

But what about her non-realist forms? George Eliot's turn to poetry in the mid-1860s is often explained as a consequence of the writer's desire to access the intellectual and cultural capital that accrued around the image of the poetess; to tap into the cultural heritage that continued to value the form over its younger sibling, the novel; and, relatedly, to claim a less evanescent presence in literary culture. Critics have explored how George Eliot's poetry strives to articulate dimensions of her own spirituality and femininity as 'poetess' and prophet and to solidify her celebrity.[41] It has been less common to address ways that her poetry is preoccupied with the elsewheres of imperial annexation and planetary exhaustion as a type of counterfactual imagining.

George Eliot Imagining Elsewhere

George Eliot's personal views on America may have been influenced by her antipathy to intrusive questions about her personal life, which seemed to flow from North America to such an extent that she twice paid for a notice to be inserted in the *New York Tribune* declaring that requests for autographs or biographical details were unwelcome.[42] She writes to Sara Hennell on 26 December 1862 that George Henry Lewes had just finished reading William Howard Russell's *My Diary North and South* (1862), reporting it was 'interesting—full of strange pictures', in terms that collapse layers of indigenous and settler colonist habitation and habits into one mass of difference. Her ironic follow-up captures something of her unease with the navigation of associations between race and nationhood: 'Some one told me on oracular authority that if I had to be born again, I ought to pray to God to be born as an American. I should sooner pray to be born a Turk or an Arab' (*GEL*, 4: 72). Her correspondence with Harriet Beecher Stowe suggests her ongoing contestation with her own earlier views though she stays within familiar territory: a critique of English ignorance of religious and cultural histories. With specific reference to her portrayal of Jews in *Daniel Deronda*, her focus on English obligation to Jewish people reinscribes the invisibility of specific communities the British have in fact colonised, the indigenous peoples that settler projects have annihilated, and people whose ongoing exploitation fuelled the imperial project:

> But precisely because I felt that the usual attitude of Christians toward Jews is—I hardly know whether to say more impious or more stupid when viewed in the light of their professed principles, I therefore felt urged to treat Jews with such sympathy and understanding as my nature and knowledge could attain to. Moreover, not only towards the Jews, but towards all oriental peoples with whom we English come in contact, a spirit of arrogance and contemptuous dictatorialness is observable which has become a national disgrace to us. There is nothing I should care more to do, if it were possible, than to rouse the imagination of men and women to a vision of human claims in those races of their fellow-men who most differ from them in customs and beliefs. But towards the Hebrews we western people who have been reared in Christianity, have a peculiar debt and, whether we acknowledge it or not, a peculiar thoroughness of fellowship in religion and moral sentiment. Can anything be more disgusting than to hear people called 'educated' making small jokes about eating ham, and showing themselves empty of any real knowledge as to the relation of their own social and religious life to

the history of the people they think themselves witty in insulting? They hardly know that Christ was a Jew.

(GEL, 6: 301–2)

George Eliot does write about an American, if not actually America, namely the speaker who dominates the first half of her ironic vision of Utopia as conceived in 'A Minor Prophet'. That American is presented as a mockery of the assimilative aggressions of the imperialist who claims the world as his own in his totalising vision of 'perfection'. The achievement of such vision refracts questions of racial extermination in animal and fairy-tale analogues and aspirations to global dominance through the avaricious banality of Britain's former colony, the as-yet underdeveloped nation-in-formation that is America. It is a diversionary tactic that avoids direct critique of colonising Britain in this heated period of resistance to British imperialism.[43]

The poem comprises two monologues, parallel, never converging into full dialogue. The first asserts global domination of space (the vision of the 'minor' prophet), Elias Baptist Butterworth. The other voice, also a minor prophet, is an unnamed, ungendered person and our framing speaker. They listen to Butterworth's proclamations and aver a non-linear and fluid flow of time shaped by memory's circuitous layering that is positioned as the purposeful opposite to the bullish momentum of Butterworth's vision. The poem is a deeply sarcastic take on cosmopolitanism as type of prescriptive and persecutory idealism, and on projected utopias that make the world one of borderless occupation on the presumptive ideology that the human species can absorb all 'elsewheres' into a global 'here'. Butterworth's vegetarian utopia requires the annihilation of animals, birds, and reptiles that are deemed not beautiful or useful, to make room for the increasing presence of people (though some dogs are permitted to continue to exist, once their digestive tracts adapt to their all-plant diet). Butchers will become redundant.

'New Jerusalem' puritanical zealots are the target of scorn, those who see land as blank canvas and the making of their version of utopia a morally sanctioned global project. The erasure of boundaries, and the dangers of such, is achieved stylistically in the opening lines: we are disoriented in terms of both time and place as the poem begins with little sense of the speaker's context and the subject's situatedness. However, there is an immediate registering of colonisation and enforced plantation in the early mention of Cromwell (the Lord Protector of the so-called Commonwealth and persecutor of vicious military campaigns in Ireland) and 'America' as 'new-found' land and providential destination occupied by Elias' ancestors:

> I have a friend, a vegetarian seer,
> By name Elias Baptist Butterworth,
> A harmless, bland, disinterested man,
> Whose ancestors in Cromwell's day believed
> The Second Advent certain in five years,

But when King Charles the Second came instead,
Revised their date and sought another world:
I mean—not heaven but—America.[44]

The caesura created by the dash underscores the unevenly distributed ironies of the poem. The framing speaker reports all to us and editorialises to comic effect to undercut 'harmless, bland, disinterested' Elias. And we wonder, as one contemporaneous critic put it of the one-dimensional targets of Theophrastus' irony in *Impressions*, why such a large sharp sword is needed for such soft bodies: is it really worth bothering with Butterworth's pronouncements?[45] But our guide speaker is not without ironic framing. The poem remains fascinating for the weirdly multidirectional irony that pings between these associated but disconnected 'friends'.

Their blank verse account fizzles off into incoherence and Eliot's critique resonates outward against the flattening anthropogenic annihilating vision offered by Butterworth. But it also diffuses through the looping, direction-less fantasy of coeval contentment with which our guide, the unnamed second speaker, counters. The poet provides very little visual sense of the American base in which Butterworth is now situated since his ancestral replanting. Instead, we are given a vision of a globalised world premised on the advancement to perfection of the human species: 'when all Earth is vege-tarian—/When, lacking butchers, quadrupeds die out' ('MP', ll. 53–4). It is a totalising vision (as with all utopic elsewheres), with intriguing predictive aspects on George Eliot's part, when looked at from our future elsewhere:

'Tis on this theme—the vegetarian world—
That good Elias willingly expands:
He loves to tell in mildly nasal tones
And vowels stretched to suit the widest views,
The future fortunes of our infant Earth—
When it will be too full of human kind
To have the room for wilder animals.
Saith he, Sahara will be populous
With families of gentlemen retired
From commerce in more Central Africa,
Who order coolness as we order coal,
And have a lobe anterior strong enough
To think away the sand-storms. Science thus
Will leave no spot on this terraqueous globe
Unfit to be inhabited by man.
('MP', ll. 62–76)

The poem has been read as a critique of faddish thinking, unreflective zealotry (of Puritans, vegetarians, idealists whose fervour leads them to abandon any sense of historical perspective or respect for tradition save for that framed by the narrow exegesis of the bible).[46] But the buoyant expansionist vision of the white coloniser, self-presenting as a progressive champion of advanced civilisation and preserving the planet for the future of mankind, is the overt surface of the text and cannot be ignored. Whether or not the implicit critique is of those who 'civilise' without respect for tradition (superficial Americans? ignorant British imperialists?) in terms that are consonant with George Eliot's critical cosmopolitanism, it is worth pointing out how the vision expressed, for all the exaggerated ironies, is nonetheless emblematic of the casual violence and speciesism that undergirded what Eliot knew of British settler colonialism. As Henry, Lovesey, and others have made clear in different contexts, this understanding prefigures versions of what she reads in her letters from her stepsons, and even echoes the words of her life partner, Lewes. No supporter of what he saw as the false and faddish physiological theories underpinning vegetarianism, Lewes was no stranger either to the jingoistic when it came to anthropocentric annexation of the planet. In a review article in the *Westminster Review* in 1858, he observes: 'Missionary zeal, trading enterprise, and love of sport, together with the native restlessness and spirit of adventure animating the Anglo-Saxon race, will soon bring us acquainted with the whole habitable surface of our globe', adding that the English are 'gradually mapping the whole earth; and our children may live to see railroads across the desert'.[47]

Such smooth, capable ownership of the terraqueous globe, Butterworth concludes, will require the annihilation of species, which will not be problematic because of their stupidity:

> Earth will hold
> No stupid brutes, no cheerful queernesses,
> No naïve cunning, grave absurdity.
> Wart-pigs with tender and parental grunts,
> Wombats much flattened as to their contour,
> Perhaps from too much crushing in the ark.
> ('MP', ll. 114–21)

The acoustic shimmer of 'native' in 'naïve' here is given additional amplification in the litany of exotic creatures of elsewhere, of empire's farthest corners (wombats) and those native species hunted to extinction in Britain in the middle ages (wart-pigs). It is, of course, not insignificant that this vision of perfection follows from ongoing debates about biological evolution fomenting before and after the publication of Darwin's *Origins of Species* (1859). The perfection of the human species is just one dimension to this unrelenting forward momentum in terms that anticipate eugenicist movements of the end of century.

> All these rude products will have disappeared
> Along with every faulty human type.

By dint of diet vegetarian
All will be harmony of hue and line,
Bodies and minds all perfect, limbs well-turned,
And talk quite free from aught erroneous.
('MP', ll. 128–33)

George Eliot's comic satire thus provides a deflective, if deadly serious, take on what Mukherjee observes is pervasive in work from the period: 'Endemic in Victorian writing was also the nagging feeling that there was something drastically wrong with the mode of this sense of entitlement, with how the earth became possession.'[48] This catastrophist consciousness provides the keynote for her verse drama in tragic mode, *The Spanish Gypsy*. Thematic, formal, and temporal anxieties underscore both works. 'A Minor Prophet' was originally conceived as a prose piece, entitled 'My Vegetarian Friend'. Eliot rewrote it as a long blank verse poem around the time she was struggling to make headway with her new drama based in Spain, provisionally entitled 'Fidelma'. Though George Eliot habitually changed working titles, it is worth pausing on the shift from prose to verse for both of these works over which George Eliot laboured, then abandoned, but returned to again in overlapping months. Both 'A Minor Prophet' and *The Spanish Gypsy* overtly address imperial fantasies of conquering elsewhere, and both register the wide-ranging ecological destructiveness that follows such totalising aggression. In the reengineering of these works from prose to poetry, she is acting out a realisation that realist modes could not accommodate the violence of what she was describing.

At the 'climax of this prophecy' from Elias, the friend who opens the poem takes over, and turns with sadness from Elias' 'utopic' prophecies:

No tears are sadder than the smile
With which I quit Elias. Bitterly
I feel that every change upon this earth
Is bought with sacrifice.
('MP', ll. 143–6)

The jagged syllabic pulse and scrambled facial signals (a smile sadder than tears) underline the impossibility of meaningful communication between these two 'friends', and the point is structurally underscored by the fact that the speaker's part is addressed not back to his visionary friend Elias but to us readers. This is not a discussion or debate: the incompatible world views of Elias and the unnamed speaker, the poem implies, cannot be reconciled. This is a failed relationship, a forced formal grafting of discordant visions that knowingly displays its formal incoherence in its monologues of two uneven parts that never resolve into dialogue. The felt bitterness of the second speaker provides affective judgement, but it is non-directive: bitterness towards whom? And who or what is sacrificed? What follows is a garbled mesh of backward-facing nostalgia for vaguely imagined simpler times past and a forward-facing fear of future extinction. This alternative vision is premised on legend, tradition, folklore, personal memory, and, tellingly, local militaristic victories. The historical forms are absent from the modish idealism of Butterworth. The more localised but still not situated or specified views of the second speaker comprise more than half of the poem, and though this section has been read, by Charles La Porte, for instance, as presenting a vision of English habitation, moving with the rhythms of tradition and the diurnal, it presents an equally vague and unnamed elsewhere that typifies non-metropolitan-anywhere to produce an effect of spatial dislocation.

The disorientation is reinforced by the elision of gender and temporal markers. The speaker is a visionary woman, according to LaPorte, though the text is so vague on details that no gender is clear.[49] In another intriguing set of intertextual ironies, however, the speaker declares, 'Speaking in parable, I am Colin Clout' ('MP', l. 172), a malleable figure of the pastoral who features in works by John Skelton and John Gay among others. But not incidentally, Clout is perhaps best known as a recurring vehicle for the articulation of both the pastoral vision and agrarian reform in Edmund Spenser's work as he navigated his transforming relationship with the Elizabethan plantation as a settler colonist in County Limerick, Ireland. The intertextual reference seems to play on Colin Clout's immersion in the prosaic, with which our speaker identifies, exemplified by the scent of raw onion that pervades Clout ('MP', ll. 65–70). There is nonetheless a hint of the underlying pastoral critique that features in Spenser's 'Colin Clouts Come Home Againe' (1595), which, I suggest, adds an ironic layer both to the expressed parochialism of this second 'minor prophet' and to the colonising energies of Butterworth.

At the heart of this 'Colin Clout' vision is a love of the unevenness and unexpected, the misshapen and flawed. Progress of the forward moving global-dominating sort is always premised on the erasure of otherness, here figured in terms of weakness, physical difference, cracks, brokenness, and eccentricity, and also valued for that difference and romanticised:

> My yearnings fail
> To reach that high apocalyptic mount
> Which shows in bird's-eye view a perfect world,
> Or enter warmly into other joys
> Than those of faulty, struggling human kind.
> That strain upon my soul's too feeble wing
> Ends in ignoble floundering: I fall
> Into short-sighted pity for the men
> Who living in those perfect future times
> Will not know half the dear imperfect things
> That move my smiles and tears.
>   ('MP', ll. 146–56)

This vision, equally drawing on the fantastic, is shaped by the lexicon of fairy-tale and superstition:

> I cleave
> To nature's blunders, evanescent types
> Which sages banish from Utopia. ...
> But by my hearth I keep a sacred nook
> For gnomes and dwarfs, duck-footed waddling elves
> Who stitched and hammered for the weary man
> In days of old.
>   ('MP', ll. 174–6, 179–82)

This speaker's world, though, is equally muddled, an admixture of past tales, angelic vision, and the rhythms of the ordinary every day. They move from a peroration on the glories of a local military celebration to a focus on the bun in their pocket that they pass on to a child at the parade, and from there to memories of sitting at their father's knee. It is the final vision that marks a shift in George Eliot's sense of time and place, the expansion and contraction of sense of place and her place in it.

> Presentiment of better things on earth
> Sweeps in with every force that stirs our souls
> To admiration, self-renouncing love,
> Or thoughts, like light, that bind the world in one:
> Sweeps like the sense of vastness, when at night
> We hear the roll and dash of waves that break
> Nearer and nearer with the rushing tide,
> Which rises to the level of the cliff
> Because the wide Atlantic rolls behind
> Throbbing respondent to the far-off orbs.
>   ('MP', ll. 316–25)

That presentiment of better things on Earth is overlaid with a sense of future annihilation of the human species by forces of nature and the cosmos well beyond us. Our conquering of the 'terraqueous globe' premised by Elias is undermined by the powerfully operating forces of tide, ocean, and space, not place, but those 'far-off orbs' to which the Atlantic responds, rolling in to wipe away what was a cliff in the 'roll and dash' of gravity's waves. Earth will return to water.[50]

It is worth considering this scene of erasure alongside another take on potential futures post-Anthropocene, an ultimate elsewhere, imagined in George Eliot's final work, in the essay that was intended as the last of Theophrastus' impressions. 'Shadows of the Coming Race', the seventeenth of the eighteen essays or chapters that comprise *Impressions of Theophrastus Such*. 'Entertaining the fantasy of a world stripped bare of frantic, self-deluding human discourse', as Rosemarie Bodenheimer summarises, it 'makes quite a fitting conclusion to the book of fools George Eliot wrote'.[51] Here, the champion of modernity, Trost, is in dialogue with his friend, our narrator, Theophrastus the cosmopolitan cynic, in Helen Small's reading, reminding us that the first cynic, Diogenes of Sinope, 'was an exile – not because he was a citizen of the world, but because he did not identify as a citizen in the Greek cities he inhabited'.[52] Trost, we are told, no fantasist of the Elias kind, opens with an acknowledgement of future annihilation not just of the species or the planet but of the solar system. Alert to pervasive concerns about the exhaustion of the elsewhere of empire, Eliot keeps recalibrating the scales, from local to colonial to planetary to the universe: 'My friend Trost, who is no optimist as to the state of the universe hitherto, but is confident that at some future period within the duration of the solar system, ours will be the best of all possible worlds' (*TS*, ch. 17). That 'within the duration' is an important overlooked detail in George Eliot's late work, a hedging clause that chases all attempts to secure longer life and legacy. She is increasingly conscious of the inevitability of 'plot without man',[53] which, of course, would be no plot at all since it is 'man'—the scientist or the artist, historian or anthropologist—who consciously marks or records or puts order and limits on origins and ends, our heres and elsewhere.

The techno-optimism of Trost envisions a world where technology is harnessed to bring ease and efficiency to human living. It produces more precise and refined machinery to determine 'truth' (as imagined, for instance, by the accuracy with which machines can weigh currency to detect 'dud' coins). Theophrastus, the cynic, is more sceptical, foreseeing a future where the affordances of technology are outweighed by their threat to the species, robbing us of livelihoods, and ultimately developing the ability to reproduce without human intervention, thus combining their inorganic and organic strengths to wipe out human consciousness. In the Darwinian struggle for survival, only those humans who can support a mechanic universe, the scientists and calculators, can continue to exist:

> This last stage having been reached, either by man's contrivance or as an unforeseen result, one sees that the process of natural selection must drive men altogether out of the field; for they will long before have begun to sink into the miserable condition of those unhappy characters in fable who, having demons or djinns at their beck, and being obliged to supply them with work, found too much of everything done in too short a time. What demons so potent as molecular movements, none the less tremendously potent for not carrying the futile cargo of a consciousness screeching irrelevantly, like a fowl tied head downmost to the saddle of a swift horseman? Under such uncomfortable circumstances our race will have diminished with the diminishing call on their energies, and by the time that the self-repairing and reproducing machines arise, all but a few of the rare inventors, calculators, and speculators

will have become pale, pulpy, and cretinous from fatty or other degeneration, and behold around them a scanty hydrocephalous offspring.

(*TS*, ch. 17)

The instability of the category 'race' in this usage (human? English? European? non-scientist?) carries both the mobility of the term in nineteenth-century discourses—its interchangeability with species, for instance—and the specificity with which it was deployed as a political and biological category in other contexts.

This chapter, envisioned as the final one in the collection, would have been the last piece of writing published by George Eliot, and a bleak end to her creative vision. In a late change, 'Shadows of the Coming Race' was switched with 'The Modern Hep! Hep! Hep!', an overt critique of English colonial practices and anti-Semitism that also indicates her turn to Ireland, finally, at the end of her life. George Eliot did not know she was going to die in 1880. She did not consider *Impressions* her last word, her last work. She was planning another novel, after *Daniel Deronda*, after 'Shadows of the Coming Race', and it was to be partially set in Ireland.

The untitled novel exists only in brief sketches that suggest a multigenerational story based on an upper-class family in the English midlands, now in decline.[54] The narrative is partly set during the Napoleonic Wars that heralded England's reassertion of power on the global stage. A claim on the midlands estate is threatened by the newly discovered existence of a son of the current owner's eldest brother. That son was born in Ireland to the now deceased brother's secret wife. She is described as the daughter of an innkeeper from County Cork. Only paragraph fragments exist. I am not going to extrapolate more from this novel that we never saw written except to ask, why Ireland at this point in George Eliot's writing life?

Neil McCaw has written on her remarkable 'silence' on Ireland, given that from the 1840s, she demonstrated some sympathy towards Irish home rule (she attended a Daniel O'Connell rally in 1842) and, unsurprisingly, supported Catholic Emancipation.[55] I suggest that *Impressions of Theophrastus Such* provides us with some answers as to why such silence on Ireland. It does so in a way that indicates George Eliot's evolving relationship with the elsewhere of Empire, so decidedly absent from overt representation in her other works, though McCaw has argued that *Adam Bede* is an allegory for the failed so-called Union of Great Britain and Ireland in the 1801 Act of Union that ended Ireland's short-lived legislative independence in Grattan's parliament. But more explicit references to Ireland are available to us in George Eliot's published work: namely, the persistent references to Irish subordination as a damning indication of British colonial practices that can be traced through the opening and closing chapters of *Impressions*.

The opening so-called autobiographical chapters, 'Looking Backward' and 'Looking Inward', present Theophrastus in reflective mode, musing on his origins, son of a conservative English clergyman who was resistant to change and celebrated the England of Pitt:

> I gathered that our national troubles in the first two decades of this century were not at all due to the mistakes of our administrators; and that England, with its fine Church and Constitution, would have been exceedingly well off if every British subject had been thankful for what was provided, and had minded his own business—if, for example, numerous Catholics of that period had been aware how very modest they ought to be considering they were Irish. The times, I heard, had often been bad; but I was constantly hearing of 'bad times' as a name for actual evenings and mornings when the godfathers who gave them that name appeared to me remarkably comfortable. Altogether, my father's England seemed to me lovable, laudable, full of good men, and having good rulers, from Mr Pitt on to the Duke of Wellington, until he was for emancipating the Catholics; and it was so far from prosaic to me that I looked into it for a more exciting romance than such as I could find in my own adventures, which consisted mainly in fancied crises calling for the resolute wielding of domestic swords and firearms against unapparent robbers, rioters, and invaders who, it seemed, in my father's prime had more chance of being real.
>
> (*TS*, ch. 2)

The naivety of this view of the past, of England, of imperial rule and of Catholic Emancipation, is exposed in Theophrastus' own ironic tones about his slavish (and therefore, childish) adoption of his father's view. It is notable that by the final chapter of *Impressions*, we encounter a much more explicit observation about the oppression of Ireland and the Irish by English colonial rule. The suppression of national self-determination is drawn out in a comparison between the Irish and the Jewish people. We witness an oppositional turn, an antipodal positioning against the early 'Looking Backward' chapter, which, it is clear, this Theophrastus judges in its racial bias to be very backward looking, explaining how the 'medieval' English prejudice against Jewish people

> is mirrored in an analogy, namely, that of the Irish, also a servile race, who have rejected Protestantism though it has been repeatedly urged on them by fire and sword and penal laws, and whose place in the moral scale may be judged by our advertisements, where the clause, 'No Irish need apply,' parallels the sentence which for many polite persons sums up the question of Judaism—'I never *did* like the Jews.'
>
> (*TS*, ch. 18)

George Eliot's orientation towards Ireland, partial and sketchy, means she can no longer look at England in the same way. A critique of her tacitly colonial politics is offered by some of her postcolonial critics who suggest that any writing about the colonised 'elsewhere' or the exoticised other was always only about refining or renewing understanding of the centre—the here to that elsewhere. The closed-loop logic of this view is challenged, I suggest, by George Eliot's problem with endings, including how to end *Impressions of Theophrastus Such*. A defence of the Jewish right to self-determination, as many have argued, an articulation of belief in national separatism, 'The Modern Hep! Hep! Hep!' yields on the situating of that nation in a physical elsewhere. Following publisher John Blackwood's first reactions, readers have frequently complained that the journey 'East' of Daniel and Mirah is not described in *Daniel Deronda*. 'There will I know be disappointment at not hearing more of the failure of Gwendolen and the mysterious destiny of Deronda', the ever diplomatic Blackwood writes, 'but I am sure you are right to leave all grand and vague' (*GEL*, 6: 272).

The faltering sense of the impossibility of writing about 'elsewhere' because of her alertness to the fact that every nation's efforts to establish itself elsewhere will no doubt challenge someone else's 'here' underscores Eliot's most overt exploration of Empire formation—her verse drama *The Spanish Gypsy*. Its very title suggests the contradictions of here and elsewhere: what is it to be of a nomadic people with a nation-place-designating adjective, 'Spanish'? Is Fedelma the Spanish Gypsy? Or should we also look to the aristocratic Juan, who gives up his social position as agent of Spanish imperialism to live with Fedelma's gypsy tribe as another candidate for that unstable designation? The questions are unresolved.[56]

Conclusion: George Eliot Elsewhere

'Elsewhere' is an antipode that can be geographical, obviously, but integral to that designation are questions that press on the existential, experiential, and anthropological; the historical and the eschatological; as well as the commercial and the political. All incorporate the navigation of the national, colonial, and imperial formulations of place and mappings of space into imagined 'communities' across and outside activated boundaries. Crucially, these are overlapping categories. Whether an orientation, a designation, or destination, 'elsewhere' is an opportunity or a threat but rarely, if ever, neutral. The shifting boundaries of those categories are fundamental propulsions in George Eliot's work, when designation turns to desired destination, for example, when threat becomes opportunity or its reverse. However we approach it, elsewhere is entirely and always contextual and contradictory. It is at once situated yet unstable since its relationship to meaning is dependent on perspective and questions of agency, among them the key question: who speaks to whom from elsewhere and of elsewhere? In this way, it is a useful starting point for attending to the mobile interchange and reversals of a globalised nineteenth century that disrupts centre-periphery hierarchies long dominant in the field of Victorian studies, hierarchies that conjoin the formal operations of narrative point of view with cultural inscription (how George Eliot teaches us to read, to see with her eyes).[57] This chapter has sought to think instead of George Eliot unresolved, uneasy, and uncomfortably displaced.

Notes

1 Henry James, review of John Walter Cross, *George Eliot's Life*, in *The Atlantic Monthly* (May 1885), 668–78, reprinted in *George Eliot: The Critical Heritage*, ed. David Carroll (London: Routledge and Kegan Paul, 1971), 504.

2 Amanda Anderson, *The Powers of Distance: Cosmopolitanism and the Cultivation of Detachment* (Princeton: Princeton University Press, 2001), 64.

3 For the most detailed accounts of George Eliot's embeddedness in colonialism, see Nancy Henry's groundbreaking *George Eliot and the British Empire* (Cambridge: Cambridge University Press, 2002) and Oliver Lovesey, *Postcolonial George Eliot* (Basingstoke: Palgrave Macmillan, 2017). On George Eliot's many global investments, see Dermot Coleman, *George Eliot and Money: Economics, Ethics and Literature* (Cambridge: Cambridge University Press, 2014).

4 Lauren Goodlad, *The Victorian Geopolitical Aesthetic: Realism, Sovereignty, and Transnational Experience* (Oxford: Oxford University Press 2015), 7.

5 See Elizabeth Carolyn Miller's succinct articulation of a key aspect of racial capitalism: 'investment in mines necessitated investment in railways and infrastructure, to ease the removal of subsurface mineral wealth from one part of the world to another', in *Extraction Ecologies and the Literature of the Long Exhaustion* (Princeton: Princeton University Press, 2021), 89. The letters of Thornton and Bertie Lewes are discussed by Henry, *George Eliot and the British Empire*, and by Rosemarie Bodenheimer, *The Real Life of Mary Ann Evans: George Eliot, Her Letters and Fiction* (Ithaca: Cornell University Press, 1994), 189–231.

6 Nathan Hensley, *Forms of Empire: the Poetics of Victorian Sovereignty* (Oxford: Oxford University Press, 2016), 19.

7 George Eliot, *The Spanish Gypsy*, ed. Antonie Gerard van der Broek (1868; London, Pickering and Chatto, 2008), bk. 1, l. 139.

8 In addition to Henry's *George Eliot and the British Empire*, see Alicia Carroll, *Dark Smiles: Race and Desire in George Eliot* (Ohio: Ohio State University Press, 2003), which examines the ways George Eliot's work encodes and resists traditional racial and ethnic representations of otherness in her fiction in terms that critique what Carroll calls 'home culture'. Oliver Lovesey in *Postcolonial George Eliot* attends to how Eliot becomes a key figure in the colonial library and details her engagement with the colonial world into which she was born, and to which she was acutely alert, as figured, Lovesey argues, though the ways her writings registered sympathy with otherness, the marginalised, and the peripheral. All three observe that Eliot did not write from the perspective of the places of Empire.

9 See, for instance, Ruth Livesey, 'On Writing Portable Place: George Eliot's Mobile Midlands', *Mobilities*, 12.4 (2017), 559–71. For her travel journals, see *The Journals of George Eliot*, ed. Margaret Harris and Judith Johnston (Cambridge: Cambridge University Press, 1998).

10 Arjun Appadurai, *Modernity at Large: Cultural Dimensions of Globalization* (Minneapolis: University of Minnesota Press, 1996), 181.

11 George Eliot, *Daniel Deronda* (1876; Oxford: Oxford World's Classics, 1998), ch. 3. Alexander Allardyce's obituary was published anonymously: 'George Eliot', *Blackwood's Magazine* (February 1881), 255.

12 [T.E. Kebbel], 'Village Life of George Eliot', *Fraser's Magazine* (February 1881), 263–76.

13 [Leslie Stephen], 'George Eliot', *Cornhill Magazine* (February 1881), 152–68, reprinted in Carroll, *Critical Heritage*, 469.

14 Patty Townsend and Lillian Russell, *George Eliot: Her Early Home*, arranged by Emily Swinnerton (London: Raphael Tuck, 1891), 16.

15 Allardyce, 'George Eliot', 256.

16 Ian Duncan, 'The Provincial or Regional Novel', in *A Companion to the Victorian Novel*, ed. Patrick Brantlinger and William B. Thesing (Cambridge: Cambridge University Press, 2003), 322.

17 Henry, *George Eliot and the British Empire*, 6. Eliot's work was serialised in magazines in Australia, America, and New Zealand. On the global circulation of her serial fiction, see, for instance, Matthew Poland, '*Middlemarch* in Melbourne', *George Eliot-George Henry Lewes Studies*, 73.2 (2021), 131–41.

18 Henry, *George Eliot and the British Empire*, 6.

19 Goodlad, *Victorian Geopolitical Aesthetic*, 1, 169. For other accounts of this worlded dimension to George Eliot's work, see also Hensley, *Forms of Empire*, and Miller, *Extraction Ecologies*.

20 John Plotz, *Semi-Detached: The Aesthetics of Virtual Experience Since Dickens* (Princeton: Princeton University Press, 2018), 102.

21 Margaret Harris, 'George Eliot's Reputation', in *The Cambridge Companion to George Eliot*, 2nd edn, ed. George Levine and Nancy Henry (Cambridge: Cambridge University Press, 2019), 253.

22 Brian Massumi, *Parables for the Virtual: Movement, Affect, Sensation* (Durham: Duke University Press, 2002), 9.

23 Livesey, 'George Eliot's Mobile Midlands', 559.

24 Livesey, 'George Eliot's Mobile Midlands', 559.

25 John Rignall, *George Eliot, European Novelist* (Farnham: Ashgate, 2011), ch. 8. See also *George Eliot and Europe*, ed. John Rignall (Aldershot: Scolar, 1997).

26 Anderson, *Powers of Distance*, 120.

27 Bruce Robbins, 'The Cosmopolitan Eliot', in *A Companion to George Eliot*, ed. Amanda Anderson and Harry E. Shaw (Chichester: Wiley-Blackwell, 2013), 401. Robbins offers a robust reading of anti-cosmopolitanism in George Eliot's work.

28 Robbins, 'Cosmopolitan Eliot', 404. See also Charlotte Sussman, *Consuming Anxieties: Consumer Protest, Gender, and British Slavery, 1713–1833* (Stanford: Stanford University Press, 2000).

29 Gillian Beer, *George Eliot and the Woman Question* (1986; Brighton: Edward Everett Root, 2019), xviii.

30 Jason R. Rudy, 'Settled: *Dorrit* Down Under', *Nineteenth-Century Literature*, 75.2 (2020), 185. Rudy offers a brilliant contrapuntal reading of Dickens' novel that foregrounds the ways Australia functioned to reinscribe the centripetal tendencies of mid-Victorian bourgeois novels that drive back to the metropolitan 'centre'.

31 Elleke Boehmer, *Colonial and Postcolonial Literature: Migrant Metaphors*, 2nd edn (Oxford: Oxford University Press, 2005), 28, cited in Rudy, '*Dorrit* Down Under,' 201.

32 Rudy, '*Dorrit* Down Under', 185.

33 Rudy, '*Dorrit* Down Under', 186.

34 George Eliot's nephew, Edward Clarke, the eldest son of her sister Chrissey, emigrated to Australia in 1861 and later settled in New Zealand. See *GEL*, 8: 221.

35 See Henry, *George Eliot and the British Empire*, 2.

36 Lovesey, *Postcolonial George Eliot*, 18.

37 Lovesey, *Postcolonial George Eliot*, 144.

38 Lovesey, *Postcolonial George Eliot*, 19.

39 Pablo Mukherjee, 'Victorian Empire', in *The Cambridge History of Victorian Literature,* ed. Kate Flint (Cambridge: Cambridge University Press, 2012), 648.

40 Henry, *George Eliot and the British Empire*, 20.

41 On George Eliot as poetess, see Charles LaPorte, 'George Eliot, the Poetess as Prophet', *Victorian Literature and Culture*, 31 (2003), 159–79 and Wendy S. Williams, *George Eliot, Poetess* (Farnham: Ashgate, 2014); on celebrity, see Alexis Easley, 'Poet as Headliner: George Eliot and "Macmillan's Magazine"', *George Eliot-George Henry Lewes Studies*, 60/61 (2011), 107–25.

42 George Griffith, 'The Face as Legible Text: Gazing at the Portraits of George Eliot', *Victorian Review*, 27.2 (2001), 25.

43 Hensley registers the 'profusion of ... killing' that marked British imperialism during Victoria's reign with '228 separate armed conflicts during the period' and eight in 1854 alone. See Hensley, *Forms of Empire*, 2.

44 George Eliot, 'A Minor Prophet', in *The Complete Shorter Poetry of George Eliot*, vol. 1, ed. Antonie Gerard van den Broek and William Baker (London: Pickering and Chatto, 2005), ll. 1–8. All subsequent references are to this edition.

45 [Anon], 'Three Small Books by Great Writers', *Fraser's Magazine*, 115 (July 1879), 107. 'Such transparent evils, such commonplace sinners want but little pointing out' the reviewer concludes.

46 See, for example, Stella Pratt-Smith, 'Inside-Out: Texture and Belief in George Eliot's "Bubble-World"', *George Eliot-George Henry Lewes Studies*, 60/61 (2011), 62–76.

47 [George Henry Lewes], 'African Life', *Westminster Review* (January 1858), 1–16, cited in Henry, *George Eliot and the British Empire*, 33.

48 Mukherjee, 'Victorian Empire', 653.

49 LaPorte, 'George Eliot', 172. For a reading of the poem that emphasises environmental degradation, see Sophie D. Christman, 'The Rise of Proto-Environmentalism in George Eliot', *Dickens Studies Annual*, 50.1 (2019), 81–105.

50 'A distinctive Victorian move', Mukherjee explains,

> was to extend this heightened consciousness of the inevitable, even impending, death of the individual, to that of human history, and more specifically, to imperial history. Victorian writing is full of melancholic notes on the passing of human imperial civilizations ... Haunted by the globalized production of death, writers of the Victorian empire could not wipe visions of apocalypse from their eyes.

See Mukherjee, 'Victorian Empire', 658–9.

51 Rosemarie Bodenheimer, 'George Eliot's Last Stand: *Impressions of Theophrastus Such*', *Victorian Literature and Culture*, 44 (2016), 617.

52 Helen Small, 'George Eliot and the Cosmopolitan Cynic', *Victorian Studies*, 55.1 (2012), 103.

53 Gillian Beer, *Darwin's Plots: Evolutionary Narrative in Darwin, George Eliot and Thomas Hardy* (1983; Cambridge: Cambridge University Press, 2000), 17.

54 William Baker, 'A New George Eliot Manuscript', in *George Eliot: Centenary Essays and an Unpublished Fragment*, ed. Anne Smith (London: Vision, 1980), 9–20, which reproduces what is called the Canterbury copy of these notes. Another version is in Princeton University Library, entitled 'George Eliot's Notebook for an Unwritten Novel'.

55 Neil McCaw, 'Beyond "A Water and Toast Sympathy": George Eliot and the Silence of Ireland', *George Eliot-George Henry Lewes Studies*, 38/39 (2000), 3–17.

56 My thinking on these points has been shaped by David Kurnick's rich analysis of the unresolved contradictions of this verse drama, formally and thematically, which Kurnick reads in terms of George Eliot's agonised navigation of the claims of ethnic nationalism and universal cosmopolitanism. See David Kurnick, 'Unspeakable George Eliot', *Victorian Literature and Culture*, 38 (2010), 489–509.

57 This is a core argument, for example, in Philip Davis' *The Transferred Life of George Eliot* (Oxford: Oxford University Press, 2017), which echoes Edith Simcox's passionate praise of her beloved George Eliot:

> Her mind was a mirror, upon which the truth concerning all human relations was reflected with literal fidelity ... merely to read one of her books in an impressionable mood is to see such a portion of the world with her eyes and to share in the multiform influence exercised by the vision.
>
> (Edith Simcox, 'George Eliot', *The Nineteenth Century* (May 1881), 778, cited in Davis, *The Transferred Life*, 1)

2 Before *Scenes of Clerical Life*

Eliot's 1854–57 Travelogues as Poetic Practice

Julia Kuehn

Up to the 1990s, discussions of George Eliot's career tended to identify a clear divide between the Marian Evans who wrote reviews and other journalistic pieces as well as personal writings such as letters and journals, and George Eliot the writer of fiction. However, critics like Rosemarie Bodenheimer, Margaret Harris and Judith Johnston, Barbara Hardy, and Rosemary Ashton see such nonfiction writings not only as early signs of her writing talent—a talent that also predates the encounter with George Henry Lewes—but also as important preparatory work for her career in fiction. Fionnuala Dillane's *Before George Eliot: Marian Evans and the Periodical Press* analyses in detail how Eliot's working life as a journalist, editor, and writer of serial fiction shaped her multifaceted literary persona, her understanding of the audience, and the stylistic intricacies of her earliest collection, *Scenes of Clerical Life*.[1]

My chapter continues this line of enquiry into the shaping forces of Eliot's writing as it focuses on her travel writing—published and unpublished—in the years between 1854 and 1857. The travel genre has so far been largely ignored in discussions of Eliot's writings. It is precisely this turn to the margins of Eliot's oeuvre and a rereading of her work from de-centred vantage points that establishes this collection's rationale and anchors my essay's attempt to recalibrate our understanding of 'central' Eliot texts and scholarly orthodoxies. Specifically, I reject the claims of such critics as F.R. Leavis, U.C. Knoepflmacher, and Catherine Nicholl who maintain that the *Scenes* are Eliot's 'prentice-work' and that her oeuvre properly begins with her 'experimentation' in 'The Sad Fortunes of the Reverend Amos Barton', 'Mr Gilfil's Love-Story', and 'Janet's Repentance'.[2] Rather, I read Eliot's travel memoirs about Germany and North Devon alongside the *Scenes* to argue that preparatory work for the novels is done in these travel pieces. They are, just like her reviews, 'prentice work', as Eliot not only reworks her diary entries into extended prose and a publishable format but also experiments, in particular, with place and character writing, the narrator's voice and persona and—on the macro-level—realism.[3] Drawing upon her review articles of the same period, the essay argues that Eliot's early travelogues about Weimar, Berlin, and Ilfracombe also elaborate on what will emerge as the dual focus of her

DOI: 10.4324/9781003362821-3

realism: a truthful documentation of reality and the creation of sympathy for characters or issues hitherto disregarded in fiction.

A Voyage Out

Travel and travel writing occupied a prominent place in Eliot's years as a journalist and budding novelist. In Germany between July 1854 and March 1855, in Weimar and Berlin, Eliot pored over many books of travel, primarily for her reviewing work.[4] She read Goethe's recollections of his *Italienische Reise*, travels of 1786–88 (published only in 1816–17); Heine's *Reisebilder*, a collection of descriptions from the 1820s about the poet's travels in Germany, England, Poland, and Italy; and Adolf Stahr's *Ein Jahr in Italien* about his 1845 sojourn in that country. The latter two were material for reviews for the *Leader*, or reading preparation.[5] Likewise, Margaret Fuller's *Letters from Italy*, which record the American's residence between 1847 and 1849, was reviewed the following year, as were Sir John Forbes' 1856 account of *Sight-Seeing in Germany and the Tyrol*, and two accounts by minor writers of Arctic explorations and a residency in Australia and New Zealand.[6]

Eliot encountered different narrative styles and travel models in these travelogues: Goethe worked from his diary entries and letters, and over several decades smoothed his style and reworked the story of what was essentially a flight to Italy, brought about by personal and professional crises, into a Grand Tour and a young man's 'education for a lifetime'.[7] His account is carefully orchestrated and contains afterthoughts, judgement, and summative sections entitled 'Reminiscences' which align with Eliot's 'Recollections' (a term she probably borrowed from Wordsworth). In contrast, Stahr preserved the diary style and, like Goethe, celebrated both his personal cultural education and the fact that he was not a tourist in Rome, but a long-term resident traveller who could take his time to see and experience Italy.[8] Eliot's review praised Fuller's book as both informative and visually (aesthetically) stimulating: it painted 'a picture of what has hitherto perhaps been a rough diagram in [the reader's] mind; and to the historian in search of materials it is likely to contribute some valuable touches'.[9] These thoughts on the duality of form and content, or documentation and imagination, would become central facets in Eliot's emerging realist poetic.

Likewise, literature's twin responsibility to 'both think and feel forcibly'[10] and to project this agenda onto readers through carefully crafted imagery would return in Eliot's earliest conceptualisation of realism in her *Modern Painters* review, on which she worked concurrently. In this article, she defined realism, for the first time, as 'a humble and faithful study of nature', which, sincere and free from falsity and 'vague forms', did not only 'teach truth' but teaches in such a way 'as to compel man's attention and sympathy'.[11] And sympathy, which would emerge as the central feature of Eliot's realist poetic, is both an ethical and affective dynamic as a novel's reader is asked to think and feel deeply, according to the Fuller review.

Eliot's dismissals of H. Butler Stoney's memoirs of a *Residence in Tasmania* as nothing more than a 'guidebook' and, likewise, Sir John Forbes' rendering of Germany as a clichéd 're-cast[ing of] Murray' are also relevant in this context as Eliot reveals what she seeks in successful (travel) writing, namely depth and originality.[12] For instance, she appreciates that travel writer Walter White, who trekked through Tyrol like Forbes, 'trusts to his own eyes' in his descriptions rather than falling back on previously published guidebook descriptions.[13] She also opines that Arctic explorer Elisha Kane seems to be 'an actor in the scenes he describes': subjective observation that results in faithful, immediate, and visual representations, writes Eliot, is superior as it 'touches the reader's intellectual and moral enthusiasm alike'.[14]

In short, Eliot's consumption and composition of travel writing began in Germany and continued for another year as she contemplated a move to fiction. Upon her return to Britain from Germany in March 1855, Eliot reworked her diary notes for two articles for *Fraser's Magazine*, published as 'Three Months in Weimar' and 'Liszt, Wagner, and Weimar' in the summer of 1855.[15] In a parallel move, the review of Ruskin's *Modern Painters* in the *Westminster Review* of April 1856 began her more structured thinking about realism. Between May and June 1856, Eliot and Lewes sojourned in Ilfracombe, Devon, where Lewes conducted research for his *Sea-Side Studies*. It was here that Eliot wrote her *Westminster* article on Wilhelm Riehl's ethnographic method, which expanded her ideas about how realist documentation not only provided information but also invoked an ethical response in the reader. When the Riehl article was published a month later in July 1856, Lewes and Eliot had moved on to a writing holiday in Tenby, Wales, where they stayed until August. Eliot had begun her article on the poet Young in April, and she completed it in Tenby. It would be one of her last pieces for the *Westminster Review*, appearing in January 1857. In it, she criticises abstract form as devoid of power and, therefore, irrelevant to the creation of sympathy which, she argues, requires specific details. However, it was primarily 'Silly Novels by Lady Novelists' that occupied her in the late summer and early autumn of 1856. 'Silly Novels', with its attack on (some) female authors' disregard of reality in their writing, leading to both preposterous and inferior products, was finished on 12 September 1856 and published in the *Westminster Review* in October. Eliot turned to writing 'Amos Barton' on 22 September 1856, though the idea and a draft of the introductory chapter can be traced back to the 1855 Berlin sojourn. The story was published in *Blackwood's* in January 1857, the same month as the Young article, when Eliot had already turned to 'Mr Gilfil's Love-Story'. A working holiday on the Scilly Isles (26 March to 11 May 1857) and Jersey (15 May to 24 July 1857) saw the completion of 'Gilfil' and 'Janet's Repentance'.

Given the interconnectedness of reviewing, travel and fiction writing, and thinking about realism in these formative years, in the following sections, I read Eliot's early travel accounts about Germany and Devon alongside the three stories of *Scenes of Clerical Life*.[16] I will focus specifically on the texts' narrative strategies as I analyse the writing of place, character, voice, and the figure of the narrator to describe Eliot's experimentation in the travelogues before she applied certain principles to her fiction.

Place

Eliot's 'Recollections of Weimar 1854' feature, among other things, detailed descriptions of the interiors of the homes of Schiller and Goethe. These are obvious attractions for any traveller to the small Thuringian town which saw its cultural 'golden age' in the latter half of the eighteenth century as it brought forth the two poetic luminaries and also the celebrated philosophers, literary critics, and writers, Johann Gottfried Herder and Christoph Martin Wieland. When Eliot and Lewes visited Weimar, the 'silver age'—after Goethe's death in 1832—continued with Romantic composer Franz Liszt who became the Grand Ducal court conductor. Eliot met Liszt on several occasions and published impressions about him and the Schiller and Goethe homes in two *Fraser's* articles.[17]

Comparisons between Eliot's diary entries, the 'Recollections', and the published 'Three Months in Weimar' reveal Eliot's 'prentice' work and processes of rewriting. The succinct facts in the journal ('Afternoon, went to Schiller's house.', 'Goethe's House. Study and Bedroom.' *JGE*, 23) first become an extended prose account in the 'Recollections', with detailed descriptions of all places and objects, actors who move within the space ('we'), and a (female) narrator who comments and reminisces. In the published account, all personal information—about living with Lewes, ill health, relationship bliss, and personal friendships—is eliminated, better bridges are built between episodes, and the narrator's voice becomes gender-neutral. The descriptions of place are copied verbatim from the 'Recollections' though the narrative and chronological order is changed to create a sequence and coherence that begins with the traveller's arrival, continues with various site visits (Belvedere, Goethe's Gartenhaus) leading to the description of the poets' homes, which are then completed by general observations on Weimar customs. On occasion, however, Eliot also returns to her original diary entry: for instance, she includes in the publication but not the 'Recollections' the fact that she played on Schiller's 'little claveçin', which was 'queer and feeble' in tone, prompting her to think about how the human voice, too, loses vigour with age.[18] Here, we see an additional meta-level of reflection in the process of rewriting for publication.

Describing Schiller's study, Eliot moves from the outside to the inside and the impersonal to the personal:

> It is a cheerful room with three windows, two towards the street and one looking on a little garden which divides the house from the neighbouring one. The writing table, of which he notes the purchase in one of his letters, and in one of the drawers of which he used to keep rotten apples, stands near the last-named windows. On the opposite side of the room near the stove is his little claveçin with his guitar lying on it.
>
> (*JGE*, 234)

The desk and musical instruments are evoked by Eliot as symbols of (the man's) refinement. '[S]ome ugly prints of Italian scenes' on the walls (*JGE*, 234) are dutifully noticed but dismissed due to their obviously unsophisticated nature which clashes with the idea of genius. Instead, Eliot's attention moves to the part of the house that has now become a gift shop. Here, her attention is arrested by a sketch of Schiller on his deathbed. Turning to the principles of phrenology, she expresses surprise at seeing how small Schiller's 'skull' and his 'intellectual region' are in this drawing (*JGE*, 234). Eliot declares that she cannot admire this representation because—having heard Schiller acquaintances profess that the sketch beautifies his forehead—she deplores its 'untruthfulness' (*JGE*, 235).

Two things become apparent: first, Eliot favours a faithful documentation and imposes this principle on herself and other artists. Second, we begin to see what Lewes meant by Eliot's descriptive abilities. In Berlin, shortly after the Weimar sojourn, Eliot would read to him her introductory chapter of 'Amos Barton', and as she recalls in 'How I Came to Write Fiction', he was positively 'struck' with it as 'a bit of pure description' (*JGE*, 289). Her eloquence was apparent to him, but he reminded her that only description combined with 'dramatic power' would make a novelist (*JGE*, 289), a point to which I will return.

In comparison with the terse sketch of Schiller, the one of Goethe's study not only reveals more of Eliot's ability to record 'trivial details' (*JGE*, 233) but also her growing experimentation with narrative and semantic layering. Certainly, Goethe is 'more important looking' for Eliot because of Lewes' research and Goethe's higher social position in Weimar (*JGE*, 235), but the description also shows a complexity absent in the Schiller sketch.

The depth comes from Eliot's detailed knowledge about Goethe's life—she read Lewes' biography of Goethe in Berlin and subsequently reviewed it for the *Leader*—and also affect. While she is distant in the Schiller account, she is emotionally involved in the Goethe one. Eliot describes the entrance hall to Goethe's house as imposing, with a broad staircase and statues displayed in niches. Context is added through the information that the Grand Duke presented the house to the poet for continued governmental services after his Italian journey, and that the poet was allowed to 'model [the interior] after his own taste', which resulted in 'an aftershine of Italian taste' (*JGE*, 235). Eliot's reaction to seeing the 'Römische Elegien' manuscript—'one likes to look at it'—inserts affect (*JGE*, 235). This emotional involvement then climaxes in the descriptions of Goethe's private rooms which 'deeply moved' her, Eliot writes (*JGE*, 235). Her prose uses more adjectives than before as she contrasts the rooms' modest interior with the author's poetic talent. There are 'two small windows' in the study that do not provide much light; a 'plain deal table' in the middle of the room; a 'high basket' in which Goethe kept his pocket handkerchiefs; a 'long sort of writing table and book case united', above which hangs the 'pin cushion, just as he left it, with visiting cards suspended on threads' (*JGE*, 235). A high writing desk on the opposite side of the room, with a Napoleon statue on it, completes the work space. Eliot adds further depth through reflection when she writes that these 'trifles' have been made 'sacred' by Goethe's 'greatness and death' (*JGE*, 235).

Next, Eliot's narration turns Goethe's bedroom into a lived space when she notices a 'tiny washing table with a small white basin on it and a sponge' (*JGE*, 235) and an armchair next to the bed. Eliot knows that Goethe adopted the habit of drinking his morning coffee in this armchair late in life. She creates a vivid image of the old poet, civil servant, and genius who, in the winter of a life devoted to poetry, service, and study (Eliot also refers to his mineralogical collection and library), sleeps, washes, and breakfasts in his bedroom. Her prose no longer just records information but is layered with signification as a place becomes a home and site of a person's life.

We reencounter the description of an interior in 'Mr Gilfil's Love-Story', the second story in the *Scenes* and the earliest in the collection's inner chronology. It begins with a death in the 1820s: Mr Gilfil, the well-liked, jovial old clergyman of Shepperton, has passed away, and even irregular churchgoers flock to his funeral to pay him their respects. Gilfil is described as a vicar who in life and in his profession placed human interactions and sympathies above 'the pure Gospel' and any doctrinal strictures.[19] In terms of philosophy, Eliot, the translator of Strauss' *Life of Jesus* and Feuerbach's *The Essence of Christianity*, celebrates humanism in this story: Gilfil's sermons do not preach about the metaphysical but are simple exhortations to his parishioners to show kindness, charity, and love towards others. Regarding plot and drama, the revelation about the clergyman's life, remembered only by the oldest parishioners, is his brief marriage to an Italian woman, Caterina Sarti, who died shortly after Gilfil accepted the Shepperton living.[20]

The account of Gilfil's house and, specifically, his deceased wife's room takes us back to the Weimar travelogue. The two pieces of writing are connected through the way in which the narrator makes people—whether a genius or a common man—and their lives accessible through mundane details. Such details, the narrator suggests in both the 'Recollections' and 'Mr Gilfil', are the key to understanding humanity, its sites, actors, and stories. In narrative terms, the focus on human detail for insights into humanity is not gendered—both the narrator in Eliot's published Weimar essays and in 'Mr Gilfil' are gender-neutral[21]—but particularities are crucial for the documentary and 'truthful' agenda of the travelogue and of realism.

Gilfil's sitting room is plain like Schiller's and Goethe's rooms. '[B]are tables', 'large old-fashioned horse-hair chairs', and a 'threadbare Turkey carpet' constitute the main pieces of furniture, described by the narrator in straightforward fashion.[22] There is, adds the narrator, no hint of a female presence: no portrait, no piece of embroidery, 'no faded bit of pretty triviality, hinting of taper-fingers and small feminine ambitions' ('Gilfil', ch. 1). Yet this gesture towards absence and bareness in the sitting room—as in the description of Goethe's study—points to something deeper and hidden, namely, the wife's private room which most parishioners would not have known to exist. Here, a 'little' dressing table with a 'dainty' mirror 'in a carved and gilt frame' signals the female sphere; the 'bits of wax-candle [which] were still in the branched sockets on the sides' of the dressing table imply former use and a life that is no more. The 'faded satin pincushion' signals the years gone by, as do two gowns by the door, which are 'of a fashion long forgotten'. The 'unfinished baby-cap, yellow with age' speaks of a death in childbirth, and the watercolours of Naples on the walls hint at Caterina's Italian heritage. The black lace kerchief, the perfume bottle, the green fan, and the 'tarnished silver embroidery' on 'tiny red slippers' reveal a liking for pretty things but also a class position that, perhaps, was left behind upon marriage to a vicar (all 'Gilfil', ch. 1). These items were precious to the wife in life and therefore remain meaningful to the widower. Two miniatures of the young couple complete the sketch of the room. Overall, as in the Goethe description, the place speaks of the underlying lived story and its actors: it is said that Gilfil's portrait captures his sanguine expression and clear eyes and Caterina's shows her beauty but also her fragility and melancholy in 'small features, thin cheeks … and large dark eyes' ('Gilfil', ch. 1). Between the Schiller house, the Goethe account, and the *Scenes*, Eliot increasingly adds meaning to her descriptions of place and demonstrates a more sophisticated understanding of fictional strategies. In the Weimar descriptions, she adds human touches to what she assumes her audience knows of the great men Schiller and Goethe; in 'Mr Gilfil', character has to be fully created, and Eliot shows how a detailed depiction of place can be further developed to achieve historical, characterological, and narratological depth.

Similar reworking with increased sophistication can be seen in the depictions of Belvedere, the Duke of Weimar's summer residence, and Cheverel Manor in 'Mr Gilfil'.[23] In the traveller's account of the *Lustschloss*, Eliot relates many details about the castle's vista, its garden, and its importance in people's lives. Most important, however, is that Eliot combines her truthful detail with an eye for aesthetics, especially, in the interplay and contrast of colours. In a salon inside the castle, green ivy plants and 'beautiful ferns arranged in tasteful baskets' contrast with the white walls and the canework furniture (*JGE*, 224). The firs and pines at the far end of the estate, with their 'fine mass of dark green', contrast in colour with the 'various and light foliage' of the limes, plane trees, and weeping birches closer to the castle (*JGE*, 224). The aim to provide a visual image in writing then becomes evident in Eliot's suggestion that glass globes placed on a pillar and bench in the garden reflect, 'like a pre-Raphaelite painting', the landscape 'in perfect miniature' (*JGE*, 224). Eliot's words are suggestive: the mention of the Pre-Raphaelites brings to mind Eliot's *Modern Painters* review but also evokes the Brotherhood's principle that art imitates nature, its colours and detail in complex compositions while gesturing towards a deeper, spiritual dimension. Eliot's words remain unexplored in the 'Recollections', an omission that renders the *Scenes* almost a belated analysis and application of Eliot's nascent aesthetic thinking first apparent in Weimar.

In 'Mr Gilfil', the idea of painting, and painting in words, is taken up as the narrator introduces Cheverel Manor. Assessed as a 'charming picture' and worthy of 'some English Watteau', the narrator plays with various painterly aspects: form (the house is built in the revival Gothic style surrounded by a landscaped garden), colour (there are trees and a lawn in all shades of green, multicoloured flowers, and a pond with a white swan), and perspective. Caterina and Lady Cheverel who, in a painting, 'would [be] represent[ed] with a few little dabs of red and white and blue' are also seen from a vantage point other than that used by the narrator, namely, from the dining room from where Sir Christopher, Mr Gilfil, and Captain Wybrow watch the women in the distance (all 'Gilfil', ch. 2).

Scholars have discussed the painterly quality of Eliot's writing.[24] The corpus for such analyses often consists of Eliot's reviews, including those on Ruskin, her repeated use of the words 'picture' or 'portrait' in the novels, and her rare aesthetic asides, like chapter 17 of *Adam Bede*, in which she likens her mode of writing to the 'rare, precious quality of truthfulness ... in many Dutch paintings'.[25] In short, narrative visuality is linked—by Eliot and subsequent scholars—to realism. Molly Youngkin brings Eliot's realistic 'word-painting' (the term used by Ruskin) into the context of the travel journals, a connection otherwise only made by Harris and Johnston.[26] She calls the travelogues important 'first attempts' in the genesis of Eliot's novelistic power and reads the Liszt portrait in the Weimar publication against the protagonist's character in 'Janet's Repentance', suggesting that, in the latter, Eliot develops her skills from a 'narrative-based painting to ... a more dynamic portrait' which she would perfect in Dorothea Brooke and Gwendolen Harleth.[27] I share Youngkin's assessment of the importance of Eliot's travelogues but make a larger claim about its preparatory nature for her work in fiction, beyond the realm of portraiture, and for representational issues more broadly. Yet Eliot's visualisation of character must also be addressed, and my analysis of the depiction of Amos Barton will show how it builds on character sketches in the German 'Recollections'.

Character

The Weimar travelogue is focused mostly on land- and cityscapes and even the chief living celebrity—Liszt—receives only a brief mention as a 'splendid' looking conductor of Wagner operas in the theatre and a 'grand fascinating' host and acquaintance (*JGE,* 233, 236).[28] However, the extended commentary on the man in the *Fraser's* article shows both Eliot's interest in and experimentation with character depiction, and, once more, the interconnected and mutually enabling nature of various published and unpublished writings during Eliot's apprenticeship, including the correspondence. A letter to Bessie Parkes of 10 September 1854 includes a brief but forceful description of Liszt which appears to have formed the basis for the published article.[29] It describes the composer as 'friendly' and 'a glorious creature in every way – a bright genius, with a tender, loving nature, and a face in which this combination is perfectly expressed. He has that "laideur divinisée" by the soul that gleams through it' (*GEL,* 2: 173). The publication then develops the character sketch of 'a glorious creature' further as Eliot salutes the man's musical genius and also celebrates 'Liszt the man'. She highlights the 'originality of his conversation and the brilliancy of his wit' and paints him as 'a man of various thought, of serious purpose, and of a moral nature which, in its mingled strength and gentleness, has the benignest influence on those about him'. As with Schiller's deathbed sketch, she focuses on Liszt's face as she seeks an echo of his genius in his features which, she says, have 'at once so strong and clear an outline and so rich a gamut of expression'.[30] Youngkin links the Liszt description to Eliot's realist poetic;[31] I would add that a comparison with the diary entries, letters, and 'Recollections' also reveals Eliot's increasing sophistication in writing character.

The Berlin travelogue of 1854–55 offers further evidence. It differs in tone and focus from the Weimar one, not only because Berlin affords new opportunities but because Eliot employs another register to describe what she sees. For example, she reports meticulously on the art in Berlin's museums and, more importantly, includes multiple character sketches. The depiction of the sculptor Rauch repeats the phrenological search for artistic genius and the refocussing on human attributes in the descriptions of Goethe and Schiller. Again, his 'harmonious' features, his complexion with its 'delicate freshness', his 'silky white hair' waving gracefully around his 'high forehead', and his benevolent and intelligent brown eyes are signs of the sculptor's superior mind but also his kindness (*JGE,* 248). Rauch's personality is further explained when Eliot observes the artist teaching his pupil a technique that will render a sculpture more lifelike by giving the impression that its 'head is thinking and that the eyes are seeing' (*JGE,* 249). The scene can be read as a comment on the representation of people in the different artistic media of sculpture and writing: the key is to show the life and humanity behind one's appearance.

The description of Professor Gruppe takes Eliot's experimentation with character to another level as she uncovers contradictory traits which render the man more complex, and her representation of him more realist. Gruppe is described as a scholar of drama, a poet, a political writer, Goethe's friend, a keen hunter, and an inventor. Even more remarkable to Eliot than his learning are his family circumstances—his wife is 30 years his junior and he has young children—and his inconsistent character. Gruppe displays '[t]alent, fertility and versatility' in his speech and manner but while this suggests a 'fervid temperament', that impression is countered by an astonishing slowness at apprehending other people's ideas and the 'childish naïveté' with which he enjoys poor jokes and other trivialities (*JGE*, 246).

Gruppe's delight in unscholarly pleasures is elaborated by Eliot with reference to a day when Lewes entertained Gruppe's family and friends with card tricks. At this point, Eliot moves from description to dramatisation; from telling to showing; from watching to witnessing and participating; from sketch to analysis.[32] In the 'Recollections', Gruppe's character becomes three-dimensional through the ambiguities that create layers but also establish his ordinariness: he is a respected intellectual but also a father; he knew Goethe but likes bad jokes; he is inspiring but also trying when he fatigues his guests with a long recital in a warm room without noticing anyone's discomfort. In short, Gruppe displays aspects of distinction but is also a recognisable human being with many foibles. The 'Recollections' show Eliot's attempts to portray a common but remarkable humanity.

Eliot concurrently began to theorise realism in her reviews. The article on Wilhelm Riehl—written a year after Berlin, in Ilfracombe—praises an ethnographic work method: careful observation and study lead to the truthful representation of all aspects of life. Her article on 'Silly Novels', completed shortly after Ilfracombe, highlights concerns about a want of real and relatable characters and themes in some authors' novels. Eliot argues in the Riehl review that the realist representation of the strenuous nature of farmyard labour, the farmers' coarse jokes and bad teeth, carrot-scraping old women and 'people as they are' is not only truthful but, importantly, creates 'our sympathies'.[33] In a linked argument, Eliot rejects (personified) abstractions, which she discusses in relation to Edward Young's poetry, as she sees them lead to falsification. Abstraction, she maintains, is a 'want of genuine emotion' because affect is linked to 'particulars, and only in a faint and secondary manner [to] abstractions'.[34] An absence of emotion keeps the writer from achieving sympathy.

If the Gruppe portrayal succeeds in creating a fellow feeling, the novelistic portrayal of Amos Barton deals with compassion and understanding on the levels of both content and form. Barton's most prominent feature, Thomas Noble writes, is his 'lack of distinction'.[35] The opening descriptions of the Shepperton curate, who is active some decades after Gilfil's death, are far from encouraging: about 40, Barton is bald, 'with features of no particular shape, and an eye of no particular expression' ('Barton', ch. 2).

He is descended from an unimpressive blood line and has enjoyed a mediocre education. He lives, with his wife and six children, on a curate's small income. In terms of his professional and personal life, the narrator says with both humour and lament, Barton 'resembled rather a Belgian railway-horn, which shows praiseworthy intentions inadequately fulfilled' (ch. 2). In his preaching, as his workhouse sermon shows, he fails to connect his religious message (a low-church doctrine about man's sinful nature which requires salvation) with his audience's needs and intellectual level. However, he is not a bigot like Dr Cumming, whom Eliot criticised harshly in her review on 'Evangelical Teaching' which came out just prior to the *Scenes*.[36] Unlike Gilfil, though, Barton places dogma above common sense and human nature. Tone deaf to his congregation's needs, he fails to respond to and appreciate his wife's attentions, domestic labour, and sacrifices that ensure his comfort. He also does not realise that it is Milly's personality rather than his which assures the Bartons' social network.

As Eliot's narrator elaborates, it is precisely the 'humble experience of an ordinary fellow-mortal' and his or her 'commonplace troubles' which modern (realist) fiction must represent faithfully because these 'stir ... sympathy' and 'win [the readers'] tears for real sorrow' ('Barton', ch. 7).[37] The fictitious Mrs Farthingale, who prefers the ideal and comedic in novels, is reminded by the chronicler that most Britons are commonplace like Barton and neither ideal, exceptional or heroic, nor vicious or mysterious. Realism's task is to show that the life stories of those human souls 'that loo[k] out through dull grey eyes and ... spea[k] in a voice of quite ordinary tones' contain 'sacred joys', 'unspoken sorrows' and, overall, as much poetry and pathos as anyone else's (ch. 5). And if this does not please, the narrator urges the reader to pick up last season's sensationalist and sentimental novels instead. The echoes of Eliot's 'Silly Novels' review of October 1856, finished a fortnight before Eliot started 'Amos Barton', are unmistakable as the reviewer also dismisses novels by female authors who lack technical writing competencies, 'genuine observation, humour, and passion', but still manage to find a publisher and readership.[38]

In 'Amos Barton', Eliot combines the description of circumstances, the illumination of her poetic principles, and the dramatisation of character with plot. Problems arise as Barton commits a blunder, rather than a sin, by admitting the selfish Countess Czerlaski into his home. The Countess is encountering financial difficulties after her half-brother elopes with her maid, and she is too proud to forgive him or ask for his continued support. Milly is touched by the Countess' apparent affection for her and feels pity for the friendless widow while Amos believes he has risen into aristocratic circles. The curate's punishment for his hubris arrives when Milly, over-exerting herself because of the Countess' increasingly inconsiderate demands for comforts, dies after giving birth to a stillborn child. Amos loses his wife and, by a cruel stroke of fate soon after, his parish as the vicar gives the living to his own brother-in-law.

The sympathy Eliot's narrator spoke of in chapter 5 takes effect on the level of plot but also vis-à-vis reader reactions. The parishioners who never warmed to Barton are now moved by his grief as they collect money and look after his children while the curate torments himself that he did not love Milly the way she deserved. Barton and his children move to an industrialised part of Britain. The story ends years later when Amos visits Milly's grave in Shepperton, accompanied by his adult daughter Patty who has inherited her mother's capacity for selfless love and now cares for her ageing father. Eliot experiments in this story with readerly sympathy and the way in which particularities generate affective power. We see in Eliot's first published story and her 'Riehl' and 'Young' reviews of the same period the author's aesthetic and moral principles which Knoepflmacher calls the double aim and twin pulls of realism: the documentation of a temporal actuality along with permanent ethical values.[39]

Eliot, having experimented with characterisation in her Berlin travelogue, develops her technique in 'Amos Barton'. Her publisher John Blackwood raised her method of characterisation, and specifically the matter of psychological realism during the publication of the three *Scenes*. Concerning 'Amos Barton', Blackwood wondered whether Eliot had not 'fallen into the error of trying too much to explain the characters of [her] actors by description instead of allowing them to evolve in the action of the story' (*GEL*, 2: 272). Lewes' original concerns about Eliot's dramatic powers, compared to her descriptive ones, resonate with this comment. Eliot was demoralised by Blackwood's criticism, as Lewes communicated to the publisher, urging him to tread more carefully with the first-time author (*GEL*, 2: 273). Her reaction and response, however, was confident and even fiery when three months later Blackwood queried whether Gilfil's noble character and love for Caterina were sufficiently credible given Caterina's frank infatuation with Wybrow. 'I am unable to alter anything in relation to the delineation or development of character', Eliot wrote to Blackwood, 'as my stories always grow out of my psychological conception of the dramatis personae' (*GEL*, 2: 299). Eliot had argued a similar point in Berlin in 1855, in a discussion with the scholar Adolf Stahr, whose work she read and reviewed: the debate with him was about the denouement of Goethe's *Wahlverwandtschaften* which Stahr thought far-fetched while Eliot argued for it as a logical consequence of individual character portrayals (see *JGE*, 247). In this spirited Blackwood reply two years later, we see evidence of Eliot's growing dramatic ability together with her renewed defence of real 'mixed human beings' (*GEL*, 2: 299). She relied on showing rather than telling and had begun to let a story or character develop the way the internal laws of narrative, human nature, or 'truthfulness' required. Weaknesses, inconsistencies, and complexities, she wrote, make characters and plots 'true' and elicit the reader's 'tolerant judgment, pity, and sympathy' (*GEL*, 2: 299). In this endeavour, the narrator plays an important role too, as my next section shows.

Voice(s) and the Narrator Figure

My principal concern in discussing 'Janet's Repentance' is with Eliot's realist poetic and, in particular, the narrator's role in concurrently relaying knowledge and creating sympathy. In other words, the narrator's task is twofold as he—and the narrator is explicitly male in the third story of *Scenes*—moves between the epistemological and ethical realms. Like Rae Greiner, in 'Sympathy Time: Adam Smith, George Eliot and the Realist Novel', I want to think about how 'distance' and 'identification' in the text are created by and through the narrator. Unlike Greiner, however, I return to Bakhtin's concept of the novel's dialogic multivoicedness to suggest that Eliot's writing strategies for 'Janet's Repentance' are foreshadowed in 'Recollections of Ilfracombe, 1856', the most accomplished and stylistically varied piece of her early period. Once more the travelogue, in combination with the contemporaneous review articles, especially those on *Modern Painters* and Riehl's ethnography, expounds the principles of a detailed observation of particularities as it experiments with affective writing.[40]

'Ilfracombe' is the writing exercise that accompanies the theory, and various strategies concerning voice, modality, mood, and style are explored as Eliot thinks through realism's truthfulness and ethical responsibility. Of particular note are the contrasts and conflicts that start the essay. Arriving in Barnstaple, Lewes and Eliot meet a sexton and ask him whether they can 'see the Cathedral', though they demur when the man tells them he can only '*show* [them] the Cathedral'. Eliot regrets taking a seat inside the stage coach because of disagreeable travel companions while Lewes 'had a pleasanter journey outside'. Ilfracombe is an 'ugly' town with 'beautiful' surrounding hills. The accommodation recommended by a previous traveller has a 'shabby ill-furnished parlour and bedroom' while a 'smart and expensive' looking house the Leweses stumble upon turns out to be both pleasant and affordable (*JGE*, all 263). Impressions can be deceptive, acknowledges Eliot, and seeing 'correctly' has to be learned: what Eliot and Lewes believe to be polyps on their first sea-side specimen hunt are actually bits of coralline (*JGE*, 264). Eliot continues that ignorance can only be countered through observation that enhances understanding: it is necessary 'for the eye to be educated by objects as well as ideas' (*JGE*, 266). Realism requires many voices and perspectives and a narrator who can portray this heteroglossia adequately, so that perspectives are not just opposed but enter into dialogue. 'Call us not weeds—we are flow'rs of the sea', Eliot quotes from the Elizabeth Aveline poem, directing her implied reader's attention to the fact that truth is hardly found in a single viewpoint but requires checks by examination and oftentimes correction.

The description of a walk to Chambercombe shows, once more, the power of observation and an awareness of viewpoint as Eliot describes farmhouses surrounded by gates, bridges, streams, woods, 'wild verdure and flowers [in] the hedgerows', and guarded by a 'quiet' donkey or a 'great awkward puppy which came flopping after us' (*JGE*, 268). And on her return, Eliot thinks that the sea stretching over the horizon now looks 'all the finer to us because we had been turning our backs upon it, and contemplating another sort of beauty' (*JGE*, 269).

The account also reveals shifting perspectives between distance and proximity. This oscillation is not only created literally as Eliot's roving eye moves from near to far sights but also metaphorically as the writing moves between information-giving and affect-producing. There are the 'fact[s]', 'distinctive' and 'definite' ideas (*JGE*, 272), but also the picturesque landscape images and short dramatisations which add visuality and presentism. One example is the anecdote of the black pig which possesses such 'an amiable and sociable disposition' that it decides to accompany the Leweses on their walk—'without the formality of an introduction', Eliot adds humorously (*JGE*, 271). Overall, like the traveller's final vista from the 'Ladies' Cove', knowledge and information denote a 'brilliant distance', while affect, which can be invoked via the aesthetic or comical route, creates proximity through feelings of 'warmth and love' (*JGE*, 272). In the end, Eliot seems to say, affect is also a sort of knowing.

This is Eliot's experiment with realism and novelistic writing which is truthful and comprehensive through a dialogic agenda and changing perspectives (distance, proximity) and modalities (information, affect). The Ilfracombe travelogue ends with Eliot's reference to 'two "Cockle women"', who 'would make a fine subject for a painter ... treading the earth with unconscious majesty ... They are weather-beaten and wizened', while '[t]he grander of the two' has 'bright' and 'piercing' eyes that belie her humble attire (*JGE*, 273). Here are the forebears of the carrot-scraping old women in the Riehl review, and the link to Janet Dempster's tall and unconscious majesty.

'Janet's Repentance', set in Milby in the early 1830s, tells the story of a woman's conversion to Evangelicalism. Once a beautiful and intelligent young woman, Janet has in recent years become an alcoholic trapped in a verbally and physically abusive marriage with the lawyer Robert Dempster, once a promising man and a desirable marriage match but now an argumentative drunkard. Janet is initially on the side of her strong-willed husband who believes the Reverend Tryan's evangelical ways to be those of a dissenter, but changes her mind when she witnesses Tryan's sympathetic behaviour and hears his story. Robert evicts Janet from their house one drunken night and the woman finds shelter with a female friend and solace through Tryan's emotional support. When Robert suffers an accident a few days later, Janet returns to nurse him until his death. Her friendship with Mr Tryan, who is suffering from the long-term effects of consumption, continues, and Janet offers him a comfortable home until his inevitable death. The story forwards to the present where Janet, having adopted the daughter of a distant cousin after the events recounted, is now a grandmother.

As long ago as 1961, W.J. Harvey pointed out that Eliot's narrators are crucial in the reading process as they are the 'bridges between our world and the world of the novel'.[41] Harvey moves from this brief suggestion to focus on the artistry of Eliot's omniscient narrator, but we may use his observation as a starting point to explore the other aspects of the relationship between narrator, characters, and reader I suggested earlier. Specifically, I will explore how a narrator's knowledge, ideologies, and empathies shape the readers' cognitive and affective responses to the story. The narrator in 'Janet's Repentance' identifies himself as male and in his late thirties. He is educated (he speaks Greek, ch. 13), informed in religious controversy (ch. 3), and often philosophical in his comments (ch. 5, ch. 9). He has access to the women's sphere (ch. 3) and speaks out in favour of a woman's equal access to education (ch. 5). There is humour in his first description of the Tryanite women's circle (ch. 3). As a Milby insider and acquainted with the people and events described, he considers himself a 'faithful' chronicler of events and a 'copy[ist]' of facts (ch. 9).[42]

The narrator may be a witness of a larger religious shift, as evidenced by Janet's conversion story, but he also sees and understands human character. He speaks a Feuerbachian discourse of how 'divine' human sympathy and a secular humanism help suffering individuals more than abstract doctrine ('Janet', ch. 19, ch. 22), a point Eliot scholars have elaborated.[43] Eliot generates this fellow feeling through narratological methods and devices she explored in the 'Ilfracombe' travelogue. At the heart of this endeavour sits a dialogism, embodied by the narrator, that asks the readers to observe and think as well as judge and feel. The narrator's central characteristics are empathy and judgement as no character is idealised, spared criticism, or seen as anything but human. While some people, writes the narrator, might see the curate as '[n]ot a remarkable specimen', with a limited intellect and a 'too narrow doctrinal system', he sees a man who 'struggles his way along the stony road' and who therefore deserves our sympathy because he 'pushes manfully on, with fluctuating faith and courage, with a sensitive failing body' ('Janet', ch. 10). The narrator endeavours to tell his story with nuance, impartiality, and multivoicedness.

The first two chapters of 'Janet's Repentance' are largely dialogue. In the first chapter, Robert Dempster leads an intoxicated rant against Tryan's new Evangelical initiative, an additional evening lecture, by arguing that it insults the existing pastor who has served the community for 50 years. The miller Tomlinson thinks Sunday school morally suspect because to him it is a place for 'wenches to meet their sweethearts, and brew mischief' (ch. 1). The educated Luke Byles adds a philosophical note to the debate—that sectarianism destroys the Church—but is silenced by Dempster when he corrects the lawyer's misinformation. More voices come in, literally and figuratively, when Doctor Pilgrim enquires how Dempster's petition lobbying the vicar to forbid the evening lecture is progressing. The churchwarden Mr Budd then gives an update on how many and which congregation members are likely to support the petition.

Knowledge, this episode suggests, can only be found in the debating of different, even conflicting, viewpoints and by providing contextualised facts. Though sadly (as Foucault would argue much later), truth is not the same as discursive power: Dempster maintains the upper hand when Byles walks out of the argument in which he had the facts but the bully Dempster the louder voice. Two chapters later, the debate structure appears again, between the Tryanite side and the female, domestic sphere, when the Miss Linnets, Miss Pratt, Miss Eliza Pratt, and Mrs Pettifer work on Tryan's lending library project and discuss the curate and his work.

Knowledge also requires context, as the contributions of Byles and Pilgrim show. In the second chapter—between two debates—the narrator offers perspective and background as he urges the reader in a direct address to 'dismiss from your mind' all preconceived ideas and 'transport your imagination' to the different time and place represented in this story ('Janet', ch. 1). In a method that anthropologist Clifford Geertz would call 'thick description' and literary scholars the building blocks of realism, the narrator sketches Milby's 'not inconveniently high' moral standards, its 'very abundant supply of stimulants', and the adoption of Evangelicalism in the town's middle-class homes not only as 'a nuisance' but a force to reckon with (all ch. 2)

Janet's story is told by a combination of knowledge, one pillar of the realist poetic, and the other pillar, sympathy. The narrator thus paints a complex image of the woman, describing her through the eyes both of himself and others. The villagers comment on her beauty, her hair, her 'superior education' (ch. 3), and they regard the marriage to Dempster as due to the excessive pride of Janet and her mother in catching the eye of a professional man. They think Janet's abuse by her husband regrettable but consider it, like her turn to alcohol 'to blunt her feelings' (ch. 3) and her continued charity in town, as unalterable facts.

Before long, the narrator himself describes Janet. In an act of showing rather than telling—enhanced by a rhetorical move to the present tense—Janet is seen awaiting the return of her inebriated husband while having drunk herself into a 'leaden stupor' too (ch. 13). Robert arrives and turns violent as his 'heavy arm is lifted to strike her. The blow falls—another—and another. ... "O Robert! pity! pity!"' (ch. 4). The complexity of the relationship of Janet and Robert cannot be shown here: Janet reminiscences about their happy courtship and early years and forgives Robert on his deathbed; Robert's mother, to whom he is a good son, blames Janet for remaining childless and caring more for other peoples' welfare than her husband's; Mrs Raynor, Janet's mother, accepts her daughter's misery and alcoholism rather stoically as typical of a wife's lot. Thus, sympathy for the eponymous heroine arises in the story through scenes of told *and* shown characteristics.

In addition, sympathy is generated in narratorial asides, which become more frequent. In these, the narrator reiterates that sympathy requires particularities: '[i]deas are often poor ghosts', but when they 'are made flesh', 'breathe upon us with warm breath, … touch us with soft responsive hands' and 'look at us with sad sincere eyes', they manage to 'speak to us in appealing tones' (ch. 19). Once more we must cross-reference Eliot's review article 'Worldliness and Other-Worldliness: The Poet Young' and her Feuerbach translation, where there is also the proposition made in 'Janet's Repentance' that the 'act of confiding in human sympathy, the consciousness that a fellow-being [is] listening … with patient pity' is an expression of 'faith' and a 'divine' act (ch. 25). The narrator concludes that sympathy has its own transcendental reward system, which 'refuses to be settled by equations' (ch. 32): the angels, says the narrator, are touched more by the misery and salvation of one erring individual than by the uncomplicated bliss of ninety-nine others. The story of Janet's flaws, errors, wretchedness, and ultimate repentance and salvation is novelistic material, and the reader, who feels empathy and satisfaction at the outcome, is rewarded too, having his own ethical faculties tested, and either reoriented or confirmed.

Overall, these narratorial comments are paradoxical. They disconnect and distance as intrusive insertions while they simultaneously draw in the reader through a discussion of sympathy on the level of the story and the act of reading. In the same way that Eliot experimented with distance and proximity in the 'Ilfracombe' travelogue, 'Janet's Repentance' shows what Fredric Jameson calls the 'antinomies of realism', which work through a perpetual pull and push of opposing gravitational forces.[44] The narrator's are mature comments about the great dynamics of life as Janet's story is established as that of a 'scented geranium' in a gin-drenched, 'noisy pot-house' ('Janet', ch. 2). Through 'Janet's Repentance', the realist representation takes the reader into the realm of timeless moral values.

Conclusion

It is important to note that in 'How I Came to Write Fiction', Eliot maps her recollections onto particular places: in Berlin, she read the introductory chapter of 'Amos Barton' to Lewes (*JGE*, 289). The idea for the eventual title of her first story came to her in Tenby, and the idea for the *Scenes of Clerical Life* in Richmond. In Richmond Park, Lewes expressed his enjoyment of Eliot's 'good dialogue' and pathos in the new parts of 'Amos Barton' (*JGE*, 290). And 'Janet's Repentance' was begun at Scilly and sent to Blackwood from Jersey. Although Eliot briefly mentions in 'How I Came to Write Fiction' that the 'Silly Novels' review postponed her work on 'Amos', she largely avoids referring to her other writing of the period. Perhaps this was deliberate, and Eliot might have thought that the image of a 'prentice' author who drafted, revised, and even carried out writing exercises would tarnish the image of the writing genius.

This essay has made the case for reading the Germany and Devon travelogues as preparatory work at a time when Mary Ann Evans contemplated a move from reviewing to fiction and to becoming George Eliot. These travel recollections—begun in diary entries and letters and reworked into extended prose narratives that would in some cases also be published—reveal how Eliot experimented with place writing, character, and the narrator figure while also thinking about an audience. Reading Eliot's *Scenes of Clerical Life* alongside her travelogues of the years 1854 to 1857 and with reference to the aesthetic reflections in her reviewing work provides important insights into how Eliot conceptualised and gradually honed her narrative skills and realist poetic. She may not have liked the thought, and neither might we: yet we cannot deny that George Eliot was a novice and beginner once, too.

Notes

1 See Rosemarie Bodenheimer, *The Real Life of Mary Ann Evans: George Eliot, Her Letters and Fiction* (Ithaca: Cornell University Press, 1994); Margaret Harris and Judith Johnston, 'Introduction', in *The Journals of George Eliot*, ed. Margaret Harris and Judith Johnston (Cambridge: Cambridge University Press, 1998), xvi–xxv; Barbara Hardy, *George Eliot: A Critic's Biography* (London: Continuum, 2006); Rosemary Ashton, 'How George Eliot Came to Write Fiction', *The George Eliot Review*, 40 (2009), 7–13; Fionnuala Dillane, *Before George Eliot: Marian Evans and the Periodical Press* (Cambridge: Cambridge University Press, 2013). I will use 'George Eliot' throughout the essay even though the journeys to Germany and Devon occurred before her adoption of the pseudonym.

2 See F.R. Leavis, *The Great Tradition: George Eliot, Henry James, Joseph Conrad* (New York: Stewart, 1950), 36; U.C. Knoepflmacher, *George Eliot's Early Novels: The Limits of Realism* (Berkeley and Los Angeles: University of California Press, 1968), 86; Catherine Nicholl, '*Scenes of Clerical Life*: George Eliot's Apprenticeship', PhD dissertation (University of Minnesota, 1971).

3 Consequently, my question is not so much whether Eliot's travels left an imprint on her writing, a question that McCormack, Röder-Bolton, and David answer in the affirmative, while Rignall concludes that Eliot's journeys had 'no novels as their direct product' (139). My question is, rather, whether her travel *writing* provided ideas about, or even blueprints for, the form of her novels. See Kathleen McCormack, *George Eliot's English Travels: Composite Characters and Coded Communication* (New York and London: Routledge, 2005); Gerlinde Röder-Bolton, *George Eliot in Germany, 1854-55: 'Cherished Memories'* (Aldershot: Ashgate, 2006); Deirdre David, '"Getting out of the Eel Jar": George Eliot's Literary Appreciation', in *Creditable Warriors, 1830-1876*, ed. Michael Cotsell (London: Ashfield, 1990), 257–72; John Rignall, 'George Eliot and the Idea of Travel', *Yearbook of English Studies*, 36 (2006), 139–52.

4 See Avrom Fleischman, 'George Eliot's Reading: A Chronological List', *George Eliot-George Henry Lewes Studies*, 54/55 (2008), 1–106.

5 [George Eliot], 'The Art of the Ancients', *The Leader*, 6 (March 1855), 257–8; [George Eliot], 'Heine's Poems', *The Leader*, 6 (September 1855), 843–4.

6   [George Eliot], 'Margaret Fuller's Letters from Italy', *The Leader*, 7 (17 May 1856), 475; [George Eliot], 'Sight-seeing in Germany and the Tyrol', *The Saturday Review* (6 September 1856), 424–5; [George Eliot], 'History, Biography, Voyages and Travels', *Westminster Review*, 67 (January 1857), 288–306.

7   Johann Wolfgang von Goethe, *Italian Journey [1786-1788]*, tr. W.H. Auden and Elizabeth Mayer (London: Penguin, 1970), 128.

8   Adolf Stahr, *Ein Jahr In Italien* (Oldenburg: Schulze, n.y.), 152: 'Welch Glück, dass ich nicht dazu verdammt bin, Rom als Tourist zu sehen!' (12 June 1845)

9   Eliot, 'Fuller's Letters', 475.

10 Eliot, 'Fuller's Letters', 475.

11 [George Eliot], 'John Ruskin's *Modern Painters, Vol. III*,' *Westminster Review* (April 1856), reprinted in George Eliot, *Selected Critical Writings*, ed. Rosemary Ashton (Oxford: Oxford University Press, 2000), 248–9.

12 Eliot, 'Sight-seeing', 424.

13 Eliot, 'Sight-seeing', 425.

14 Eliot, 'History', 166, 167.

15 [George Eliot], 'Three Months in Weimar', *Fraser's Magazine* (June 1855), 699–706; [George Eliot], 'Liszt, Wagner, and Weimar', *Fraser's Magazine* (July 1855), 48–62.

16 The 'Recollections of the Scilly Isles and Jersey' are of lesser importance than the earlier travel journals for my argument about the intellectual and actual shaping of Eliot's writing. They contain beautiful descriptions of land- and seascapes which resemble, narratively, those of Ilfracombe, yet it is obvious that these 'Recollections' are not writing exercises or experiments, like the earlier travel memories. The Scilly Isles account is a rather perfunctory write-up of Eliot's journal entries: the personal (illnesses and deaths in her family) merges with the professional (a list of books she read) as Eliot mainly summarises events in a matter-of-fact way. The report about Jersey is more poetic, as it contains affective passages in which Eliot conveys, like Lawrence Sterne's Sentimental Traveller, impressions certain places made on her.

17 See note 15 for details of *Fraser's* publication. In this chapter, I quote from the more complete *Journals of George Eliot*, ed. Margaret Harris and Judith Johntson (Cambridge: Cambridge University Press, 1998): hereafter *JGE*, cited in-text with reference to the page number. Especially in the 'Three Months' art-icle, this edition preserves the personal comments and observations that Eliot cut for publication.

18 *JGE*, 23 and 'Three Months', 704.

19 George Eliot, *Scenes of Clerical Life*, ed. Thomas A. Noble (Oxford: Oxford World's Classics, 2015), ch. 1. Further references to this edition appear paren-thetically in text.

20 Incidentally, Caterina dies in the same room and under the same circumstances—childbirth—as Milly Barton dies two generations later, which Josie Billington highlights in her Introduction to the World's Classics edition of *Scenes of Clerical Life* (xxv). This subtle cross-reference connects the two stories and provides Eliot's social world with temporal and spatial depth and human interconnectedness.

21 The gender of Eliot's narrator has generated a lot of debate, also in the context of Mary Ann Evans' pseudonym. See Gillian Beer, *George Eliot* (Sussex: Harvester, 1986); Rosemary Ashton, *George Eliot: A Life* (London: Penguin, 1996). Beer

sees the (allegedly) male narrator in *Scenes* as used by Eliot to 'reinforce the "masculine" provenance of the writing and playfully to dramatise that persona' (39). In contrast, Ashton suggests that the narrator of *Amos Barton* is androgynous because of his knowledge of domesticity (171). I will return to the issue of the narrator's gender later.

22 Again, Eliot's desire for precision expresses itself here: her first readers, according to Blackwood, thought the author of the *Scenes* a clergyman and/or 'a *man of Science*', because of his knowledge and the 'precision of expression'. Eliot's reply—that this was realism, although she did not use the term at this point but only referenced the Dutch School of painting—begins her poetic thinking. See *The George Eliot Letters*, 9 vols, ed. Gordon S. Haight (New Haven and London: Yale University Press, 1954–78), 2: 291–4.

23 The Belvedere description was also published in the latter section of 'Liszt, Wagner, and Weimar', *Fraser's Magazine* (July 1855), 48–62.

24 Daniel P. Deneau, 'Imagery in *The Scenes of Clerical Life*', *Victorian Newsletter*, 28 (1965), 18–22; Hugh Witemeyer, *George Eliot and the Visual Arts* (New Haven: Yale University Press, 1979); Darrell Mansell Jr., 'Ruskin and George Eliot's "Realism"', *Criticism*, 7 (1965), 203–16. Deneau points in general terms to Eliot's interest in 'imagery' and argues for her increasingly complex ability to visualise scenes between the early and mature fiction (22). Witemeyer tracks the paintings she saw, the genres and styles she encountered (portraiture, history painting, genre painting, landscape), and gives examples of how this interest in visuality, perspective, and focus reveals itself in her writing. More interesting for my purposes is the line of argument begun by Mansell, which relates Eliot's reviewing of Ruskin's *Modern Painters* for the 1856 *Westminster Review* to her formulating a realist aesthetic. Eliot had earlier reviewed Ruskin's *Stones of Venice* for the 1854 *Leader*.

25 George Eliot, *Adam Bede*, ed. Carol A. Martin (Oxford: Oxford World's Classics, 2008), ch. 17.

26 See Molly Youngkin, '"Narrative Readings of the Images She Sees": Principles of Nineteenth-Century Narrative Painting in George Eliot's Fiction', *George Eliot-George Henry Lewes Studies*, 67 (2015), 1–29; Harris and Johnston, xx.

27 Youngkin, '"Narrative Readings"', 8, 11.

28 Critics later credited Eliot's article with having popularised Wagner in Britain.

29 Eliot's diary merely records meetings and a pleasant conversation with Liszt (e.g. 10 August, 17 August, 18 September, 27 October, 2 November) but does not elaborate on his character (*JGE*, 21–9).

30 All references to [Eliot], 'Liszt', 48.

31 Youngkin, '"Narrative Readings"', 10.

32 The poetic move is also significant when one compares Eliot's description of Gruppe in a letter to Sara Hennell of 9 January 1855, which describes but does not dramatise, as the letter merely lists his diverse professional accomplishments (*GEL*, 2: 192–3).

33 [George Eliot], 'The Natural History of German Life', *Westminster Review* (July 1856), reprinted in *Essays of George Eliot*, ed. Thomas Pinney (London: Routledge, 1963), 270.

34 [George Eliot], 'Worldliness and Other-Worldliness: The Poet Young', *Westminster Review* (January 1857), reprinted in Pinney, *Essays of George Eliot*, 371.

35 Thomas A. Noble, *George Eliot's Scenes of Clerical Life* (New Haven: Yale University Press, 1965), 66.

36 [George Eliot], 'Evangelical Teaching: Dr Cumming', *Westminster Review*, 64 (October 1855), 436–62.

37 See Noble's ch. 3 on sympathy in *Scenes of Clerical Life*.

38 [George Eliot], 'Silly Novels by Lady Novelists', *Westminster Review* (October 1856), reprinted in Pinney, *Essays of George Eliot*, 324.

39 Knoepflmacher, *Early Novels*, 1, 87.

40 See Rae Greiner, 'Sympathy Time: Adam Smith, George Eliot and the Realist Novel', *Narrative*, 17 (October 2009), 291–311. Incidentally, I believe that the dialogic, multivoiced character and dual aims of knowledge and sympathy—visible in 'Ilfracombe' and 'Janet's Repentance'—also explain the diverse, conflicting interpretations of Eliot's narrator figure. Older assessments included calling Eliot's narrator figure a clever fictional device (Huggins) as well as 'lazy', overbearing, or obtrusive (Steiner, Pascal). Concerning 'Janet's Repentance', Mossman calls the narrator a 'controlling' one who is 'often sexist and snobbish, always conservative and didactic' (12), while Nicholl finds it 'a pleasant surprise' to find the narrator and his comments if not 'completely absent', then at least at the narrative's 'fringes' (8–9). See Cynthia Huggins, '*Adam Bede*: Author, Narrator and Narrative', *The George Eliot Review*, 23 (1992), 35–9; George Steiner, 'A Preface to Middlemarch', *Nineteenth Century Fiction*, 9 (1955): 262–79; Roy Pascal, *The Dual Voice: Free Indirect Speech and its Functioning in the Nineteenth-Century European Novel* (Manchester: Manchester University Press, 1977); Mark Mossmann, "Violence, Temptation and Narrative in George Eliot's 'Janet's Repentance' ", *Journal of the Short Story in English*, 35 (Autumn 2000), 9–20. Note that my focus shifts from analyses of the narrator's artistry into the ways in which they create and intellectual and affective bond with characters and the readers.

41 W.J. Harvey, *The Art of George Eliot* (London: Chatto and Windus, 1961), 83.

42 As Newton stresses, the world the narrator presents is real to him, which in turn imbues the novel with realism. See K.M. Newton, 'The Role of the Narrator in George Eliot's Novels', *The Journal of Narrative Theory*, 3 (1973), 101.

43 Jumeau, Noble, and Lerner have called 'Janet's Repentance' a story about the 'human dimension of religion . . . converting Christian charity into human sympathies'. Human sympathy possesses a 'sacred quality', and Janet's religious conversion is a result of Tryan's 'pure humanity'. Respectively Alain Jumeau, 'Scenes of Clerical Life: George Eliot's Own Version of Conversion', *The George Eliot Review*, 40 (2009), 23; Noble, *Scenes*, 88; Lawrence Lerner, *The Truthtellers: Jane Austen, George Eliot, D.H. Lawrence* (London: Chatto and Windus, 1967), 30.

44 See Fredric Jameson, *The Antinomies of Realism* (London and New York: Verso, 2013).

3 George Eliot and 'the Case of Wagner'

Fabrications and Speculations

Robert Dingley

On 1 May 1877, Richard and Cosima Wagner arrived in London, where Wagner was to direct eight concert performances of his own music at the Royal Albert Hall—a project designed to redeem the Festspielhaus at Bayreuth from looming insolvency. With them they carried a letter of introduction from Cosima's father Franz Liszt to his old acquaintances George Henry Lewes and George Eliot, and the two couples met on at least a dozen occasions during the following month. Eliot attended several rehearsals and performances at the Albert Hall (weeping plentifully, Cosima told Hubert Parry, during Act Two of *Die Walküre*)[1] and, according to a titled informant of Gordon Haight's, 'seemed to find much to talk about to Wagner in the intervals'.[2] What was perhaps their closest encounter, however, took place on 17 May, when the Leweses and the Wagners dined together at the Chelsea home of the music critic Edward Dannreuther with whom the Wagners were staying—'no one else present', noted Lewes in his Diary 'until the evening when a small party gathered to hear Wagner read "Parzival" which he did with great spirit and like a fine actor'.[3] Eliot, too, briefly recorded the evening in a letter to Barbara Bodichon (*GEL*, 6: 374), and Cosima's diary cursorily notes 'Lewes for dinner, then some others, to whom R. reads *Parsifal*'.[4] Unfortunately, none of the principal participants at the dinner left any record of the table-talk, but there is an intriguing hint in a rather less obvious source. The naturalised German critic Francis Hueffer was also present at Dannreuther's soirée (presumably as one of the after-dinner arrivals) and in his book *Half a Century of Musical Life in England* he recalls that during the course of her 'friendly and animated' dialogue with Cosima, Eliot, 'with that straightforwardness which was so conspicuous and so lovable in her character', remarked '"Your husband does not like Jews; my husband is a Jew"'.[5]

Although the story sounds almost too good to be true, there is no reason to doubt its essential veracity. Hueffer was among the most ardent champions of Wagner's music in Britain (and the Leweses owned a copy of his pioneering 1876 monograph *Richard Wagner and the Music of the Future*).[6] All too aware of the generally adverse reaction among English intellectuals to the composer's egregious anti-Semitism, Hueffer made a

DOI: 10.4324/9781003362821-4

strenuous effort to palliate Eliot's assertion by announcing that, 'needless to add', the great man's 'aversion to the Hebrew race was of a purely theoretical kind, and did not extend to individuals'.[7] It seems improbable that he would have invented a story discreditable to his hero for which he would at once feel called upon to enter a plea in mitigation.

Assuming, then, that Eliot made some such remark as Hueffer recalled, the anecdote raises a number of questions, of which, of course, the most immediately pressing is posed by Eliot's conscious fabrication—for that is what it was—of a Semitic ancestry for her partner. Rosemary Ashton records that in the 1870s unfounded rumours were circulating, both in Britain and America, that Lewes was indeed a Jew—rumours founded partly on his dubious social origin, partly on his physiognomy, and partly on what was felt to be his partner's otherwise unaccountably intimate knowledge of Jewish life and customs.[8] Eliot's remark, even so, has the appearance of a spontaneous improvisation. Although Nicholas Dames suggests that she was consciously provoking Cosima,[9] a more plausible explanation, I would propose, is that, having detected vitriolic anti-Semitism in someone for whom she felt both affection and admiration (both women had, after all, set social convention at defiance to be with their chosen partners), Eliot was seeking to short-circuit the possibly acrimonious discussion of a deeply divisive, and perhaps friendship-ending, topic.

But tantalising as such speculations are, I want to address a rather different question that seems to me to be posed by Hueffer's account. Just how detailed was Eliot's knowledge of Wagner's racial beliefs, and what was its source?

Some clue to an answer is to be gathered from *Daniel Deronda*, completed less than a year before Dannreuther's dinner party (and the catalyst for much of the gossip about Lewes' ancestry). There is general agreement that the principal (though not necessarily the only) model for Eliot's portrait of the 'great pianist' Julius Klesmer[10] was the Russian Jewish musician Anton Rubinstein, whom the Leweses had encountered through Liszt during their stay in Weimar in 1854 and whom they met again in London in 1876 as Eliot was putting the finishing touches to her novel: 'We shall so like to renew our acquaintance with Klesmer', Lewes wrote,[11] thus apparently putting the matter beyond doubt.[12] But when Klesmer is first introduced in chapter 5 of the novel, he is described as 'a felicitous combination of the German, the Sclave, and the Semite', and only the last two of those terms apply to Rubinstein. Moreover, the text immediately goes on to describe Klesmer 'speaking in an odious German fashion' and with 'an assertion of superiority' unprecedented 'before the late Teutonic conquests'—a reference to Prussia's successive defeats of Denmark, Austria, and France in the 1860s and in 1871 (ch. 5). And just which stridently German musician Eliot has in mind is strongly suggested in chapter 10 when young Clintock, after hearing Gwendolen sing, observes that at least her kind of music, unlike Klesmer's, is not 'addressed to the ears of the future'—an allusion, of course, to the phrase 'music of the future' which was derived from the title of Wagner's 1850 essay *Das Kunstwerk der Zukunft* and which was generally and inescapably associated with him. The term, Eliot noted as early as 1855, had become the subject of much 'cheap ridicule' among 'adherents of the old [musical] faith'.[13]

Again, in chapter 22, Klesmer's mature relationship with Catherine Arrowpoint, founded in a compatibility of taste and intellect (and perhaps suggesting to Eliot the appropriateness of conferring a Jewish identity on Lewes), is positively contrasted with the purely sensual, and therefore fugitive, grand passions of the legendary past: 'Tannhäuser, one suspects, was a knight of ill-furnished imagination, hardly of larger discourse than a heavy Guardsman'. Other ironically diminished figures from mythology—Merlin, Ulysses—follow in this rather Thackerayan passage, but that Tannhäuser, the protagonist of an opera which Eliot knew and admired, should head the list in immediate juxtaposition with a musician of the future can hardly be coincidental. Nor can an allusion, at one of the novel's climactic moments, to the only other Wagner opera which Eliot knew well. At the end of chapter 54, Gwendolen, finally yielding to Grandcourt's psychological coercion, agrees to go sailing with him: 'I think we shall go on always, like the Flying Dutchman' she says 'wildly'. But Gwendolen's faulty memory has rendered the reference, once again, ironic. Instead of hurling herself into the sea, like Senta, in order to rescue or redeem the Dutchman from his eternal wandering, after which, as Eliot puts it in her summary of the opera's plot, 'they are seen hovering above the waters in light and glory',[14] Gwendolen fails to jump in after her drowning husband until it is too late to save him— or so she guiltily convinces herself. She has been unable to rise to the self-sacrificial role of operatic heroine, just as, in Klesmer's judgement, she would be unable to meet its vocal demands.

These oblique hints and glancing allusions—and there may be others[15]— contrive to signal Wagner's shadowy presence not so much in, as behind, Eliot's novel, which seeks to engage with, but never names, him—a notable omission, surely, in a novel which does name Schubert, Liszt, Schumann, Mendelssohn, Weber, Bellini, and Meyerbeer. And I speculate that Wagner remains an implied rather than explicit presence because Eliot has appropriated ideas from a source which she at the same time wishes to disclaim and whose basic premise her novel seeks to refute. While, that is, she nowhere makes any specific reference to Wagner's notorious essay 'Das Judenthum in der Musik', there is at least some circumstantial evidence that she had read or perhaps re-read it in the course of her characteristically strenuous preparatory research for a text which is, after all, preoccupied with both music and Jewishness.

Wagner's article, which attracted international controversy both when it was first published pseudonymously in the *Neue Zeitschrift für Musik* in 1850 and again when it was defiantly reissued in an expanded version in 1869, is, like so much of his writing, grotesquely overdetermined. Coarse anti-Semitic rant and personal special pleading are slung together in a text whose calculated offensiveness can all too easily obscure its claimed status as cultural analysis. Essentially, Wagner argues that the legal and social emancipation of European—and especially German—Jewry in the opening decades of the nineteenth century has had the effect of disrupting the evolutionary imperative, the 'wirkliches organisches Lebensbedürfniss', of Western music.[16] On one hand, he asserts, whatever Judaic music may originally have been, its jealously-guarded preservation in the enclosed world of the ghettoes has caused it to stagnate so that it is no longer a living form; conversely, westernised Jewish musicians, newly liberated into their host communities, can feel no essential connection with the national cultures from which their race has become alienated by centuries of segregation and are consequently able only to learn and repeat the musical idioms of the past. Even a supremely talented composer like Mendelssohn, Wagner claims, exemplifies a tragic impasse ('einem völlig tragischen Konflict' [*Gesammelte Schriften*, 5:79]) because his music can only recycle an existing tradition rather than contributing to its next phase of development. And if Mendelssohn is ultimately a noble failure, Meyerbeer (unnamed but unmistakable as 'the widely renowned Jewish composer')[17] is beneath contempt for his tasteless operatic concoctions, in which 'various shocks and effective emotional situations' are cunningly substituted for coherent musical drama, deceiving their audiences into accepting 'as a smart, modern utterance something which was utterly foolish and trivial'.[18] To be sure, Meyerbeer's chic productions are 'profitable',[19] and they therefore epitomise and help to consolidate an increasingly materialistic civilisation which has lost any vital connection with its own past. Since, moreover, this deadening materialism is underwritten by a distorted Judaeo-Christian ideology, the necessary corollary of Wagner's analysis is a reassertion of distinctive national values and a full absorption, both of Jews and non-Jews, into a revitalised German culture.[20]

Wagner's argument, stripped of its inflammatory language and its implicit positioning of its author as the culmination of Western musical development, is, in its essentials, a fairly familiar one in early nineteenth-century German thought. Passionate anti-Semitism pervades the whole spectrum of political opinion from the ultra-nationalist Fichte to the young Marx (whose 1843–44 essay 'On the Jewish Question' Wagner may have read and would certainly have endorsed).[21] Wilhelm Heinrich von Riehl's *Naturgeschichte des Volks*, for example, characterised Jews as a rootless and disruptive element which threatened to contaminate the organic purity of the traditional peasant community (a prominent aspect of his work that Eliot, as Bernard Semmel notices, significantly failed to mention in her generally admiring review).[22] Similarly, Ludwig Feuerbach, the philosopher who meant most to Wagner before his discovery of Schopenhauer in the mid-1850s, wrote disparagingly, as Eliot puts it in her own translation of *The Essence of Christianity*, about 'the personified selfishness of the Israelitish people' whose 'taste for Nature lay only in the palate'.[23] What is distinctive, however, about Wagner's essay, apart from the hateful crudity of its rhetoric, is its specific application to music's cultural role, and I propose that it is this application that Eliot has partially appropriated for her last novel.

Eliot had, of course, been familiar with aspects of Wagner's thought as early as 1855, when she wrote in her *Fraser's Magazine* essay on 'Liszt, Wagner, and Weimar' of the 'grand object' of Meyerbeer's operas being 'to produce a climax of spectacle, situation, and orchestral effects', and noted, following Wagner, that 'there is no attempt at the evolution of these from the true workings of the human character and human passions'.[24] It is, however, unclear how much of Wagner's prose she had read at this time. Most commentators assume that her information was based largely, as Eliot herself acknowledged, on a number of recent essays about the composer by Liszt published in the *Neue Zeitschrift für Musik*,[25] and on a piece evaluating Meyerbeer's *Robert le Diable* in which Liszt refers briefly to Wagner and which Lewes paraphrased for an article in *The Leader*.[26] None of that, of course, need preclude the possibility that she had examined some of Wagner's own writings at first hand, and her *Fraser's* article, in which she notes that Liszt's contributions constitute the *Neue Zeitschrift's* 'chief value', might be taken to imply a broad acquaintance with the journal where 'Das Judenthum ...' and other articles by Wagner first appeared.[27]

But whatever the extent of her direct familiarity with Wagner's theoretical writing, in 'Liszt, Wagner, and Weimar' Eliot was principally concerned, as was Lewes in *The Leader*, with the semi-autonomous history of musical drama 'from the warbling puppets of the early opera to the dramatic effects of Meyerbeer',[28] and she omits more than minimal reference to the larger cultural argument in which Wagner situates his critique in 'Das Judenthum ...' and elsewhere. That wider perspective, however, which Eliot may anyway have encountered in later reading, is necessarily present in *Daniel Deronda*, where discourse about music is largely embedded in conversational exchanges between and about characters the worth of whose judgement we are invited to assess. When, for example, in chapter 11, Klesmer authoritatively describes the odious Thomas Cranmer Lush to Gwendolen as 'an amateur ... too fond of Meyerbeer and Scribe—too fond of the mechanical-dramatic', his dismissive verdict suggests a close affinity between Lush, the embodiment of amoral self-gratification, and the undemanding, indeed *lush*, music he favours. Moreover, the brilliant phrase 'mechanical-dramatic' further compounds the indictment, since it hints that music of this kind, instead of transcending the deadening homogenisation of industrial process, can fully participate in it and indeed can be manufactured like any other expensive product, a source of agreeably escapist sensation. This association of grand opera with commodity culture nowhere appears so starkly in Eliot's *Fraser's* article but, perhaps significantly, it is made, again with specific reference to Meyerbeer, in Wagner's *Oper und Drama* (1850–51), which complains that works like *Le Prophète* 'come not at all into the province of drama but into that of sheer mechanics', so that 'the whole of art is resolved into its mechanical integers', requiring no active response from listeners but serving only as a sort of upmarket Muzak.[29]

That point has already received theoretical elaboration in chapter 5 when Klesmer counsels Gwendolen to stop singing arias by Bellini because such music 'expresses a puerile state of culture ... the passion and thought of people without any breadth of horizon' and with 'no sense of the universal'. Klesmer here is arguing that, as in the specific case of Lush and Meyerbeer, there is a symbiotic relationship between any audience and the music they approve. And since Gwendolen's audience has just enthusiastically approved the sort of music she performs, Klesmer's aspersion is as much about them as it is about Bellini. These leisured denizens of country houses, obsessed with status and form, sunk in what Theophrastus Such was to call a 'grosser mental sloth',[30] and treating music as a luxury postprandial entertainment, are presented in the novel as without moral purpose or direction, seeking only for ways in which to relieve the tedium of their well-heeled existences. Their general condition is supremely epitomised, indeed, in Henleigh Mallinger (malinger?) Grandcourt, who is bored by everything except occasional yachting excursions and recreational sadism. 'Bore', indeed, is among the most frequent terms in Grandcourt's admittedly limited vocabulary, and he measures his gentlemanly superiority by the number of things, people, and places he contrives to find tedious. But the condition of chronic boredom which Eliot diagnoses in the English ruling class is also, Wagner argues in his essay, the endemic condition of modern operagoers, and he deploys the term 'Langeweile' and its variants with insistent repetition throughout the paragraph in which he seeks to explain the current vogue for Meyerbeer, whose operatic concoctions pander to a 'bored audience' which longs 'desperately' for something to alleviate its debilitating lethargy but which no longer has what Klesmer would describe as the 'breadth of horizon' to respond to true music drama[31]. It was precisely, for Wagner, the vocation of the authentic artist to restore that 'breadth of horizon' by assuming a spiritually and politically transformative role in the redemption of European civilisation from its slavish worship of wealth and status. As Klesmer grandiloquently insists to the hapless Mr Bult, musicians 'help to rule the nations and make the age as much as any other public men' (ch. 22).

But if Klesmer's remarks on music and its relationship to the wider culture of which it is symptomatic but which it also helps to form echo, or at least closely resemble, Wagner's own, there is, of course, a fundamental difference. Eliot may largely have accepted Wagner's critique of current musical taste (she had certainly done so in her essay of 1855), and she may have concurred in relating that taste to the spiritual inertia of contemporary elites, but she vehemently rejects the anti-Semitic premise on which Wagner's argument is founded. Indeed, she implicitly refutes it by making Klesmer (whose very name denotes the musical tradition of the

Ashkenazim) the proponent of Wagnerian ideas. For Klesmer, after all, reconciles precisely those qualities that Wagner held to be incompatible: he is both Jewish and an exponent of the Music of the Future, both Semitic, as Eliot announces when she first introduces him, and assertively Germanic. Moreover, his insistence on his status as a creative artist within a Gentile world co-exists with a proud refusal to accept full assimilation—racial, social, or cultural. Wagner's essay, at least in its original version, ends with a characteristically opaque rhetorical flourish in which he exhorts Jews (and, if it comes to that, Gentiles) to 'remember that your redemption from the curse laid on you can be achieved by only one thing, and that is the redemption of Ahasuerus—decline and fall!'[32] Ahasuerus, the Wandering Jew, obsessed Wagner throughout his creative life as a figure for the deracinated individual. Variants recur in the protagonist of *The Flying Dutchman*, in the itinerant Wotan of *Siegfried*, in the female penitent Kundry in *Parsifal*; and the term which the standard English translation renders as 'decline and fall'—'der Untergang', literally a 'going under' or submergence—has, despite its ominous resonance, more to do with a willed and redemptive abnegation of the self ('Selbstvernichtung') than with physical destruction.[33] Effectively, it is an exhortation to Jewry to strive for total absorption into the mainstream of Western culture, to abjure its own distinctiveness. And that, quite explicitly, is an exhortation that Klesmer rejects: responding to Mr Bult's guess that he is 'a Panslavist', Klesmer defiantly announces: 'No; my name is Elijah. I am the Wandering Jew' (ch. 22). His assertion is doubly emphatic because, in calling himself Elijah rather than the more familiar Ahasuerus, the name by which the Wandering Jew had been known in Europe since the sixteenth century,[34] Klesmer obliquely alludes to a rabbinical tradition—unfamiliar to the vast majority of Eliot's readers—which identifies the Wanderer with the transfigured prophet of the Old Testament, who returns to earth after his miraculous apotheosis in order to provide help and wise counsel to the Jewish people and who is a harbinger of their eventual return to the Holy Land.[35]

Klesmer's self-identification as the Wandering Jew, then, far from implying, as Catherine Arrowpoint chooses, perhaps wishfully, to believe, 'cosmopolitan views' about the 'fusion of races' (ch. 22), rather foreshadows the assertion of the Jew of Smyrna in *Impressions of Theophrastus Such*, who, in a city 'where a whip is carried by passengers ready to flog off the too officious specimens of his race, can still be proud to say, "I am a Jew"' (ch. 18). Such an insistence on solidarity with 'a great historic body' is, Theophrastus argues, 'a humanizing, elevating habit of mind' (ch. 18), and it constitutes implicitly a repudiation of any 'submergence' of Jewish particularity of the sort envisaged by Wagner. But it also constitutes a repudiation of assumptions once held by George Eliot herself. In 1848, in her well-known epistolary critique of Disraeli's *Tancred* addressed to John Sibree, Eliot had remarked that 'Extermination seems to be the law for the inferior races ... for the rest, fusion for both physical and moral ends'. 'The fellowship of race', she goes on, is 'an inferior impulse which must ultimately be superseded', and 'Some great revolutionary force' ensures that 'the genius of a particular nation becomes a portion of the common mind of humanity'. 'My Gentile nature', she adds on a less speculative note, 'kicks most resolutely against any assumption of superiority in the Jews', for, after all, 'Everything *specifically* Jewish is of low grade' (*GEL*, 1: 245–246). Wagner would have been in enthusiastic agreement.[36]

That Eliot had earlier thought along broadly similar lines to Wagner about the desirability of 'fusion' (which for Jews would effectively entail submission to a hegemonic Gentile culture) may help to explain the insistence with which she sought to distance herself from such views in *Daniel Deronda*—and even, perhaps, in her assertive fabrication of a Jewish identity for her husband. But whether or not the speculation with which I set out—that Eliot had read 'Das Judenthum in der Musik'—is a credible one, it may serve to draw attention not only to obvious discords but also to lingering affinities between her own *later* thought and Wagner's. Both, after all, were preoccupied with what they saw as a rupture in the natural evolution of their respective cultures—the supersession of value and purpose by the absence, as Theophrastus Such puts it, of 'aims larger and more attractive ... than the securing of personal ease and prosperity' (ch. 18). For both Wagner and Eliot, the solution to moral and cultural decline lies primarily in the reassertion of distinctive national identities—German in Wagner's case, Jewish, and, by implication, English in Eliot's. Both writers, moreover, succumb to that fatal elision (or confusion) of historically transmitted cultural traditions with inherited racial characteristics which bedevils nineteenth-century (and later) ethnographic thought. In 1848, Eliot had scornfully rejected the insistence of Disraeli's omniscient Jewish capitalist Sidonia that 'All is race; there is no other truth';[37] by 1876, she had come largely to accept it—and so found herself dealing in much the same intellectual currency as Wagner. 'Who', Wagner rhetorically inquires of his presumed Gentile reader, 'has not been convinced that the musical service in a popular synagogue is a mere caricature?' and who has not experienced visceral 'feelings of repulsion, horror and amusement' at the vocal expression of a degraded racial otherness?[38] Daniel Deronda, conversely, listening to divine service in the 'popular synagogue' in Frankfurt, wonders 'at the strength of his own feeling' which seems 'beyond the occasion' (ch. 32) because in responding to the Sabbath music, he is intuitively responding to his own descent from the noble race whose history it embodies.[39]

When Eliot and Wagner finally met, then, they may indeed have found, as Haight's informant noticed, 'much to talk about', but on the specific implications of their shared belief in the ontological centrality of racial difference, they remained at antipodean variance, crusading philo-Semitism in polar opposition to pathological Judaeophobia. We should not, even so, forget that antipodes are not only hateful contraries but are also inverted mirror reflections of one another.

Notes

1 See Anne Dzamba Sessa, *Richard Wagner and the English* (Rutherford: Fairleigh Dickinson University Press, 1979), 37. If Cosima's report is true, it suggests that Eliot's responsiveness to Wagner's music had developed considerably since her lukewarm reaction to *Lohengrin* in 1854. She herself left no indication of her later views and the widespread belief among Eliot biographers that she uniformly disliked Wagnerian opera is based almost wholly on Lewes' own distaste for it and his assumption that he and Eliot were in full agreement. So far as I am aware, Lewes' final published judgement on what he called, anticipating Nietzsche, 'the case of Wagner' occurs in *On Actors and Acting* (London: Smith, Elder, and Co., 1875), where he wonders whether 'a longer acquaintance' may teach him 'to admire what is now not admirable' (233) but remains sceptical. However, in a letter of June 1877 thanking Cosima for Wagner's signed photograph, he talks of 'the stirrings of the soul which the Meister's music and your personality excited in us' and remarks that 'we are deep in the Poems and catching *faint* echoes of the Music from the Piano' (Geoffrey Skelton, 'George Eliot and Cosima Wagner: A Newly Discovered Letter from George Henry Lewes', *George Eliot Fellowship Review*, 13 [1982], 27–30). Perhaps, then, Lewes was finally converted at the Albert Hall concerts (or perhaps he was just being unctuously polite).

2 Gordon S. Haight, *George Eliot: A Biography* (Oxford: Oxford University Press, 1968), 502.

3 *The George Eliot Letters*, ed. Gordon S. Haight, 9 vols (New Haven and London: Yale University Press, 1954–78), 6: 373.

4 *Cosima Wagner's Diaries*, ed. Martin Gregor-Dellin and Dietrich Mack; tr. Geoffrey Skelton (New York and London: Harcourt Brace Jovanovich, 1978), 1: 964.

5 Francis Hueffer, *Half a Century of Musical Life in England 1837-1887* (London: Chapman and Hall, 1889), 72.

6 See Delia da Sousa Correa, *George Eliot, Music and Victorian Culture* (Basingstoke: Palgrave Macmillan, 2003), 206n.

7 Hueffer, *Musical Life*, 72.

8 Rosemary Ashton discusses the sources of this allegation and cites a letter written by Lewes to Richard Owen in December 1876 in which he notes with amusement that 'in America it is positively asserted that *I* am of Jewish origin!'; see *George Eliot. A Life* (London: Penguin, 1996), 355–6; see also *G. H. Lewes: An Unconventional Victorian* (London: Pimlico, 2000), 6–10, in which Ashton provides details of Lewes' 'unusual, but not obscure' and apparently non-Semitic antecedents. Eliot's knowledge of Jewish history and traditions derived, of course, not from her partner but principally from the wide-ranging research recorded in her *Daniel Deronda* notebooks (see note 35 below); for a study of Eliot's preparatory reading for the novel, see William Baker, *George Eliot and Judaism* (Salzburg: Universität Salzburg, 1975), 143–80.

9 See Nicholas Dames, *The Physiology of the Novel: Reading, Neural Science and the Form of Victorian Fiction* (Oxford: Oxford University Press, 2007), 38.

10 George Eliot, *Daniel Deronda*, ed. Graham Handley (Oxford: Oxford World's Classics, 1988), ch. 37. Further references to this edition appear parenthetically in text.

11 Haight, *George Eliot*, 490.

12 Gordon Haight suggests Liszt as a possible model, though he is able to adduce scant evidence for the claim (see 'George Eliot's Originals and Contemporaries', in *Essays in Victorian Literary History and Biography*, ed. Hugh Witemeyer [Basingstoke: Macmillan, 1992], 68–77); Delia da Sousa Correa reviews the various candidates and adds E.T.A. Hoffmann's fictional Johannes Kreisler to the list ('George Eliot and the Germanic "Musical Magus"', in *George Eliot and Europe*, ed. John Rignall [Aldershot: Scolar, 1997], 98–112).

13 George Eliot, *Essays of George Eliot*, ed. Thomas Pinney (New York: Columbia University Press, 1963), 99. See also Lewes' well-known remark, in a letter written to Charles Lee Lewes after attending a performance of *Tannhäuser* in 1870, that 'The Mutter and I have come to the conclusion that the Music of the future is not for us' (Eliot, *GEL*, 6: 85n.); but see note 1 above.

14 Eliot, *Essays*, ed. Pinney, 110.

15 See David A. Reibel, 'Hidden Parallels in George Eliot's *Daniel Deronda*: Julius Klesmer, Richard Wagner, Franz Liszt', *George Eliot-George Henry Lewes Studies*, 64/65 (2013), 16–52 for other possible allusions, some of them more plausible than others.

16 Richard Wagner, *Gesammelte Schriften und Dichtungen* (Leipzig: E. W. Fritzsch, 1897-98), 5: 84. Unsurprisingly, given her own intellectual preoccupations, Eliot responded positively to the organicist terminology in which Wagner regularly couched his ambitions for the music of the future, commenting that, in place of a 'succession of ill-prepared crises', he aspired to create an 'organic whole' and judging that, in *The Flying Dutchman*, he had 'admirably fulfilled his own requisition of organic unity' (*Essays*, ed. Pinney, 102, 104).

17 Richard Wagner, *Stories and Essays*, ed. Charles Osborne (London: Peter Owen, 1973), 36. I have used Osborne's translation of 'Das Judenthum...' in preference to the standard, but notoriously unreadable, version by William Ashton Ellis.

18 Wagner, *Stories and Essays*, 37.

19 Wagner, *Stories and Essays*, 36.

20 For a fuller, and admirably balanced, account of Wagner's position, see Bryan Magee, *Aspects of Wagner* (London: Panther, 1972), 29–44.

21 See Paul Lawrence Rose's controversial study *Wagner: Race and Revolution* (London: Faber and Faber, 1992), 2–22 for a useful and accessible account of the growth of anti-Semitism among the 'Young German' thinkers with whom Wagner was closely associated in the early 1840s; see Alex Ross, *Wagnerism: Art and Politics in the Shadow of Music* (London: Farrar, Straus and Giroux, 2020), 234–5 for Marx's possible influence on Wagner.

22 See Bernard Semmel, *George Eliot and the Politics of National Inheritance* (Oxford: Oxford University Press, 1994), 53. Wagner, like Eliot, approved in principle of Riehl's celebration of *völkisch* culture, but in a sarcastic review of his *Neues Novellenbuch* which appeared in the *Süddeutsche Presse* in 1867, he denigrated Riehl's exclusive focus on the virtues of traditional peasant life as a form of sentimental philistinism: Riehl had made the fatal mistake of writing about modern music and finding it altogether too sophisticated and insufficiently attuned to the simple, wholesome tastes of the *Volk*; see Wagner, *Art and Politics*, tr. W. Ashton Ellis (Lincoln: University of Nebraska Press, 1995), 252–60.

23 Ludwig Feuerbach, *The Essence of Christianity*, tr. Marian Evans [George Eliot] (New York: Harper, 1957), 114.

24 Eliot, *Essays*, ed. Pinney, 101.

25 See Eliot, *Essays*, ed. Pinney, 110n.

26 Lewes' article, like the Liszt essay on which it draws, discusses Wagner only cursorily in order to contrast Meyerbeer's concentration on 'situations and musical effects' with a musical drama in which 'the presentation of characters and their mutual relations necessarily evolved situations' (Lewes, 'The Romantic School of Music', *The Leader* [28 October 1854], 1027–8).

27 Eliot, *Essays*, ed. Pinney, 99. Eliot appears, on her own admission, to have used the Liszt articles she cites, as well as his 1851 pamphlet on *Tannhäuser* and *Lohengrin*, as aids to assist 'recollection' of the operas she had seen, as 'paraphrase' rather than 'analysis' (*Essays*, 110n), and neither they nor the article she translated for Lewes seem to me to explore Wagner's conception of music drama in sufficient detail to account fully for her own critical engagement with his ideas in the *Fraser's* essay. For the relevant articles by Liszt, see his *Gesammelte Schriften*, 6 vols, ed. Lina Ramann (Leipzig: Breitkopf und Härtel, 1880–83), 3, Part One, 48–67; 3, Part Two.

28 Eliot, *Essays*, ed. Pinney, 101.

29 *Wagner on Music and Drama: A Selection from Richard Wagner's Prose Works*, ed. Albert Goldman and Evert Sprinchorn, tr. H. [*sic*] Ashton Ellis (London: Gollancz, 1977), 121; *Gesammelte Schriften*, 3: 304–5.

30 George Eliot, *Impressions of Theophrastus Such*, ed. Nancy Henry (Iowa: University of Iowa Press, 1994), ch. 18.

31 Wagner, *Stories and Essays*, 36–7; *Gesammelte Schriften*, 5: 81–3.

32 Wagner, *Stories and Essays*, 39.

33 Wagner, *Gesammelte Schriften*, 5: 85. For a useful survey of interpretations of this passage, see Mark Berry, *Treacherous Bonds and Laughing Fire: Politics and Religion in Wagner's* Ring (London: Ashgate, 2016), 256n.; see also Ross, *Wagnerism*, 236–7.

34 See George K. Anderson, *The Legend of the Wandering Jew* (Providence: Brown University Press, 1970), 50.

35 Eliot found this tradition in Sabine Baring-Gould's *Legends of Old Testament Characters from the Talmud and Other Sources* (1871); see *George Eliot's* Daniel Deronda *Notebooks*, ed. Jane Irwin (Cambridge: Cambridge University Press, 1996), 350.

36 In November 1878, Cosima started reading *Tancred* to Wagner in the evenings. They agreed with Eliot (and most subsequent readers) that it was 'vapid' and rapidly began to skip, but Wagner at an early stage commented of Disraeli's discussion of Jewry, 'here at any rate they have been emancipated a generation too soon' (*Cosima Wagner's Diaries* 2, 210). As with so many of his *obiter dicta*, the implication is unclear, but he may have meant that if the opening up of the German ghettoes had occurred later in the century, the possibility of a separate homeland might have seemed a more practicable (and preferable) alternative solution to the Jewish 'problem' than assimilation. If that is so, Daniel's project might have met with his wholehearted approval. For a suggestive, if somewhat wayward, discussion of Wagner and Disraeli, see L.J. Rather, *Reading Wagner: A Study in the History of Ideas* (Baton Rouge: Louisiana State University, 1990), 139–46.

37 Benjamin Disraeli, *Tancred, or the New Crusade* (1847; Bradenham edn, London: Peter Davies, 1927), 153.

38 Wagner, *Stories and Essays*, 32.

39 For an excellent account of this passage and its sources, see Beryl Gray, *George Eliot and Music* (New York: Palgrave Macmillan, 1989), 114–7.

4 *The Mill on the Floss* and the Novel in Bengal

Sneha Kar Chaudhuri and Debashree Dattaray

This chapter will engage with the reception and re-interpretation of George Eliot's *The Mill on the Floss* (1860) by two major canonical novelists in Bengal: Saratchandra Chattopadhyay (1876–1938) and Bibhutibhushan Bandyopadhyay (1894–1950). Saratchandra Chattopadhyay imitated and indigenised the English provincial novel, so that his novels reflect the community values and experiences of colonial Bengal. By contrast, Bibhutibhushan Bandyopadhyay's *Pather Panchali* (*Song of the Road*, 1929) can be treated as an intertext to *The Mill on the Floss*. We will discuss how George Eliot's intellectual influence emerged in the cultural transformations made by these Bangla writers, including in how they imagine culture in relation to the environment. As a prelude, we provide a brief outline of the Bengal Renaissance that nurtured Saratchandra Chattopadhyay and functioned as a historically important intellectual legacy for Bibhutibhushan Bandyopadhyay.

Nineteenth-century British culture profoundly influenced the intellectuals of the Bengal Renaissance. Relevant figures include social reformer Raja Rammohan Roy, educationist and scholar Pandit Iswarchandra Vidyasagar, novelist Bankimchandra Chattopadhyay, poet and novelist Michael Madhusudan Dutt, religious reformers Keshab Chandra Sen and Swami Vivekananda, and poet-novelist and playwright Rabindranath Tagore, among others. S.L. Ghosh discusses the specific ways in which Western thought influenced the Bengal intelligentsia in the long nineteenth century:

> The nineteenth century renaissance which centred mainly on Bengal was the result of the impact of Western culture on the traditional Indian culture. While its leaders went back beyond the current traditions to rediscover high philosophical values in the ancient heritage of India, they adapted some ethical values from the West and advocated the necessity of looking at tradition from the viewpoint of rational humanistic logic. … The humanism they preached was, however, essentially different from the Western concept in that it was founded on belief in a universal God. Their social reform programmes encountered heavy opposition from the orthodox sections which were strongly for the traditional ways.[1]

DOI: 10.4324/9781003362821-5

In other words, what the Bengal Renaissance intellectuals were trying to achieve was an amalgamation of the Western (mainly British) history of ideas with Indian philosophical traditions, but often these values were at odds with each other. The acceptance of British polity, culture, and literature was widespread, with the exception of the indigenous purists and traditionalists who endorsed the Aryan Sanskritic tradition. British influences left an indelible mark on the career and achievements of Bengali Renaissance scholars, thinkers, and activists. David Knopf, in his seminal book, points out that

> With respect to Indian accommodation of British Orientalism, the same years [1772–1830] witnessed the genesis of what has not infrequently been called the Bengal renaissance. The literature of the nineteenth-century Bengal renaissance falls into two broad categories: the popular image of the Bengalis proud of their recent heritage and the scholarly notion of renaissance as a problem in British Indian historiography. ... Though it is by no means certain when the term renaissance was first used in nineteenth-century Calcutta, Rammohun Roy referred to recent events in Bengal as being analogous to the European renaissance and reformation.[2]

The term Bengal Renaissance implies an incipient Westernisation or Britishisation, but as Homi Bhabha has pointed out, what he calls 'colonial mimicry' was not necessarily imitative and secondary, but deconstructive and subversive in its fractured cultural hybridity.[3] Cultural tropes and conventions were not copied passively. Rather there was an active sense of resistance and appropriation through re-contextualisation, making the process of transculturality ambiguous and complicated. Writers such as Saratchandra Chattopadhyay came towards the end of this intellectual movement and took the legacy of 'colonial mimicry' to a whole new level by incorporating indigenous elements and intimately Bangla domestic experiences into the project of colonial re-writing and cultural translation.

Bankimchandra Chattopadhyay (1838–94)[4] and Rabindranath Tagore (1861–1941)[5] are senior figures in the Bengal Renaissance. If Walter Scott was a major inspiration for the historical novels of Bankimchandra Chattopadhyay with their mix of romance and patriotism against the background of rural and feudal Bengal, then Rabindranath Tagore's novels were influenced by the domestic novels of Jane Austen and later nineteenth-century novelists like Charles Dickens, William Thackeray, Elizabeth Gaskell, and George Eliot and can be categorised as classic realist texts. Bankimchanda Chattopadhyay and Tagore were both preoccupied by issues concerning women's empowerment, changing dimensions of heterosexual relationships, domestic politics, the Swadeshi movement against the British following the partition of Bengal in 1903, and the burning political consciousness of young Bengal affecting both the public sphere and the struggles of daily existence in the private sphere. These novelists strove to indigenise the form and content of the nineteenth-century British novel. The writings of Michael Madhusudan Dutta (1824–73), particularly historical pastiches in the contemporary Western mould, followed the same tradition.

Saratchandra Chattopadhyay, though much younger than Bankimchandra Chattopadhyay, Tagore, and Madhusudan Dutta, is one of the last thinkers associated with the intellectual legacy of the Bengal Renaissance.[6] He is one of the most popular, if not the most popular, Bangla novelists of all time, and there are innumerable film adaptations of his novels and short stories. His novels are unlike the elitist, abstruse, and recondite novels of Bankimchandra Chattopadhyay or Tagore. Sarat Babu wrote in a letter that 'Rabindranath writes for readers of my caliber whereas I write for readers like you'.[7] The influence of the Victorian realist novel supported his belief in the power of the novel as a means of serious social criticism and commentary, and as an agent of social transformation. Sarat chronicled in fiction the political and cultural turmoil of the late colonial period. Like the Victorian sages, he believed in the creative power of the novel as a literary form and the importance of the authoritative and didactic voice of the novelist. Accordingly, although he knew and enjoyed the folk traditions of *jatra* (opera), *kathak* (rural songs), and *kabir gaan* (poet's duel), he chose to write in the foreign literary form of the novel as domesticated and modernised by Bankimchandra Chattopadhyay and Rabindranath Tagore, aligning with the high Victorianism associated with the British rulers of colonial India.

Saratchandra Chattopadhyay wrote extensively in the Victorian subgenre of provincial novels and short stories. Vishnu Prabhakar (the author) and Jai Ratan (the translator) of *Great Vagabond: Biography and Immortal Works of Sarat Chandra Chatterjee* (1990), and Narasingha Prasad Sil (in *The Life of Sharatchandra Chattopadhyay: Drifter and Dreamer* [2012]) have claimed that he read the novels of George Eliot appreciatively, and his realist narratives were modelled on the form, ideology, and content of the English provincial novels for which George Eliot was renowned.[8] Sarat resembles George Eliot because both have regard for the natural beauty of the provincial world and its traditional appeal, together with the economic forces controlling it. At the same time, both were critical of the social, human, and psychological environment of provincial culture. There are evident similarities in their representation of the provincial natural world and the life of the people related to it, with a critical emphasis on the pros and cons of the values of a traditional society. Noted Bengali critic Narayan Chaudhuri describes this quality of Saratchandra's fiction as

> Villagism ... a marked trait of his works ... embedded in religious and social conservatism. ... [H]e had a far deeper acquaintance with the rural segment of society than with the urban and that is why his city-centric books paled into shade before his village-based tales.[9]

Particular examples of Saratchandra's fiction are *Pallisamaj* (*The Homecoming*, 1916) and the four *Shrikanto* novels (1917–33) together with short stories such as 'Bindur Chele' ('Bindu's Son'), 'Abhagir Swargo' ('The Unfortunate's Heaven'), and 'Mamlar Phol' ('The Result of the Case'). John Plotz has examined the fine balance between emotional attachment and detachment that Victorian novelists maintained towards provincial life.[10] Both George Eliot and Saratchandra Chattopadhay had this 'semi-detached' outlook. They were insiders to the provincial world in their early lives, but by virtue of the fuller intellectual exposure enabled by their education, they took their distance from the narrow values of the provincial community, and so gained insight into the strengths and limitations of traditional community ethics. They described the rural world and its people with a sense of assured and intimate awareness, yet ironically displayed a partly detached approach in criticising the rustic old-world values and ideologies. The social distancing they achieved allowed them to imagine the agrarian rustic world as an idyllic utopian space flawed by problems of economic decline, social prejudices, and moral backwardness.

Saratchandra did not engage in intertextual re-workings of George Eliot's novels, nor did he translate any of her works. Their similarities lie in terms of their articulation of the interactions of the rising urban classes and the vanishing importance of the rural world in the transitional phase between the feudal agrarian world order and the industrial world order that ushered in modernity. Both writers persistently focused on the effects of class transitions. Their characters mirror their complex and layered communities in terms of their class, gender, and social status. Like George Eliot in *Middlemarch* (1871–72), Saratchandra experimented with multiple protagonists in his *Shrikanto* novels, where the lives of the protagonist Shrikanta and the outcast woman Annadadidi unfold in parallel as in the case of Dorothea and Lydgate. The male protagonist of *Pallisamaj*, the urbanised and highly educated Ramesh Ghoshal, is much like Eliot's Lydgate in that their visions of philanthropy, modernity, and emancipation appear advanced in comparison with the norms of the provincial milieu they inhabit. In both instances, the authors show how these characters suffer because their generosity and visions of social change are completely unacceptable to the limited minds of the communities in which they live.

Saratchandra Chattopadhyay's works also explored the inheritance and property rights within patriarchy that affected women negatively, along with the legal status and social rehabilitation of widows, and familial conflicts involving law and women's rights. Thus, like George Eliot's Dorothea Casaubon in *Middlemarch*, most of the women characters in Saratchandra Chattopadhyay's novels such as *Baikunther Will* (1916), *Datta* (1918), and *Grihadaha* (1923) grapple with issues of discriminatory practices of property rights which victimised and disempowered women and put them at the mercy of male whims and prejudices. Saratchandra Chattopadhyay's gender ideology, with particular focus on the essays of *Narir Mulya* (*The Worth of*

Women, 1918), is sympathetic and enlightened. Like George Eliot, he used women characters in provincial settings as his protagonists to articulate the various problems and challenges for women in a narrow provincial world. The issues he identified include women's struggles to come to terms with the stringent gender norms set by patriarchy, the demands of running a family, economic breakdown affecting the domestic world, and motherhood, surrogacy, and childlessness. In his prose works such as *Narir Mulya* and *Narir Itihaas (The History of Women)*—the latter was lost in a fire at his ancestral house—he drew on J.S. Mill's arguments from *The Subjection of Women* (1869) and Herbert Spencer's *Descriptive Sociology* (1898).[11] Like Eliot, he was influenced by views on human evolution such as Herbert Spencer's concept of 'Social Darwinism' which were examined extensively in their novels. Saratchandra Chattopadhyay's analysis addressed what was known as 'the Woman Question' in Victorian England. Although Eliot did not engage with the movement for women's rights as a gender activist, her struggles as a woman writer and her unconventional personal life were examples of how educated Victorian women were defying gender norms, adopting new professional roles, and setting new personal and professional goals.

Saratchandra Chattopadhay's engagement with the issue of women's empowerment and freedom was liberal and unambiguous. He criticised women's subjugation in scathing terms exposing the hypocritical sexual morality of traditional patriarchy.[12] His discourse combined the duties of motherhood with the formation of an ideal nation and inspired the Bangla intelligentsia intent on achieving freedom from their British rulers. Thus, the empowerment of women was connected with the empowerment of the nation against the oppression of foreign rulers. He uses this nationalist discourse in arguing for women's emancipation in novels such as *Parineeta* (1916) and *Pather Dabi* (1926). He writes on the first page of *Narir Mulya* (1918): 'Manimanikaya mahamulyaban bostu kenona taha dushprapya. Narir mulya beshi nohe—karon songsare ini dushprapya nohen. Jol jinishti nityaprojoniyo, othocho etir daam nai' ('Precious stones are very valuable as they are rare. But women's worth is not much as they are not rare in society. They are like water which is indispensable, but not much valued'—our translation). He adroitly compares the importance of precious stones and water in our daily lives: women are precious as water but not as rare as valuable stones. Men must learn to understand women's constructive contribution to social progress. But within the confines of a Brahminical and Hindu patriarchy, Saratchandra could not advance Bangla women's economic independence and vocational rights. His focus was rather on demonstrating the acute problems of women's deprivation within the private sphere and the maladies occasioned by patriarchal dicta against women's empowerment.

There are also many discontinuities and dissimilarities between George Eliot and Saratchandra Chattopadhay because they were dealing with two different topographical and geopolitical worlds. Bengali critics of Saratchandra's novels have always compared him with Charles Dickens: for instance, Gopal Halder claims that 'the emotional surge that carried him away reminds us of Charles Dickens'.[13] Amalendu Bose expresses a similar view,[14] while critic and biographer Subhash Chandra Sarker maintains that

> [In his early life Saratchandra] was very much under the influence of three English writers—Charles Dickens, [Mrs] Henry Wood and Marie Corelli. His story 'Abhimaan' reflected one of [Mrs] Henry Wood's stories and the story 'Pashan' (The Stone) imitated Marie Corelli's novel *[The] Mighty Atom* (The manuscript of' 'Pashan' was irretrievably lost). For a period Sarat Chandra even took an English pen name St. C. Lara— St. being an abbreviation of his name Sarat, C. for his middle name Chandra and Lara being his own pet name to the nearest relation.[15]

However, any influence of Dickens, Corelli, and Wood was overtaken by the influence of George Eliot as he adopted her model of 'provincial novels' to write his 'village' novels located in the Bengal provinces. Saratchandra represented the domestic and public spaces of colonial Bengal with photographic fidelity. The Bengali environment was fundamentally much more regressive than English provincial life. His works are a record of British oppression and injustice in colonial Bengal, and the conflicting dynamics of a Bengali everyman, the quintessential Bengali *bhadralok* (gentleman) with his fractured middle-class and colonised subjectivity, opposed to the aggressive, exploitative, and domineering British rulers. He also recorded the dissimilar social norms for women and their double repression under Bengal patriarchy and British colonisation, producing highly layered and complex fictional accounts of the attendant socio-cultural and aesthetic problems of colonial modernities.[16] Saratchandra Chattopadhyay displays sensitivity about caste divisions and their damaging impact upon communities, and about impervious hierarchies as well as the blatantly exploitative practices of foreign regimes. His works are enriched with narratives of pain, suffering, and trauma engendered by caste and racial politics in late colonial Bengal.

By contrast, Bibhutibhushan Bandyopadhyay, from a village in Bengal's Nadia district, marks a departure from the bestselling novels of Saratchandra in terms of his depiction of nature. His oeuvre was diverse, eclectic, and prolific. He produced more than a dozen works of fiction, hundreds of short stories, and a handful of memoirs and essays. The innovation of his fiction was to capture the hinterland of Bengal in a way no one had previously done. In *Ichamati* (1950), a novel named after a river, he examines caste dynamics within a rural setting. In *Asani Sanket (Distant Thunder)*, he evokes the gradual decline of a rural economy caught in the aftermath of World War II and the devastating famine of 1943 that ravaged Bengal's countryside.[17]

Our discussion will concentrate on *Pather Panchali* (1929), specifically through a comparison of Maggie Tulliver in *The Mill on the Floss* and Durga in *Pather Panchali*. The contrast is framed by the notion of nature as simultaneously a disruptive and reassuring 'text'. Maggie desires and despairs aloud: 'I begin to think that there can never come much happiness to me from loving ... I wish I could make myself a world outside it as men do'.[18] In *The Mill on the Floss,* traditional modes of interpreting the world are shown to be breaking down irrevocably. According to Tim Dolin:

> There is an undeniable nostalgia in Eliot for the rural landscapes of her childhood (even in *Daniel Deronda*) even as there is an intense awareness of the dangers of nostalgia (as in *The Mill on the Floss*). At the same time, the industrial present—the informing condition of Eliot's fiction, is always just out of sight, away from the rural tranquillity.[19]

The persistence of semiotic codes of the 'linguistic and nonlinguistic cultural'[20] authoritarian presence in Maggie's life seems omnipresent in the novel. In much of *The Mill on the Floss*, Maggie is perceived as a wild animal, incapable of being tamed. Nancy Henry writes: 'in the first chapter alone Maggie is compared to a Skye terrier, a long-tailed sheep, and a Shetland pony',[21] drawing attention to her affinity with the natural world. An ecocritical reevaluation of Victorian literature posits the historical emergence of ecology 'as both a scientific and a social philosophy' in relation to evolutionary theory.[22] As John Parham observes further, 'evolutionary theory and energy physics ... allowed for the development of an understanding, albeit incomplete, [of ecosystems as] characterized by the complex, dialectical—cooperative and competitive—interrelation between species'.[23] Consequently, the Victorians began to expand upon 'a broadly materialist awareness that "human being", as molded by social and political institutions, ultimately resides in the nature and quality of humanity's relationship with other species and its surrounding physical environment'.[24] Maggie's ability to nurture moments of joy with the family dog Yap is indicative of the existence of a framework of animal relationships and metaphors. The pivotal importance of such relationships in Maggie's life takes cognisance of the tensions in the narrative and Maggie's resistance to normative structures.

Maggie's efforts to reach beyond Victorian gender constructs, especially in the Red Deeps sequences, offer rich possibilities of narrative reconfigurations. From her childhood, Maggie has been true to her non-normative nature despite attempts to cultivate her as an English garden is shaped and pruned. Her meetings in the Red Deeps with Philip Wakem pave the way for unprecedented intellectual and personal expansion, providing for Maggie 'a pleasure she loved so well, that sometimes in her ardours of renunciation, she thought she ought to deny herself the frequent indulgence in it' (bk. 5, ch. 1). The natural world of the Red Deeps is a space that is stripped of artifice and convention. Maggie's relation to nature bestows on her immediate sexual power, but also exposes her to potential commodification and hence to the risk of being 'denaturalized'.[25] Maggie's affinities to

Scotch firs and wilderness, and her later struggle with colonising forces (like Tom, Stephen Guest, and the community at large), render the text a compelling indictment of a mindset that encloses, encumbers, and even enslaves her in parallel with what another discourse shows as the ruling British mindset in colonial India.

Here, we turn to Bibhutibhushan Bandyopadhyay's Bangla novel, *Pather Panchali* (1929), better known beyond Bengal by its English title *Song of the Road* after Satyajit Ray's 1956 film of that name achieved international recognition. Though Rabindranath wrote on the Bengal hinterlands, notably in *Chhinapatrabali* (first published in 2012 and translated into English in 2014 by Rosinka Chaudhuri as *Letters from a Young Poet*), it was Bibhutibhushan who delineated the magical landscape of rural Bengal in a manner reminiscent of both the English Romantic poets and the pristine beauty of the Vaishanava Padavali in Bengal. The Vaishanava Padavali was a movement that flourished from the fifteenth to the seventeenth centuries, reflecting an earthly view of divine love. Bibhutibhushan found peace and fulfilment in a natural landscape, acknowledging the simple ecopoetic joys of life.

The Norwegian philosopher Arne S. Naess writes on ecosophy in the following terms:

> By an ecosophy, I mean a philosophy of ecological harmony or equilibrium. A philosophy as a kind of sofia (or) wisdom, is openly normative, it contains both norms, rules, postulates, value priority announcements, and hypotheses concerning the state of affairs in our universe. Wisdom is policy wisdom, prescription, not only scientific description and prediction. The details of an ecosophy will show many variations due to significant differences concerning not only the 'facts' of pollution, resources, population, etc. but also value priorities.[26]

Pather Panchali and its sequel, *Aparajito* (1931), may be read as a two-part Bildungsroman which narrates the story of a young boy named Apu living in a remote village of Bengal—the fictitious Nishchindipur. The novel not only delineates Apu's journey but also narrates his story in relation both to his immediate family and to the microcosmic and macrocosmic forces that nurture and change his life from early childhood in rural Bengal to young adulthood in the burgeoning metropolitan and colonial city, Calcutta. The childhood of the siblings Apu and his elder sister Durga can be interpreted in terms of ecosophy, as Bibhutibhushan depicts the joys of nature through their ramblings. They spend a childhood of poverty and joy in the rural landscape of the Ichhamoti River, the autumnal clear blue skies resplendent with the fragrance of the *chatim* flowers and echoing with the folk songs and rituals that usher in a new season.

Apu's relationship with Durga is crucial. They share a deep-rooted emotional connection, unlike the difficult and tangled relationship of Maggie and Tom Tulliver. However, while Apu's imaginative life is always directed towards the world outside, Durga's world is firmly embedded in the village, physically and mentally. Durga's imagination is earthbound—her perceptions are sensory—in touch and taste. She has a remarkable ability to empathise with the weak and the persecuted (the widowed old aunt, the uncouth street dog, the neighbour's wife being beaten by her abusive husband). Durga also collects heterogeneous objects in a broken chest—bits of a broken mirror, beads from a string, a gold sindoor box. The chest is broken by her mother, Sarbajaya, in a fit of anger, an episode that in many ways marks a ritualistic end of Durga's childhood. The barefooted waif with tangled hair may be seen as a free spirit, who cannot be held by the prosaic constraints of gender roles, and as such Durga cannot grow to adulthood and be bound to a marriage. Her death, therefore, is inevitable. On one of her solitary walks in the fields, Durga witnesses a young peasant bride wailing in a bullock cart making her way to her new 'home', and she wonders:

> If I go away from here, leaving my parents and Apu behind, will I ever be allowed to come back? She could not conceive that she will have to leave for ever the garden, this grove of *basak* flowers, this copper-coloured cow, the shade of her favourite jackfruit tree, the smell of dry leaves and path to the river.[27]

According to Meenakshi Mukherjee, Apu is permitted to widen his physical and mental horizons, but Durga's desires and her mobility are constrained as she grows up. In fact, her 'untamed spirit' is akin to 'the unkempt overgrown bushes and swamps of Nishchindipur—or with Vishalakshi Debi, the neglected local deity of the village'.[28] Just before her fatal illness, Durga is shown running through green orchards, chirping birds, and open grounds, trying to 'touch' nature:

> She was so happy she felt like running right across the open fields, from one end to the other. She could not of course, but she did run around in a wide circle flashing her arms up and down like wings. If only she could fly! Her body was light enough. If only she could spread her arms like wings and breast the wind with the birds.[29]

The spatial movement facilitates emotional recapitulation of precious moments of childhood, freedom, and innocence. The memory of Durga's memory becomes ensconced in Apu's mind as a tangible part of a distant past, when he was closer to nature. Durga Chew Bose discussing Ray's film based on the novel writes:

> For most of *Pather Panchali,* we experience Durga in her role as older sister to her younger brother, Apu. She is his compass: the first face he sees when he wakes up in the morning, the hand that slaps him when he borrows tinsel from her toy box without asking, the tongue that sticks

out and makes him smile … Durga is the water-skaters, the dragonflies, the lilies. Durga is the train passing through the kaash field; she is the show of black smoke that lingers in its wake. She is the leftovers of a family forced to move on, the home once the home is no more. She is also there with Apu, a boy no longer in possession of his compass but equipped instead with a stare that is already wiser. Apu continues, alone but not exactly, because there she is. Look.[30]

The discourse of memory is concerned with representation and the present. It subverts absolutist assertions of historical truth and approaches the past in a more qualified manner. In 'Notes on Filming Bibhuti Bhusan', Satyajit Ray writes further on the cinematic process:

One can be entirely true to the spirit of Bibhuti Bhusan, retain a large measure of his other characteristics—lyricism and humanism combined with a casual narrative structure—and yet produce a legitimate work of cinema. Indeed, it is easier with Bibhuti Bhusan than with any other writer in Bengal. The true basis of the film style of *Pather Panchali* is not neo-realist cinema or any other school of cinema or even any individual work of cinema, but the novel of Bibhuti Bhusan itself.[31]

The narratives of Durga and Maggie are framed through a juxtaposition of collective memory and popular imagination, thereby creating a narrative of exclusion, extermination, and resistance.

Apu's gradual movement towards a larger world is juxtaposed to the open fields of Sonadanga and the ghat of Kadamtala Sahib of Nishchidipur. The Song of the Road continues as the Deity of the Road beckons Apu:

The deity of the eternal road smiles benevolently and asserts, Foolish boy, the path of life does not end in the bamboo grove of your village, or under the peepul tree of Biru Roy, the Thug, or near the ferry ghat of the village Dhalchita. The road proceeds endlessly forward from one country to another, from the land of sunrise to the sunset, from the known to the unknown … days pass by, birth and death pass by months and years pass by … my path never ends … goes on, on and on. Eternal is its harp heard by the eternal time and eternal space. Putting the unseen mark of wonderful pleasure trip of the road on your forehead, I have drawn you out of home. Let's go ahead.[32]

Pather Panchali does not end in catastrophe like *The Mill on the Floss*. Rather, it engages with a continued understanding of the world through the eyes of both Durga and Apu. The cycle of seasons in Nishchindpur is echoed in the rhythm of the novel rooted both in European Romanticism and also in an oral storytelling tradition of mythical tales in India. Durga and Apu may be seen as young environmental activists in extremely adverse conditions who find a unique voice through the mode of the *panchali*. According to Meenakshi Mukherjee,

> Perhaps unknown to the author himself, the structure of the novel is modified by a concept of time quite different from what underlies realistic fiction as it originated in the west. The word *panchali* in the title refers to a ritualistic narrative song which continues at length without any perceptible climax or a cause and effect relationship connecting the sequences.[33]

Each of Eliot, Saratchandra, and Bibhutibhushan articulates a dialogic exchange within the cultural and geographical ecotones of their writings. The 'Conclusion' of *The Mill on the Floss* repeats the phrase 'Nature repairs its ravages', referring not just to the flood at St. Ogg's but also to Maggie herself. The Victorians responded to their changing world with a 'multiplicity' of different arguments drawing on 'a bewildering array of influences: Romanticism, Christianity, mysticism and spirituality, Darwinism, feudalism, [and] socialism', influences that articulated themselves through the discourse of government reports, newspaper accounts, and literary fiction.[34] Maggie resists the nature of the world in which she lives. She is indeed a 'thing out of nature'. Kyle McAuley draws attention to the 'estuarial form' of Eliot's novel that

> structures the area's [St Ogg's'] ecological change in two entangled ways: first, its status as a global mercantile gateway makes the terraforming of rural development possible; and more broadly, the continual opposition of the interflowing currents and tides portends the ecological catastrophe spurred by this development's catastrophic inexorability.[35]

Tom and Maggie's fatal 'embrace never to be parted' is emblematic of their intertwining fates at St. Ogg's and their diverse conditions of existence.

Scholars like Ramachandra Guha and Rob Nixon have drawn attention to the 'environmentalism of the poor' which focuses on the nuanced environmental activism beyond the ambit of industrialised nations.[36] In contradistinction to the 'environmentalism [conceived of] in largely mental terms as a question of values affirmed or denied, "post-materialist" or "anti-materialist"', the 'environmentalism of the poor' has an unmistakable material context.[37] Such a context 'originate[s] in social conflicts over access to and control over natural resources'.[38] The 'truth claim' of the narrative challenges established hierarchies with nature, gender, or race. The blurred and fluid boundaries of 'otherness' create a collective story or what Ronald Takaki refers to as a community of memory.[39] The novelists anticipate ecological concerns by interrogating the linkages between racism, colonialism, and sexism that play in our imaginings of, and relationships to, the changing histories of the environment. The authors examine the conventions of reading landscape, including the implied expectations of the reader, the question of the gendered narrator, and how place defines the kind of action and characters in the novels of these versatile writers. Each writer defines the relevance of landscape in creating mood and the pastoral as a moral marker for readers in terms of paradigmatic shifts in aesthetic theory. In the process, they draw our attention to the significance of such references in the evocation of cultural and environmental history in their novels. Thus, the novelists facilitate a much-needed engagement around the complex and historically situated ways in which the literary world imagines and inhabits the environment in their oeuvre.

Notes

1 S.L. Ghosh, 'An Introduction to Modern Bengali Fiction', *Indian Literature*, 12 (1969), 75.
2 David Knopf, *British Orientalism and the Bengal Renaissance: The Dynamics of Indian Modernization 1773-1835* (Berkeley: University of California Press, 1969), 2–3.
3 Homi K. Bhabha, 'Of Mimicry and Man: The Ambivalence of Colonial Discourse', in *The Location of Culture*, ed. Homi K. Bhabha (London and New York: Routledge, 1994), 85–92.
4 Bankimchandra Chattopadhyay (1838–94) was one of the most successful Bangla novelists of the Bengal Renaissance, and also wrote poems, songs, satires, and non-fiction. His first novel, *Rajmohan's Wife* (1864), was written in English. He wrote very well-known Bengali novels like *Durgeshnandini* (1865), *Vishabriksha* (*The Poison Tree*, 1873), *Anandamath* (1882), *Debi Choudhurani* (1884), and *Sitaram* (1887), among others.
5 Rabindranath Tagore (1861–1941) is Bengal's most notable poet, novelist, dramatist, and prose writer. He won the Nobel Prize in 1913 for his book of poems *Gitanjali* (*Song Offerings*). He was a prolific novelist, author of canonical novels such as *Choker Bali* (*Eyesore*, 1903), *Gora* (1910), *Noukadubi* (*The Boat Drowning*, 1906), *Ghaire Baire* (*The Home and the World*, 1916), and *Char Adhay* (*Four Chapters*, 1933), among others. Saratchandra and Tagore enjoyed great mutual respect.
6 Saratchandra Chattopadhyay (or Chatterjee) wrote shorter novels such as *Biraj-Bau*, *Palli Samaj*, *Arakshaniya*, *Pandit Mashai*, *Niskriti*, and *Bamuner Meye*, and short stories such as *Mahesh*, *Abhagir Swarga*, *Ekadashi Bairagi*, *Bilasi*, *Mamlar Phal*, *Ramer Sumati* and *Bindur Chhele*, as well as essays and other works.
7 Narasingha Prasad Sil, *The Life of Sharatchandra Chattopadhyay: Drifter and Dreamer* (Madison, New Jersey and British Columbia: Fairleigh Dickinson University Press, 2012), 8.
8 See also Vishnu Prabhakar, *Great Vagabond: Biography and Immortal Works of Sarat Chandra Chatterjee*, tr. Jai Rata (New Delhi: B. R. Publishing, 1990). Saratchandra Chattopadhyay and Sarat Chandra Chatterjee are different spellings and surnames used to denote the same author. 'Chatterjee' is the British version of the Bengali Brahmin surname 'Chattopadhyay'.

9　Narayan Chaudhuri, 'Social Changes as Reflected in Bengali Literature', *Indian Literature*, 14 (1971), 93.

10　John Plotz, 'The Semi-Detached Victorian Novel', *Victorian Studies*, 53 (2011), 408.

11　Critic Narayan Chaudhuri similarly observed in 'Social Changes as Reflected in Bengali Literature', *Indian Literature*, 14 (1971), 48:

> It is not for nothing that Saratchandra wrote the book *Nareer Mulya* (tr. *The Worth of Women*), espousing the cause of women in general. In this respect he was greatly influenced by the writings of Herbert Spencer and possibly also of John Stuart Mill.

12　See also Sil, *The Life of Sharatchandra Chattopadhyay*, 6–7.

13　Gopal Haldar, 'Tradition of Saratchandra in Bengali Novel', *Indian Literature*, 19 (1976), 66.

14　Amalendu Bose, 'Saratchandra: His Novelistic Technique', *Indian Literature*, 19 (1976), 75.

15　Subhash Chandra Sarker, 'Sarat Chandra Chatterjee: The Great Humanist', *Indian Literature*, 20 (1977), 56.

16　See Kirsten Holst Petersen and Anna Rutherford, eds., *A Double Colonization: Colonial and Post-colonial Women's Writing* (Mundelstrup and Oxford: Dangaroo Press, 1986), 1–12.

17　Bibhutibhushan Bandyopadhyay is best known for his novels, such as *Pather Panchali, Aparajito, Aranyak, Adarsha Hindu Hotel, Ichhamati, Drishti Pradeep, Chander Pahar, Hire Manik Jale, Bipiner Sangsar, Anubartan, Ashani Sanket, Kedar Raja, Dampati, Sundarbane Sat Batsar* (not completed by him), *Dui Bari, Kajol*—sequel of *Aparajito* (completed by his son Taradas), *Maroner Danka Baje, Mismider Kabach, Aam Antir Bhenpu*, and many more prose narratives.

18　George Eliot, *The Mill on the Floss*, new edn, ed. Gordon S. Haight (1860; Oxford: Oxford World's Classics, 2015), bk 6, ch. 7. Further references to this edition appear parenthetically in text.

19　Tim Dolin, *George Eliot* (Oxford: Oxford University Press, 2005), 247.

20　Douglas Kellner, *Media Culture Cultural Studies, Identity, and Politics in the Contemporary Moment* (New York: Routledge, 2020), 35.

21　Nancy Henry, *The Cambridge Introduction to George Eliot* (Cambridge: Cambridge University Press, 2008), 57.

22　John Parham, 'Was there a Victorian Ecology?', in *The Environmental Tradition in English Literature*, ed. John Parham (Aldershot: Ashgate, 2002), 156.

23　John Parham, 'Editorial: Victorian Ecology', *Green Letters: Studies in Ecocriticism*, 14 (2011), 5.

24　Parham, 'Editorial', 5.

25　M. Melissa Elston, '"A World Outside": George Eliot's Ekphrastic Third Sphere In "The Mill on the Floss"', *George Eliot-George Henry Lewes Studies*, 62/63 (2012), 35.

26　Arne Shewry Naess, *Ecology, Community, Lifestyle: Outline of an Ecosophy* (Cambridge: Cambridge University Press, 1989), 9.

27　Bibhutibhushan Bandyopadhyay, *Pather Panchali: Song of the Road*, tr. T.W. Clark and T. Mukherji (London: George Allen and Unwin, 1968), 184.

28 Meenakshi Mukherjee, 'An Analysis of *Pather Panchali*', *Journal of Arts and Ideas*, 3 (1983), 22.

29 Bandyopadhyay, *Pather Panchali*, 183.

30 Durga Chew Bose, 'Constant Compass: Uma Das Gupta in *Pather Panchali*' in *The Criterion Collection* (Features, 8 May 2017), www.criterion.com/current/posts/4535-constant-compass-uma-das-gupta-in-pather-panchali, accessed 3 April 2020.

31 Satyajit Ray, 'Notes on Filming Bibhuti Bhusan', in *Satyajit Ray on Cinema*, ed. Sandip Ray, Satyajit Ray, Dhritiman Chatterji, Arup K. De, Deepak Mukherjee, Debasis Mukhopadhyay, and Shyam Benegal (New York: Columbia University Press, 2011), 10.

32 Bandyopadhyay, *Pather Panchali*, 208.

33 Meenakshi Mukherjee, 'The House and the Road: Two Modes of Autobiographical Fiction', *Journal of Caribbean Literatures*, 5 (2008), 63.

34 Parham, 'Editorial', 6.

35 Kyle McAuley, 'George Eliot's Estuarial Form', *Victorian Literature and Culture*, 48 (2020), 189.

36 Ramachandra Guha and Joan Martinez-Alier, *Varieties of Environmentalism: Essays North and South* (London: Earthscan, 1997), 55–9; Rob Nixon, *Slow Violence and the Environmentalism of the Poor* (Cambridge: Harvard University Press, 2011), 47; and Rob Nixon, 'Environmentalism and Postcolonialism', in *Postcolonial Studies and Beyond*, ed. Ania Loomba and Suvir Kaul (Durham: Duke University Press 2005), 233–51.

37 Guha and Martinez-Alier, *Varieties of Environmentalism*, 5.

38 Guha and Martinez-Alier, *Varieties of Environmentalism*, xxi.

39 Ronald Takaki, *Strangers from a Different Shore: A History of Asian Americans* (Boston/New York: Little Brown, 1998), 89.

5 A Roar of Sound

George Eliot on Sympathy and the Problem of Other Minds

Moira Gatens

> One cannot give a recipe for wise judgment: it resembles appropriate muscular action, which is attained by the myriad lessons in nicety of balance and of aim that only practice can give.[1]

Recent scholarship leaves no room for doubt concerning George Eliot's scientific and philosophical credentials.[2] She translated dense and challenging works by David Strauss, Ludwig Feuerbach, and Benedict Spinoza, assisted her partner-in-life, George Henry Lewes, with his biography of Goethe, and completed Lewes' massive five-volume magnum opus, *The Problems of Life and Mind*, after his death.[3] In addition to being Lewes' valued interlocutor, Eliot exchanged scientific and philosophical ideas with Herbert Spencer and influenced countless other intellectual luminaries of the time through her clandestine editorship of the *Westminster Review*, to which she also contributed many essays and reviews.[4] Virginia Woolf captured something of Eliot's exceptional status when she wrote: 'She knew everyone. She read everything'.[5] However, Eliot's fame and influence are not of only historical interest. Contemporary scholars judge that the contributions made by her novels to moral philosophy have yet to be fully appreciated. Her novels explore complex philosophical themes around issues such as determinism, self-deception, and responsibility. In this essay, I will focus on her nuanced account of the role of sympathy in our cognitive and moral life.

The central role of sympathy in Eliot's theory of mind and morality is well known, with Melissa Raines going so far as to state that '"sympathy" is at the heart of any work by George Eliot'.[6] Less appreciated by her critics is the philosophical subtlety of her account of the sympathetic imagination and her acute awareness of its limitations and potential abuses in the moral arena. Contemporary neuroscience and moral psychology count the capacity for sympathetic identification as crucial to the human ability to engage in complex and reciprocal processes of intersubjective exchange essential to even the most basic forms of sociability, for example, 'mindreading'. Two prominent contemporary philosophers of mind, Shaun Nichols and Stephen Stich, have remarked that in addition to its importance to the lofty endeavours of philosophical research, mindreading is also at work in

DOI: 10.4324/9781003362821-6

everyday 'mundane chores, like trying to figure out what the baby wants, what your peers believe about your work, and what your spouse will do if you arrive home late'.[7] They further remark that the concepts central to the phenomenon of mindreading—belief, desire, intention—refer to 'unobservable states'.[8] When we form a view about the other's state of mind, we necessarily exercise our imagination and powers of inference. Through intonation, body language, and context, most of us are able to 'read' the attitudinal states of others beyond the bare factual content conveyed by an ambiguous statement like: 'My supervisor is very friendly'. As will become evident, such exercises of the sympathetic imagination involve reciprocal perspective-taking and should not be confused with a mere 'reflex' action. Eliot wrestled directly with the problem of other minds, sympathy, and moral judgement in 'The Lifted Veil' (1859), which was published more than a decade before *Middlemarch* (1871–72).

Even casual students of Eliot know that she devoted an extraordinary amount of time to detailed research concerning the medium in which her characters act and suffer (the dialects they would have spoken, their historical and political context, geography, mode of dress, social mores, and so on). 'The Lifted Veil' and *Middlemarch* are no exceptions, but it should be noted that both works present especially clear instances of Eliot's profound knowledge of contemporary science and its contested boundaries. 'The Lifted Veil' treats 'double consciousness', phrenology, mesmerism, mindreading, and prevision, alongside the then dubious procedure of blood transfusion (it is noteworthy that it was not until 1901 that Karl Landsteiner discovered the three blood types). Likewise, *Middlemarch* considers the existence of a 'primitive tissue' underlying organic life, new hygiene medical procedures, innovative treatments for fever, and so on. Eliot always gets her facts right, and given the complexity and range of the issues she deals with, this is impressive. However, the more philosophically important point is that she sees that such facts, although crucial, do not determine the human meanings and significances that inevitably shadow facts and science. For that more subtle work, we require skill in reading context, nuance, an active imagination, and an affective awareness. Consider what Eliot wrote in a letter after she had read Charles Darwin's *Origin of Species* (1859): 'the Development theory and all other explanations of processes by which things came to be, produce a feeble impression compared with the mystery that lies under the processes'.[9] At the close of this chapter, I will return to this statement and put it in a light that resists a mystical interpretation.

Eliot's vast knowledge of science, and her strict respect for facts and veracity, are what make her deliberations on the *meaning* of science and facts so philosophically valuable and enduring. On her view, the moral imagination, rightly configured, imbues facts with a sympathetic perspective that acknowledges not only the facts of the matter, but also the context, the affective force of those facts, and a certain ineffability intrinsic to human life. Undergirding Eliot's exploration of the moral imagination is a distinction that animates all her work: between stupidity and morality, or put more fully, between what she calls an inborn egoism, on one hand, and hard-won moral wisdom, on the other. For her, wise judgement is an art attained only through attention, experience, and practice, as the epigraph to this chapter suggests.

The title of her novella, 'The Lifted Veil', likely refers to a sonnet, 'Lift Not The Painted Veil', by Percy Bysshe Shelley, which reads, in part:

Lift not the painted veil which those who live
Call Life: though unreal shapes be pictured there,
And it but mimic all we would believe
With colours idly spread,—behind, lurk Fear
And Hope, twin Destinies; who ever weave
Their shadows, o'er the chasm, sightless and drear.[10]

The painted veil refers to the screen between self and others, the present and the future, ignorance and knowledge, and ultimately, life and death. 'The Lifted Veil' is a first-person narrative by Latimer, an apparently delicate, introverted, and hypersensitive character who presents himself as possessing 'the poet's sensibility without his voice', that is, a poet who fails to create any works.[11]

After a serious illness in his late adolescence, Latimer discovers that he has acquired two uncanny powers: *insight* (into the minds of others) and *foresight* (into the future), which he refers to as his 'double-consciousness'. Thus, the 'twin destinies' that on Shelley's description serve to frame human experience—hope and fear—are foreclosed to him. Without hope or fear, Latimer cannot experience mystery, doubt, or anticipation (ch. 1). The shadowy but nevertheless protective veil, woven out of hope and fear, has been lifted for him, and he is left pitifully exposed to the 'sightless and drear' abyss. Consider Latimer's description of the foresight of his own death that includes reference to the 'Unknown Presence' (ch. 2) lurking within the abysmal darkness that awaits him and is 'something unknown and pitiless' (ch. 2).

Latimer views his mindreading, which is perhaps more accurately described as 'mindhearing', as a power that cuts through the pretence involved in everyday sociability. He doesn't just hope or fear that his inferences about others' thoughts are correct, he actually hears their thoughts, and he knows some of what the future holds. What the narrator refers to as the breath of life of the soul, namely, its capacity to doubt, hope, and so have reason to strive, depends upon life's contingencies remaining 'hidden and uncertain' (ch. 2). Latimer's soul is deprived of this life breath with one significant exception: a young woman named Bertha, a cold figure described as having 'pale grey eyes at once acute, restless, and sarcastic' (ch. 1). She becomes the fiancée of Alfred, Latimer's robustly masculine, older half-brother. However, in one of his visions of the future, Latimer sees Bertha not as his sister-in-law but as his own wife; he sees also that her future self utterly despises him, wishes him dead, and that their marriage is a torture for them both. This knowledge does not cancel his desire for her in the present, and after his brother dies in a horse-riding accident, Latimer does, indeed, become her husband.

Does Latimer's superordinate power of insight give rise to an equally superordinate power of sympathetic understanding? Does it furnish him with self-knowledge and compassion? Latimer's exceptional involuntary powers appear to be more akin to having privileged access to facts about the thoughts of others rather than a genuine grasp of what Nichols and Stich referred to as the 'unobservable states', that is, the beliefs, desires, and intentions of others that mindreading aims to grasp. Latimer's extraordinary hearing power is closer to an intellectual reflex than to an imaginative sympathetic engagement with a different other, and it has the effect of alienating him from others and from himself. He finds his access to the thoughts of others exhausting, and his insight merely serves to reinforce his melancholic and reclusive nature. What Latimer finds nesting in the minds of others is petty egoism. In a compelling passage, Latimer tells the reader that he found his knowledge of the interiority of strangers annoying, but when it came to hearing the thoughts of those close to him, it was worse than an annoyance: it was intensely painful because

> when the rational talk, the graceful attentions, the wittily-turned phrases, and the kindly deeds, which used to make the web of their characters, were seen as if thrust asunder by a microscopic vision, that showed all the intermediate frivolities, all the suppressed egoism, all the struggling chaos of puerilities, meanness, vague capricious memories, and indolent make-shift thoughts, from which human words and deeds emerge like leaflets covering a fermenting heap.
>
> (ch. 1)

Suzy Anger claims that all of Eliot's novels 'are centrally about the persistent problems of knowing the world and other minds'.[12] 'The Lifted Veil' is Eliot's philosophical thought experiment concerning what mere knowledge of the other's mind might entail: not sympathy and concern but antipathy and repulsion. This 'slight story', a '*jeu de melancolie*', as she described it to her publisher John Blackwood (*GEL*, 3: 41), provides clear evidence of Eliot's scepticism concerning the power of either purely intellectual knowledge, on one hand, or a basic human sympathetic mechanism, on the other, to yield genuine moral knowledge. Rather, the novella gives body to her view that

> there is not a more pernicious fallacy afloat in common parlance, than the wide distinction made between intellect and morality. Amiable impulses without intellect, man may have in common with dogs and horses; but morality, which is specifically human, is dependent on *the regulation of feeling by intellect*.[13]

As will be shown, Eliot never subscribed to a naïve theory about the role of sympathetic feeling in moral life, and the figure of Latimer demonstrates that as well as having amiable impulses without knowledge, one can also have knowledge without amiability.[14] Without the exercise of the reflective imagination, neither capacity can result in moral competence. For her, as for Adam Smith, sympathy is a necessary but not a sufficient component of moral agency. The misanthropic Latimer embodies the philosophical problem posed by a lack of sympathy, but a detailed consideration of its complexity was not offered until the publication of *Middlemarch*. Rather than turn to contemporary philosophers in order to elaborate these themes, I prefer to consult those philosophical resources that Eliot herself drew upon in working through this cluster of problems: Adam Smith, Ludwig Feuerbach, and Benedict Spinoza.[15]

Three Problems for Mind and Morality

Eliot lays out three philosophical problems in 'The Lifted Veil', problems that cannot be adequately addressed in that brief story but to which she returns again and again in her fictional and non-fictional writings. First, she is exploring the insufficiency of either pure intellect (Kantian or deontological theory) or a sympathetic reflex (crude Sentimentalism) to alone ground moral life. Second, she sketches a theory about the difficulty of achieving moral maturity given universal inborn egoism. Third, Eliot shows that ways of knowing and ways of being are co-implicated and that this feature of human life is unable to be expressed in abstract facts alone or captured in a purely scientific language. I will treat each theme briefly in turn to show that the moral view Eliot develops through her fiction has its roots deep in the philosophies of Smith, Feuerbach, and Spinoza. Although each thinker's influence is strong in all three of the problems laid out here, for the sake of brevity, I will refer to Adam Smith to elucidate Eliot's conception of the moral imagination, Feuerbach for the problem of inborn egoism, and Spinoza for the co-implication of ways of being and ways of knowing. It should be noted, however, that the sympathetic *imagination* plays an essential role in the philosophy of mind of all three thinkers, and this role serves to unite these otherwise disparate philosophers with respect to their accounts of moral wisdom.

The Insufficiency of Intellect or Feeling to Alone Ground Morality

We have seen that Eliot rejects the basic contagion or imitative theory of sympathy as able to provide an adequate ground for morality. However, in *The Mill on the Floss*, the contrary view, where intellect and duty are taken as sufficient to ground morality, is also rejected:

> All people of broad, strong sense have an instinctive repugnance to the men of maxims; because such people early discern that the mysterious

complexity of our life is not to be embraced by maxims, and that to lace ourselves up in formulas of that sort is to repress all the divine promptings and inspirations that spring from growing insight and sympathy. And the man of maxims is the popular representative of the minds that are guided in their moral judgment solely by general rules, thinking that these will lead them to justice by a ready-made patent method, without the trouble of exerting *patience, discrimination, impartiality,* — without any care to assure themselves whether they have the insight that comes from a *hardly-earned estimate of temptation,* or from a life vivid and intense enough to have *created a wide fellow-feeling* with all that is human.[16]

Clearly then, Eliot's view of moral agency involves both feeling and intellect, both care and impartiality, and puts a premium on sympathetic judgement that is achievable only through reflection on experience. This moral stance is embodied in the Impartial Spectator, as described by Adam Smith. Some contemporary philosophers are critical of Sentimentalist moral theorists, like Smith, whom they mistakenly represent as positing an automatic sympathetic fellow-feeling as sufficient ground for moral judgement. For example, Jesse Prinz has argued that sympathy is intrinsically egoistic, biased towards those closest to us, and performs poorly when it comes to distant or different others. Prinz briefly considers Smith's device of the Impartial Spectator only to dismiss it as idealistic.[17] However, as Millicent Churcher rightly points out, this interpretation of Smith's moral stance is flawed. The Impartial Spectator undoubtedly presents a demanding figure, but it is nevertheless attainable by an embodied, situated individual who is able to engage in 'sufficiently informed (though not perfectly informed), attentive, and critically self-reflective exercises of imaginative perspective taking'.[18] Moreover, on Smith's view, a concordance of sentiments between the spectator and the agent is necessary to motivate moral behaviour and to create and sustain harmonious social relationships.

Unfortunately, when discussing the role of sympathy in her novels, some of Eliot's critics also take an overly simplistic view of its nature and its place in moral life and fail to note her deep agreement with Smith.[19] Like him, she sees that sympathy often fails and that a well-honed moral imagination involves the cultivation of reflection and deliberation on our beliefs and desires. In an exceptionally insightful paper, Rae Greiner shows how Smith's account of sympathy, 'activated by intellectual and imaginative power, coupled with will, takes a self-consciously narrative form', making it an ideal vehicle for novelistic representation.[20] It should come as no surprise, then, that Eliot shares with Smith the conviction that ethics and aesthetics are essentially connected endeavours: both engage our imaginative, affective, and deliberative capacities. Both require the passage of time if mere impulse, sensation, or desire is to be transformed into reflectively endorsed aesthetic or moral judgement. For both Smith and Eliot, it is not only a matter of feeling with, and for our fellow human beings, it also a matter of grasping the meaning and significance *that their feelings have for them* in a way that allows us to attend to and evaluate them appropriately. Before becoming a fiction writer, Eliot had remarked in an essay that the peculiar power of art stems from it 'being the nearest thing to life; it is a mode of amplifying experience' that can surprise 'even the trivial and the selfish into that attention to what is apart from themselves, which may be called the raw material of moral sentiment'.[21]

For all Latimer's claims to delicacy and sensitivity, he fails to attend to what is apart from himself. His apparent omniscience involves hearing without understanding. He fails to 'see' the other in her specificity. Indeed, he has only a patchy knowledge about the thoughts and feelings of others, and he is unable to put that knowledge into an imaginative frame that would facilitate reciprocity in relation to the feelings and judgements of others. He refers to his extraordinary powers as a 'dreary desert of knowledge' (ch. 1). His knowing is conspicuously abstract and general rather than involving feeling-with a particular other.[22] Unable to calibrate his own desires with the thoughts and desires of those around him, Latimer's thoughts and feelings are almost always firmly focused on himself and his own preoccupations and petty resentments.

It is not only what Latimer knows—or doesn't know—that matters. What matters is his manner of knowing (a theme that will be treated explicitly when we turn to Spinoza on ways of knowing, below). Lewes made a similar point when he remarked that 'The Lifted Veil' 'is only an exaggeration of what happens—the one-sided knowing of things in relation to the self'.[23] Latimer's 'one-sided knowing' not only shows a lack of charity towards others, it also forecloses any hope of achieving a 'concordance of sentiments' with them. He fails to acknowledge his own egoism and the vulnerability of others to *his* gaze and to *his* judgement of them. And this lack cannot be made good through acquiring more facts about others. The one being that can cause Latimer to experience hope and fear—Bertha, in all her opacity—provides only temporary relief from his suffering. He knows that the curtain between them will drop, and he has foreseen what it will reveal: her contempt and loathing for him. In the course of his contemplation of this future horror, he makes a direct appeal to the reader: 'Are you unable to give me your sympathy—you who read this?' (ch. 1). The rather defeatist 'are you unable' (rather than 'are you able?') is probably affirmed by many readers given Latimer's disagreeable narcissism and self-pity. In the same passage where he seeks succour from the reader, Latimer remarks that Bertha, once subjected to his 'unhappy gift of insight', will be 'no longer a fascinating secret, but a measured fact' (ch. 1). His way of knowing the other only as abstraction, a measurement, a fact, exposes his incapacity for *imaginative* fellow feeling, and imagination is the essential soil of Eliot's moral landscape. As the following section will show, Latimer's egoism prevents him from forming moral community with others. His claim, early in 'The Lifted Veil', that he was not encouraged 'to trust much in the sympathy of my fellow-men' (ch. 1) has hardened by the end of the story into a rigid incapacity to *imagine* the pains and pleasures of others as more than mere facts about them. Knowing a fact about someone does not entail understanding how that fact makes him feel, or what it means in the context of his life. Latimer's lack of imagination is what prevents him from sympathising with others, and it is also what blocks the expression of his poetic ambitions: he is morally and aesthetically barren.

Egoism and the Difficulty of Developing Moral Reciprocity

Eliot famously enthused in a letter: 'with the ideas of Feuerbach I everywhere agree' (*GEL*, 2: 153). The philosophers favoured by Eliot tend to place the imagination at the centre of their thought, or at least view the relation between imagination and reason as the central question for their theories of mind and morality. Her strong attachment to Feuerbach stems, in part, from her admiration of his analysis of religion and his constant endeavour to incarnate the ideas that have dominated human consciousness, to bring human abstractions (which have no existence outside the intellect) back to the fleshy particulars from which they developed.[24] There is an egoism at work in these abstractions, especially those that posit aspects of human excellence in exaggerated, idealised terms that are then projected onto supernatural beings (like God, Saints, or Martyrs) as qualities such as omniscience, omnipotence, and omnibenevolence. Egoism is behind the pleasure taken in the contemplation of a perfect being who is an idealised figure of humanity, as well as the motivation that drives a conception of human immortality.

Eliot, like Feuerbach, was keen to return to human beings that which they have abstracted into the heavens. She expressed as much in a letter of August 1868 when she described the aim of her novels as being

> to help my readers in getting a clearer conception and a more active admiration of those vital elements which bind men together and give a higher worthiness to their existence; and also to help them in gradually dissociating these elements from the more transient forms on which an outworn teaching tends to make them dependent.
>
> (*GEL*, 4: 472)

Although religion can provide comfort and moral guidance, human maturity must involve the recognition that love, forgiveness, and redemption are embodied in human relationships and communities. Along with Feuerbach, Eliot recognised that such enlightenment involves an inevitable blow to inborn egoism and narcissism. What we lose in forfeiting the illusions of religion we gain in the enriched and embodied I–Thou relations that Feuerbach posits as the true basis of divinity. Such a worldview, of course, places a high value on the quality of human relationships and our capacities to love and support each other. The ethical task becomes more, rather than less, important once morality loses its transcendent warrant. The efficacy of the sympathetic moral imagination now takes on an urgency that philosophy and art are obliged to address.

For Feuerbach, becoming an independent moral agent necessarily involves understanding the role of the imagination and emotion in relation to reason. In *The Essence of Christianity*, he wrote that imagination is the necessary 'middle term between the abstract and the concrete' and then adds that 'the task of philosophy ... is to comprehend the relation of the imagination to the reason,—the genesis of the image by means of which an object of thought becomes an object of sense, of feeling'.[25] In this passage, he is referring to the figure of Christ who mediates between the abstract idea of God and the world, but the analysis holds good across the human tendency to universalise particulars in a manner that cancels our capacity for moral behaviour towards our embodied fellow human beings. Instead, our capacity for love and morality is squandered on non-existent abstractions, such as the worship of God. Attending to the embodied, particular, other constrains our capacity for egoism and its tendency to universalise to the case of the other that which is, in fact, felt only by the self. This is a learned art that Dorothea Brooke, in *Middlemarch*, comes to attain after experience, pain, and several disappointments have tempered her emotions and refined her capacity for sympathy. But before spelling out what the acquisition of that art involves, it is important first to note that in *Middlemarch*, Eliot revisits the cost of being exposed to the feelings of others that so pains Latimer.

We are protected, veiled from the intensity of others' pain, by our inborn egoism and stupidity. Recall that when remarking on his 'diseased participation in other people's consciousness', Latimer describes his experience as a 'torment' where the thoughts of others

> rushed upon me like a ringing in the ears not to be got rid of, though it allowed my own impulses and ideas to continue their uninterrupted course. It was like a preternaturally heightened sense of hearing, *making audible to one a roar of sound where others find perfect stillness*.
>
> ('LV', ch. 1, emphasis added)

There is a striking resonance between this passage and the well-known passage from *Middlemarch* concerning the squirrel's heartbeat:

> That element of tragedy which lies in the very fact of frequency, has not yet wrought itself into the coarse emotion of mankind; and perhaps our frames could hardly bear much of it. *If we had a keen vision and feeling of all ordinary human life, it would be like hearing the grass grow and the squirrel's heart beat, and we should die of that roar which lies on the*

other side of silence. As it is, the quickest of us walk about well wadded with stupidity (emphasis added).[26]

It is noteworthy that these passages from 'The Lifted Veil' and *Middlemarch* are concerned not with profoundly tragic events but rather with ordinary, common, everyday pain. Both works of fiction offer accounts of bad marriages: those of Bertha and Latimer, and Dorothea and Casaubon. Unlike Latimer, Dorothea eventually achieves a degree of moral maturity. What she progressively manages to bring into focus is the egoism involved in her projections of what she has taken to be the temperament, needs, and feelings of others. She must learn about essential human difference and the limitations and dangers of her impulsively sympathetic nature.

Dorothea's excessive sympathy can inflict as much damage as Latimer's deficient sympathy. Her relationship with Casaubon is based on her own selfish projections: she 'had looked deep into the ungauged reservoir of Mr Casaubon's mind [and saw] reflected there in vague labyrinthine extension every quality she herself brought' (*M*, ch. 3). 'Mr Casaubon had been the mere occasion which had set alight the fine inflammable material of her youthful illusions' (ch. 10). Once she acquires the skill of attending to the other in his difference she does experience this as painful, but also as morally redemptive. Unlike Latimer, Dorothea does not see her newfound insight as 'diseased'.

Although, like the rest of us, Dorothea is 'well-wadded with stupidity' (*M*, ch. 20), she does possess the strength of character to emerge from the common illusion that the world is 'an udder to feed our supreme selves' (ch. 21). The narrator of *Middlemarch* tells us:

> it had been easier to [Dorothea] to imagine how she would devote her-self to Mr Casaubon, and become wise and strong in his strength and wisdom, than to conceive with that distinctness which is no longer reflection but feeling—*an idea brought back to the directness of sense, like the solidity of objects*—that he had an equivalent centre of self, whence the lights and shadows must always fall with a certain difference.
>
> (ch. 21, emphasis added)

This notion, of infusing an idea with the reality of an embodied affect with such force that the idea may now be likened to 'the solidity of objects', is at the core of Eliot's moral theory, and understanding this theory requires understanding Feuerbach on the incarnation of ideas. Compare the description of Dorothea's awakening, which involves conceiving 'with that distinctness *which is no longer reflection but feeling—an idea brought back to the directness of sense, like the solidity of objects*—that he [Causabon] had an equivalent centre of self', with Feuerbach's description of the process by which '*an object of thought becomes an object of sense, of feeling*' (emphases added). Both passages are concerned to make actual, that is, actually *sensed*, that which was abstract (the idea) without losing one or the other (hence, the notion of an *incarnate idea*). There is no ready-made method for attaining this skill precisely because each moral situation is an embodied particular. Abstracted facts fail to capture the salient features of embodied human relationships.

This reading of Eliot's indebtedness to Feuerbach's ambition to embody knowledge, infused with vital sensation, does not rely on one isolated passage concerning Dorothea's awakening to Casaubon's difference. Consider, for example, what Ladislaw says about the poet's access to knowledge through feeling (and to feeling through knowledge):

> To be a poet is to have a soul so quick to discern that no shade of quality escapes it, and so quick to feel, that discernment is but a hand playing with finely-ordered variety on the chords of emotion—a soul in which knowledge passes instantaneously into feeling, and feeling flashes back as a new organ of knowledge.
>
> (*M*, ch. 22)

To reiterate a point made in the previous section: this type of knowledge cannot be translated into the 'facts of the matter'. Some types of knowledge assume embeddedness in a particular way of life, imbued with specific values, and characterised by embodied, meaningful affective relations with others. For Eliot, this distinctive form of knowledge characterises both aesthetic and moral endeavour and is closed to those who lack sympathetic imagination.[27]

Ways of Knowing—Ways of Being

In his *Ethics*, Spinoza wrote: 'the Mind does not err from the fact that it imagines'[28], and in Eliot's handwritten translation, this phrase is underlined. For Spinoza, as for many philosophers, the imagination, the senses, and passions are the origin of all human error and folly. They make a stick in water appear bent and drive us to act in ways that we know to be foolish. Notwithstanding these pitfalls, Spinoza counts the imagination as a form of knowledge (the lowest kind of three, the others being reason and intuition) provided we are clear-eyed about what it is and what it can do. Indeed, for him the mind is the idea of the body and our basic human consciousness begins in an awareness of the affections of the body, that is, in the imagination. For both Spinoza and Feuerbach, the imagination is necessary to the development and maintenance of human knowledge, well-being, and sociability. Spinoza's theory of the imitation of the affects resonates with Feuerbach's account of the distinctively human disposition to 'feel-with' [*mitgefühl*] the other, that is, of sympathy. Spinoza states: 'If we imagine a thing like us, toward which we have had no affect, to be affected with some affect, we are thereby affected with a like affect'.[29] It is through this natural disposition to feel-with that Spinoza explains the origin of ben-evolence, love, emulation, and the other sociable emotions.[30] But caution must be exercised in relation to this reflexive sympathy and other primitive imaginative powers: in particular, we must not mistake imaginative ideas for rational ones. Like Feuerbach, Spinoza sees a primary task of philosophy as being to understand the roles of imagination and reason, and their rela-tion to each other, in human life and knowledge. The imagination, and the narratives to which it gives rise, will be features of human life for as long as human life remains *embodied* life, that is, the sociable and socialised imagin-ation is not a *stage* that scientific progress can shed but a permanent struc-ture of human life that gives rise to specific forms of worthwhile knowledge. Philosophical thought should strive to transform the destructive aspects of the imagination, but it works in vain if it aims to eradicate them.

For Spinoza, becoming a moral being necessarily involves understanding the role of the imagination and feeling (or affect) in relation to reason. From Spinoza, Eliot takes the notion that through reflection and deliberation, some of our affects can become rational or active. Our feelings cannot, he insists, be dominated or destroyed by reason, but they might be transformed, and once transformed, endorsed by reason. The key point on his view is the idea that cognition and emotion are not entirely separate faculties but can operate as complementary powers. As one commentator has put it, Spinoza proposes the 'harnessing' of affect to cognition.[31] On Spinoza's account of feeling and ethics, the moral being learns to transform passive affects into endorsed action in a manner not dissimilar to Smith's account. And the indi-vidual who has mastered this skill lives her life in a distinctively active (or in Spinoza's term, virtuous) way. Knowing in a certain way implies being in a certain way because gaining knowledge about particular things, beings, and relations can be transformative of how one exists with those things and beings, and within those relations. On this reading of Spinoza, 'knowledge is more a mode of being than of having, not something we possess but some-thing we *are* or *become*' (emphasis original).[32] For Eliot, this amounts to becoming a person capable of 'seeing truly and feeling justly' (*GEL*, 2: 362) which is the transformation in her readers that her novels endeavour to bring about: to allow them to 'be better able to *imagine* and to *feel* the pains and joys of those who differ from themselves' (emphasis original, *GEL*, 3: 111). The power to see truly and feel justly involves unique and complex modalities of both seeing and knowing. As has been shown, both intellect and feeling are necessary for moral judgement, but taken separately, neither is sufficient without the unifying and motivating power of the imagination.

Latimer neither sees truly nor feels justly. His egoism is all-consuming and even after Alfred's death he realises that he does not experience sincere regret:

> We try to believe that the egoism within us would have easily been
> melted, and that it was only the narrowness of our knowledge which

hemmed in our generosity, our awe, our human piety, and hindered them from submerging our hard indifference to the sensations and emotions of our fellow. Our tenderness and self-renunciation seem strong when our egoism has had its day.

('LV', ch. 1)

Latimer's one-sided way of knowing cannot be made good through the acquisition of further facts. Scientific knowledge is not what is at stake here. The required knowledge is not something that is able to be added to a list of 'things Latimer knows' but rather concerns the way that he knows, that is, the absence of any contextual colouring or contouring of the facts that are embedded in the specific relations that make up his life.

The introduction into the story of Meunier, Latimer's old school friend—the only friend he seems ever to have had—who in the meantime has become a doctor and famous medical researcher, allows Eliot to set up a dramatic contrast between distinct ways of knowing. Bertha's maid, Mrs Archer, has developed an intense hatred for her and plans to tell Latimer that Bertha has procured poison in order to murder him. However, before she can execute her vengeance, she contracts peritonitis. To Bertha's palpable relief, the delirious maid dies before she can impart this secret. But Meunier, who is staying in the Latimer home and treating the maid's illness, has secretly recruited Latimer to assist in an experimental blood transfusion should the maid die.[33] After she dies, the doctor transfuses his own blood into the maid, thus drawing aside the veil of death itself. Hence, the maid is presented with another opportunity at life, but this second chance is merely seen as an opportunity to express her vindictiveness—and she grasps it, before dying for a second time.

This vignette would have made challenging reading for many of Eliot's contemporaries. It spells out a secular view of life: there is no redemptive paradisiacal afterlife, no forgiving Father, with the power to make amends for our suffering. All we have is what we mere mortals are able to offer each other in the here and now. The narrator's response after the maid denounces Bertha conveys both shock and astonishment:

Great God! Is this what it is to live again ... [sic] to wake up with our unstilled thirst upon us, with our unuttered curses rising to our lips, with our muscles ready to act out their half-committed sins?

(ch. 2)

The maid's viciousness has a profound effect on Meunier, such that 'life for that moment ceased to be a scientific problem to him' (ch. 2). As Spinoza remarked, the best life is one passed in harmony with others, but he stresses that when he refers to a *human* life, he means 'one defined not merely by the circulation of the blood, and other things common to all animals, but mostly by reason, the true virtue and life of the Mind'.[34]

Eliot appropriates and develops certain resources in the philosophies of Smith, Feuerbach, and Spinoza, in her considerations of the problems generated by the complex role of sympathy in the attainment of mature moral agency. There is a type of one-sided egocentric sympathy, which grasps the being of the other only in relation to one's own being, but there is another reflective and potentially recognitive form of sympathy, which strives to imagine the other's situation as she experiences it (rather than as a projected aspect of oneself), and which, perhaps ironically, also involves recognising and respecting the other's ineffable difference from oneself.

Near the beginning of this chapter, it was noted that Eliot's respect for facts and veracity is part of what makes her deliberations on the *meaning* of facts and science so valuable. Her scepticism concerning the capacity of scientific knowledge to banish mystery from human affairs does not arise from mysticism. What Meunier comes to see after the maid has been revivified is apposite, namely, that knowledge of physiology, biology, anatomy, and the circulation of the blood, far from exhausts what there is to know about human life. What if we did possess the science that allowed us to revive the dead? What would that mean for human life and relationships and 'the true virtue and life of the mind'? Eliot's point is surely that a more complete knowledge would see that the complex phenomena associated with life and death cannot be captured by science alone. Facts are infused with meanings and values that will always remain vital to a genuinely *human* life.

Notes

1 George Eliot, *Impressions of Theophrastus Such*, ed. Nancy Henry (1879; Iowa City: University of Iowa Press, 1994), 105.
2 Gillian Beer, *Darwin's Plots: Evolutionary Narrative in Darwin, George Eliot and Nineteenth-Century Fiction*, 3rd edn (1983; Cambridge: Cambridge University Press, 2009) remains a key text. See also Sally Shuttleworth, *George Eliot and Nineteenth-Century Science: The Make-Believe of a Beginning* (Cambridge: Cambridge University Press, 1984); and more recently, Amy M. King, 'George Eliot and Science', in *The Cambridge Companion to George Eliot*, 2nd edn, ed. George Levine and Nancy Henry (Cambridge: Cambridge University Press, 2019), 175–94. For philosophy, see Suzy Anger, 'George Eliot and Philosophy', in *The Cambridge Companion to George Eliot*, ed. Levine and Henry, 215–35; and Moira Gatens, 'Philosophy', in *George Eliot in Context*, ed. Margaret Harris (Cambridge: Cambridge University Press, 2013), 214–21.
3 Before the creation of George Eliot, Marian Evans translated David Strauss, *The Life of Jesus Critically Examined* (1846), Ludwig Feuerbach, *The Essence of Christianity* (1854), and in 1854, Spinoza's *Ethics*. Her translation of the *Ethics* has now been published with excellent apparatus: *Spinoza's* Ethics, ed. Clare Carlisle, tr. George Eliot (Princeton: Princeton University Press, 2020).
4 See Nancy L. Paxton, *George Eliot and Herbert Spencer: Feminism, Evolutionism, and the Reconstruction of Gender* (Princeton: Princeton University Press, 1991), for Eliot's complex intellectual and emotional relationship with Spencer.

5 Virginia Woolf, 'George Eliot' (1919), in *A Century of George Eliot Criticism*, ed. Gordon S. Haight (Boston: Houghton Mifflin, 1965), 184.

6 Melissa Raines, 'Knowing too Much: the Burden of Omniscience in *The Lifted Veil*', *The George Eliot Review*, 43 (2012), 41. But how the concept 'sympathy' is defined in Eliot's work is incredibly varied, and this variation generates quite different interpretations of her novels. This is especially true of 'The Lifted Veil', where critics' understanding of sympathy will largely determine the contours, and the soundness, of their interpretations.

7 Shaun Nichols and Stephen Stich, *Mindreading: An Integrated Account of Pretence, Self-Awareness, and Understanding Other Minds* (Oxford: Oxford University Press, 2003), 2.

8 Nichols and Stich, *Mindreading*, 4.

9 George Eliot, *The George Eliot Letters*, 9 vols, ed. Gordon S. Haight (New Haven and London: Yale University Press, 1954–78), 3: 227.

10 Percy Bysshe Shelley, *Shelley's Poetry and Prose*, ed. Neil Fraistat and Donald Reiman (New York: Norton, 2010), 327.

11 George Eliot, *The Lifted Veil; Brother Jacob*, ed. Helen Small (Oxford: Oxford World's Classics, 1999), ch. 1. Further references to this edition appear parenthetically in text.

12 Suzy Anger, 'George Eliot and Philosophy', in *The Cambridge Companion to George Eliot,* ed. Levine and Henry, 221.

13 George Eliot, 'Evangelical Teaching: Dr Cumming', in *Selected Essays, Poems and Other Writings*, ed. A.S. Byatt and Nicholas Warren (Harmondsworth: Penguin, 1991), 44. Emphasis added.

14 Eliot's sophisticated understanding of sympathy makes me doubt the soundness of the argument offered by Thomas Albrecht in 'Sympathy and Telepathy: The Problem of Ethics in George Eliot's "The Lifted Veil"', *English Literary History*, 73.2 (2006). He asserts that the problem of egoism, inherent to human nature, cannot be resolved and so Eliot must attempt 'to protect her ethics of sympathy' (442) at the level of the plot of 'The Lifted Veil'. Thus, she projects Latimer's antipathy onto Bertha which allows him some redemption at the novella's close. On my alternative reading, Eliot's ethics of sympathy does not need protection, and her portrayal of Latimer lays bare a soul lacking sympathetic *imagination*. It is not his egoism alone that is the problem. Rather, and as I explain with reference to Eliot's reliance on Adam Smith's *The Theory of the Moral Sentiments*, Latimer's lack of imagination is the problem.

15 Patrick Fessenbecker, in *Reading Ideas in Victorian Literature: Literary Content as Artistic Experience* (Edinburgh: Edinburgh University Press, 2020), uses the work of Christine Korsgaard and Martha Nussbaum to elucidate aspects of Eliot's account of moral agency and says in reading Eliot through the prism of contemporary philosophy he 'lets her speak from her time to ours' (168). I am sceptical about this reading practice mostly because of Eliot's deep immersion in the thought of philosophers from her own time. In an earlier paper ('Sympathy, Vocation, and Moral Deliberation in George Eliot', *English Literary History*, 85.2 [2018]: 501–32), Fessenbecker presents a reading of Eliot's view of sympathy, and 'The Lifted Veil', through Kant's philosophy. Both works by Fessenbecker yield fascinating and ingenious insights into Eliot's fiction writing. However, in neither work does he consider the influence of the philosophers to whom Eliot's

thinking was most indebted. He rightly sees that for Eliot sympathy is much more than 'an impulsive feeling'; rather, sympathy 'emerges as a kind of deliberation' ('Sympathy', 504). But Fessenbecker sees this emergence as evidence of Kant's influence, despite Eliot's stated opposition to deontological morality. As I show in this chapter, Eliot's view of sympathy as a complex, emergent, deliberative exercise of reciprocal perspective taking is developed from Adam Smith's theory of the moral sentiments. Fessenbecker does not mention Smith.

16 George Eliot, *The Mill on the Floss* (1860; Oxford: Oxford World's Classics, new edn, 2015), bk. 7, ch. 2, emphasis added.

17 Jesse Prinz, 'Is Empathy Necessary for Morality?' in *Empathy: Philosophical and Psychological Perspectives*, ed. Amy Coplan and Peter Goldie (Oxford: Oxford University Press, 2011), 211–29.

18 Millicent Churcher, 'Can Empathy Be a Moral Resource? A Smithean Reply to Jesse Prinz', *Dialogue*, 55 (2016), 439.

19 Unfortunately, there are too few works that elaborate on the connections between Eliot and Smith. Dermot Coleman, a happy exception, notes Eliot's 'lifelong intellectual connections' with the works of Adam Smith. See his *George Eliot and Money: Economics, Ethics, and Literature* (Cambridge: Cambridge University Press, 2014), 10.

20 Rae Greiner, 'Sympathy Time: Adam Smith, George Eliot, and the Realist Novel', *Narrative*, 17.3 (2009), 294.

21 George Eliot, 'The Natural History of German Life', in *Selected Essays*, ed. Byatt and Warren, 110.

22 There is perhaps one exception: he feels pity in the face of his father's desolation at the death of his favoured son, Alfred (see 'LV', ch. 1).

23 Lewes made the remark to Edith Simcox in response to her puzzlement over the meaning of the novella: *GEL*, 9: 220.

24 Cristina Griffin, in 'George Eliot's Feuerbach: Senses, Sympathy, Omniscience and Secularism', *English Literary History*, 84.2 (2017), 475–502, rightly argues that Feuerbach strongly influenced Eliot's conception of the sympathetic imagination and her avoidance of abstraction in favour of 'proximate and embodied experiences' (476). I discovered Griffin's paper only after this chapter was completed. However, we reach mostly similar conclusions about Feuerbach's role in Eliot's moral philosophy, although we approach these conclusions by different paths. Griffin is less convinced of Adam Smith's influence on Eliot. In my view, this is because she takes the visual aspect of his Impartial Spectator too literally and so views this figure as abstract and disembodied. Greiner, in 'Sympathy Time', more aptly stresses that Smith's spectator is an embodied, reflective deliberator.

25 Ludwig Feuerbach, *The Essence of Christianity*, tr. Marian Evans [George Eliot] (New York: Harper, 1957), 81–2. Elsewhere he writes:

> The task of philosophy … consists not in leading away from sensuous, that is, real, objects, but rather in leading toward them, not in transforming objects into ideas and conceptions, but rather in making visible, that is, in objectifying, objects that are invisible to ordinary eyes.
>
> (*Principles of the Philosophy of the Future* [Indianapolis: Hackett, 1986]), 60

Recall here that both Lewes and Eliot viewed art as a practice which makes the invisible visible.

26 George Eliot, *Middlemarch* (1872; Oxford: Oxford World's Classics, 1998), ch. 20. Further references to this edition appear parenthetically in text.

27 Greiner rightly notes that, like Latimer, Rosamond Vincy's narcissism and incapacity to sympathise is 'keyed to a lack of imagination' ('Sympathy Time', 304). Compare Rosamond's attitude to her spouse to Latimer's attitude to Bertha: 'Rosamond, in fact, was entirely occupied not exactly with Tertius Lydgate as he was in himself, but with his relation to her' (*M*, ch. 16). Indeed, the description also resonates with Dorothea's attitude to Casaubon prior to her emerging from her egoism.

28 Benedict Spinoza, *Ethics. The Collected Works of Spinoza*, ed. and tr. Edwin Curley (Princeton: Princeton University Press, 1985), vol. 1, Scholium to Proposition 17 of Part Two, 465.

29 Spinoza, *Ethics*, in *Collected Works*, Proposition 27 of Part Three, 508.

30 For an insightful account of Eliot's reworking of Spinoza's theory of affect in 'The Lifted Veil', see Sophie Alexandra Frazer, 'George Eliot and Spinoza: Toward a Theory of the Affects', *George Eliot-George Henry Lewes Studies*, 70.2 (2018), 128–42.

31 James Arnett, 'Daniel Deronda, Professor of Spinoza', *Victorian Literature and Culture*, 44.4 (2016), 846.

32 Yirmiyahu Yovel, *Spinoza and Other Heretics: The Adventures of Immanence* (Princeton: Princeton University Press, 1989), 159.

33 Kate Flint, 'Blood, Bodies, and "The Lifted Veil" ', *Nineteenth-Century Literature*, 51.4 (1997), 455–73, has written perceptively on the obvious class and gender issues raised by Meunier's experiment. See also B.M. Gray, 'Pseudoscience and George Eliot's "The Lifted Veil"', *Nineteenth-Century Fiction*, 36:4 (1982), 407–23.

34 Benedict Spinoza, *The Political Treatise*, in *Collected Works*, ed. and tr. Curley, vol. 2 (Princeton: Princeton University Press, 2016), 530.

6 Sympathy and Alterity
The Ethical Sublime in *Romola*

Thomas Albrecht

Romola (1862–63) is a comparatively marginal work in George Eliot's oeuvre, often ignored or only cursorily discussed by readers and scholars. One reason for its neglect may be that at first glance, its overall ethical vision, and the moral development of its eponymous protagonist, are largely unremarkable, even perfunctory. They are the well-trodden trajectories from inadvertent egoism to deliberate altruism, and from religious forms to forms of secular humanism, that by this midpoint in Eliot's career are familiar places and movements, familiar from her earlier works *Scenes of Clerical Life* (1858), *Adam Bede* (1859), 'The Lifted Veil' (1859), *The Mill on the Floss* (1860), and *Silas Marner* (1861).

But on a closer look, we see that *Romola* is more complex than it first appears, and that it tells more than a single ethical story. Eliot herself intimates this greater complexity. In an 1863 letter to the critic Richard Holt Hutton, she diagnoses a kind of surplus within the novel. She claims to find in *Romola* a 'tendency to excess' and 'something excessive—wanting due proportion'. The figures of excess allude to the concept of the sublime, as Eliot also does when she tells Hutton that in the novel 'great, great facts have struggled to find a voice through me, and have only been able to speak brokenly'.[1] Victorian critical responses to *Romola* sometimes tap into this allusion, as when a review in *The Times* asserts that the novel 'impresses one with a sense of sublime power', or when Henry James singles out *Romola* as 'the one [of Eliot's works] in which the largest things are attempted'.[2]

My reading of *Romola* demonstrates that Eliot's evocations of the sublime, evocations previously unexplored, reveal a second, supplementary ethical dimension within the novel. This supplementary dimension is an ethics of otherness, an ethics of alterity that emerges alongside *Romola*'s (and Romola's) more familiar, more superficial ethics of altruism and human fellowship.

Noticing this ethics of alterity may prompt us to question our inherited assumptions about *Romola*'s insignificance. When Eliot scholars have regarded *Romola* at all, they have sometimes situated it as a transitional, midcareer pivot between two more major poles within Eliot's oeuvre: Eliot's early English Midlands pastoral fiction (*Scenes of Clerical Life, Adam*

DOI: 10.4324/9781003362821-7

Bede, and *The Mill on the Floss)* and her politically and philosophically more radical, formally more ambitious late work (*Middlemarch* [1871–72] and *Daniel Deronda* [1876]). In relation to the former pole, critics have interpreted *Romola* as Eliot's deliberate break with the limitations of her early provincial fiction, due to its unprecedented historical setting in a time and place far removed from Eliot's own. In relation to the latter pole, one might see anticipations of Eliot's late work in *Romola*'s ambitious attempt to depict a moment of profound transformation in Western European history and culture, the moment that Eliot's Victorian contemporaries were beginning to call the Renaissance. *Romola*'s historicism might be said to foreshadow the complex historicism of *Middlemarch*, devoted to pre-Victorian provincial England in the transformational period around the 1832 Reform Act; and the complex historicism of *Daniel Deronda*, devoted to understanding Eliot's own place and time, the protean cosmopolitan modernity of late Victorian London, Britain, and Europe.

This essay contends that its complex ethical vision, even more so than its distant historical setting or dynamic historical subject, makes *Romola* an important work. Much like its complex historicism, its similarly complex ethics makes the novel a pivotal (rather than merely perfunctory) *topos* within Eliot's oeuvre. Through figures of the sublime, *Romola* articulates an ethics of alterity, a more ambitious, nuanced conception of ethics that critics have generally not found in Eliot's writings until *Middlemarch* nine years later. At the same time, this ethics also makes the novel a unique and radical work in its own right. Hence, *Romola* calls for a deeper critical appreciation of how it expands and complicates our understanding of Eliot's ethical ideas in general, and of the development of those ideas at the midpoint of her career.

A recurring motif in *Romola* is the figure of someone's pain as a call that Romola hears and to which she responds. In the scene in which readers first meet her and her father Bardo de' Bardi, an aged scholar who has been disappointed in his ambition for academic recognition, 'the old man's voice, which had risen high in indignant protest, fell into a tone of reproach so tremulous and plaintive that Romola, turning her eyes again towards the blind aged face, felt her heart swell with forgiving pity'.[3] In another scene, the grey hairs of the stranger Baldassare Calvo 'made a peculiar appeal to [Romola], and the stamp of some unwonted suffering in the face ... stirred in her those sensibilities towards the sorrows of age, which her whole life had tended to develop' (ch. 24). And in the episode of the plague-stricken village near the end of the novel, the 'cry of a little child in distress ... drew Romola so irresistibly' (ch. 68), animating within her 'so energetic an impulse to share the life around her, to answer the call of need' (ch. 69). After returning from the village to Florence, she thinks of the abandoned Tessa and her children, 'pictured the childish creature waiting and waiting at some wayside spot in wondering helpless misery', and resolves 'to seek these beings ... that she was bound specially to care for' (ch. 70).

This motif of a call and response is one indication that like her fellow protagonists Dorothea Casaubon in *Middlemarch* and Daniel in *Daniel Deronda*, Romola is endowed with the power of what Eliot, her Romantic precursors, and her Victorian contemporaries call sympathy. Akin to our present-day word empathy, sympathy for Eliot means an emotional attunement to the feelings and suffering of fellow human beings, and the moral capacity to be moved by that suffering into attempting to relieve it. The narrator of *Adam Bede* calls sympathy 'the one poor word which includes all our best insight and our best love'.[4] The narrator of *Romola* calls it 'the very life and substance of our wisdom' (ch. 15). Critics frequently call the moral vision Eliot develops over the course of her career an ethics of sympathy. And they regularly posit *Romola* as exemplary and paradigmatic of this ethics. Ranging from earlier studies by Bernard J. Paris, Virgil A. Peterson, William J. Sullivan, J.B. Bullen, and Elizabeth Deeds Ermarth, to more recent studies by Melissa Anne Raines, Ilana M. Blumberg, Ariana Reilly, Mary Beth Tegan, Jacob Jewusiak, and Meechal Hoffman, commentators writing about *Romola* have near unanimously defined its ethical vision in terms of sympathy and have defined the character Romola's ethical agency as a form of sympathy.[5] Eliot herself, in her letter to Richard Holt Hutton, describes the ideal readership of *Romola* as 'minds prepared … by that religious and moral sympathy with the historical life of man which is the larger half of culture'.[6] And the novel's narrator repeatedly associates Romola with the word sympathy, as, for instance, in describing Romola as 'ardent and sympathetic' (ch. 15), in invoking Romola's 'sympathy with aged sorrows, aged ambition, aged pride and indignation' (ch. 12), or in asserting that Romola's 'sympathy with her father had made all the passion and religion of her young years' (ch. 27). As Romola attempts to commune with the solitary and abject Baldassare, he 'instinctively felt her in sympathy with him' (ch. 53).

Romola's capacity for sympathising with the feelings and pain of others, like that of Dorothea or Daniel, and like that of Adam in *Adam Bede*, or Philip Wakem in *The Mill on the Floss*, does not emerge fully formed, Athena-like at the novel's outset. Rather, her inchoate sympathies are gradually, arduously developed and refined over the course of the plot: this refinement is one trajectory of her moral *Bildungsroman*. Early in the novel, Romola's sympathies are ethically limited in two ways. First, they are overly narrow and shallow: shallow in the sense of being wholly affective, instinctive, and reactive, closely entangled with other, as yet obscure, unformed passions on her part; and narrow in the sense of restricting themselves primarily to her father Bardo, 'to my father's feeling, which I have always held to be just' (ch. 13), and to people closely associated with him, like her brother Dino de' Bardi or her godfather Bernardo del Nero. As the narrator puts this limitation, 'Her mind had never yet bowed to any obligation apart from personal love and reverence; she had no keen sense of any other human relations' (ch. 36).[7] Second, Romola's early sympathies are limited by their underlying self-reference and inadvertent egoism, as when, with respect to her father, she is 'moved with sympathetic indignation, for in her nature too there lay the same large claims, and the same spirit of struggle against their denial' (ch. 5). Even as she seeks 'to comfort him by some sign of her presence', she also has to suppress an impulse to direct some of this comfort back at herself, feeling 'too proud to obtrude consolation in words that might seem like a vindication of her own value' (ch. 5).[8]

Romola's narrator marks these early limitations in Romola's sympathy by noticing her 'need for deeper motive' (ch. 49) and by anticipating her eventual transcendence of them: 'All Romola's ardour had been concentrated in her affections ... Romola had had contact with no mind that could stir the larger possibilities of her nature; they lay folded and crushed like embryonic wings' (ch. 27). The character who helps unfold another character's 'embryonic wings', who stirs the larger possibilities of another character's nature, is a familiar *topos* in Eliot's fiction, as, for instance, when Edgar Tryan stirs Janet Dempster's nature in 'Janet's Repentance' (1857); Felix stirs Esther Lyon's in *Felix Holt, the Radical* (1866); Dorothea stirs Will Ladislaw's in *Middlemarch*; and Ezra Mordecai Cohen stirs Daniel's nature, and Daniel stirs Gwendolen Grandcourt's, in *Daniel Deronda*. As the narrator of *Middlemarch* puts this idea, 'The presence of a noble nature, generous in its wishes, ardent in its charity, changes the lights for us'.[9]

In *Romola*, the person who provides Romola with a deeper motive, who stirs the larger possibilities of her nature, who changes the lights for her, is the Dominican friar, prophet, and anti-papal reformer Girolamo Savonarola, one of many Florentine quattrocento historical personages who are characters in the novel.[10] In response to her contact with Savonarola's persona and preaching, Romola and her sympathy are qualitatively transformed. From narrowly restricted personal affection and familial loyalty, Romola's ethics broaden into 'an enthusiasm of sympathy with the general life' and 'a new consciousness of the great drama of human existence in which her life was a part' (ch. 44). Channelled by Savonarola's influence into active charity towards her Florentine neighbours, they become sharper and more delineated: 'through her daily helpful contact with the less fortunate of her fellow-citizens this new consciousness became something stronger than a vague sentiment; it grew into a more and more definite motive' (ch. 44). And in taking the form of a 'self-denying practice', 'a reason for living, apart from personal enjoyment and personal affection', and a 'flame of unselfish emotion' (ch. 44), Romola's newfound charity becomes the principal means by which she transcends her own lingering egoism.

Critics writing about *Romola* have noted Savonarola's widening and vitalising influence on Romola's ethics and being, even as many of them have also interpreted his teaching and character in the novel as a fundamentally negative influence that Romola must ultimately overcome or transcend as part of her full moral development.[11] What critics, to my knowledge, have neglected to notice is Eliot's repeated association of Savonarola with the diction and imagery of the Longinian and Romantic sublimes. The narrator refers to Savonarola's reformist ambition as a 'sublimest end' (ch. 35) and describes Romola feeling Savonarola's inspiration as 'a heroism struggling for sublime ends' (ch. 52). Romola experiences Savonarola's person and teaching as a 'roll of distant thunder' (ch. 27); as 'certain rare heroic touches in history and poetry' (ch. 27); as an 'immense personal influence' (ch. 40); as 'something unspeakably great' (ch. 40); as a 'mighty music' (ch. 52); as a 'mighty voice thrilling all hearts with the sense of great things' (ch. 55); and as a 'vision of [a] great purpose ... which could ennoble endurance and exalt the common deeds of a dusty life with divine ardours' (ch. 61). Her inner and outer responses to Savonarola similarly take sublime forms. The narrator describes Romola as 'vibrating to the sound' of Savonarola's 'strong rich voice' (ch. 15), and as feeling in Savonarola's presence 'the sense of being possessed by actual vibrating harmonies' (ch. 27). Savonarola's influence leaves her 'trembling under a sudden impression of the wide distance between her present and her past self' (ch. 40), and elsewhere inspires in her a 'sublime excitement' (ch. 55).[12]

In response to the 'subduing influences' of Savonarola's sublimity (ch. 40), Romola ultimately submits herself: 'his moral force had been the only authority to which she had bowed' (ch. 55). In her confrontation with Savonarola on the road outside of Florence, as she attempts secretly to escape from her unhappy marriage to Tito Melema, she cedes to his insistence that she return to Florence and to Tito: 'she was subdued by the sense of something unspeakably great to which she was being called by a strong being who roused a new strength within herself' (ch. 40). In Romola's response to Savonarola's call, submission to 'something unspeakably great' coincides with empowerment. This kind of double impetus, being at once subdued and strengthened, recurs frequently in the novel. For instance, Romola finds in Savonarola's presence a 'presentiment of the strength there might be in submission' (ch. 40), and that under his influence, 'all her strength must be drawn from the renunciation of independence' (ch. 41). And elsewhere, 'Her enthusiasm was continually stirred to fresh vigour by the influence of Savonarola ... her strong affinity for his passionate sympathy and the splendour of his aims had lost none of its power' (ch. 44). Her motive for living 'seemed to need feeding with greater forces than she possessed within herself' (ch. 44). In moments like these, Romola's mind is paradoxically invigorated by its submission to Savonarola's sublime influence. This kind of recuperative turn is a familiar *topos* in German Idealist and European Romantic writings on the sublime, as when Immanuel Kant in the *Critique of Judgment* (1790) affirms the transcendent, totalising power of the mind at the very verge of the mind's being overwhelmed by the forces of the mathematical and dynamical sublimes, or when William Wordsworth in Book Sixth of *The Prelude* (1805) counters the Alps' 'solitudes sublime' by affirming the 'awful promise' of his own mind and poetic imagination reflecting on those solitudes.[13]

As her 'sudden impression of the wide distance between her present and her past self' intimates, Romola's strengthening manifests itself as a figurative or literal expansion of the space around her, in pointed contrast to her confinement earlier in the novel at home and in her father's library. Savonarola's teaching has a 'widening influence' on her (ch. 52). Romola finds in Savonarola a 'deeper and more efficacious truth' and finds a 'large breathing-room ... in his grand view of human duties' (ch. 52). She begins regularly to leave the narrow confines of her house and to go into the streets, dispensing charity. And not only does space expand around Romola, but her mind also expands in turn. 'She had drunk in deeply the spirit of that teaching by which Savonarola had urged her' (ch. 56), and she attains through his teaching a 'large freedom of the soul' (ch. 36). This expansion of space around Romola, and this correlative expansion of her mind, are indicative of the 'transcendent moral life' into which Savonarola initiates her (ch. 55). What Romola transcends is the narrowness, shallowness, and inadvertent egoism of her early sympathy.

This transcendence, as critics have noted, manifests itself foremost as an outward widening of Romola's sympathies, as those sympathies coming to extend from her family to her Florentine neighbours and fellow citizens, and ultimately to humankind generally. The narrator refers to 'the inspiring consciousness breathed into [Romola] by Savonarola's influence that her lot was vitally united with the general lot ... She was marching with a great army; she was feeling the stress of a common life' (ch. 56), and positively evaluates this expanded consciousness within Romola of a human 'general lot' and 'common life': 'All that ardour of her nature which could no longer spend itself in the woman's tenderness for father and husband, had transformed itself into an enthusiasm of sympathy with the general life' (ch. 44). The narrator repeatedly uses the word fellowship to indicate Romola's newfound general sympathy for other human beings, in phrases like 'simple human fellowship [expressing] itself as a strongly-felt bond' (ch. 40), 'that new fellowship with suffering, which had already been awakened in her' (ch. 40), and 'that enthusiasm of fellowship' (ch. 43). Fellowship is shorthand here for an ethics of sympathy that is founded on feelings of a common humanity, as in Romola's 'new consciousness of the great drama of human existence in which her life was a part'. This humanist ethics into which Romola is initiated in many respects parallels Eliot's own. Eliot prefaces the 1878 Cabinet Edition reprint of her novella 'The Lifted Veil' with the epigraph, 'Give me no light, great Heaven, but such as turns / To energy of human fellowship', and in an 1868 letter to Clifford Allbutt, an Oxford friend of her husband George Henry Lewes, she similarly writes,

> the inspiring principle which alone gives me courage to write is, that of so presenting our human life as to help my readers in getting a clearer conception and a more active admiration of those vital elements which bind men together.[14]

As it is for Kant in the *Critique of Judgment*, then, the sublime for Eliot in *Romola* is an intrinsically ethical experience.[15] But the sublime expansion of Romola's world, and the correlative widening of her mind, do not manifest themselves solely in her growing sense of a general human fellowship, her newfound sense of partaking in a common life, of marching with a great army. Concurrently they also manifest themselves as a growing intuition on Romola's part of what might be called otherness or alterity, of persons or minds or things that are outside of, and heterogeneous to, her own being and consciousness. This otherness of which she only gradually, arduously becomes aware is not something she fully comprehends. As with her newfound sense of human fellowship, it is the awe she feels in Savonarola's presence that arouses her initial intuition of it. '[H]is very voice', she tells Tito, 'seems to have penetrated me with a sense that there is some truth ... of which I know nothing' (ch. 17). The narrator specifically frames Romola's intuitions of otherness in sublime imagery and diction, and causally attributes them to Savonarola's sublime effects on Romola: 'the awe which had compelled her to kneel ... seemed like a sudden opening into a world apart from that of her life-long knowledge' (ch. 36). As Romola contemplates her first escape from Tito and Florence,

> those moments in the Duomo when she had sobbed with a mysterious mingling of rapture and pain, while Fra Girolamo offered himself a willing sacrifice for the people, came back to her as if they had been a transient taste of some ... far-off fountain.
>
> (ch. 36)[16]

Romola's relationship to the otherness of which she becomes increasingly conscious is openness and curiosity, not fear, disavowal, or attempted mastery: 'It belongs to every large nature ... to suspect itself, and doubt the truth of its own impressions, conscious of possibilities beyond its own horizon. And Romola was urged to doubt herself' (ch. 27). Like her embrace of human fellowship, Romola's doubtful relationship to her own 'large nature', her open relationship to otherness, her openness to widening horizons, and her capacity for self-doubt and self-criticism are for Eliot a distinctive form of ethics.[17] As Pauline Nestor defines this ethics,

> Romola's [moral] capacity ... arises in part from her respect for, and openness to, others. Just as importantly, however, it is grounded on her capacity for doubt ... Indeed, it is a measure of the nobility and generosity of her mind that she is given to uncertainty.[18]

As with Romola's sense of broader human fellowship, the narrator uses the word sympathy to describe Romola's openness to uncertainty and otherness: 'when she heard Savonarola invoke martyrdom, she ... felt herself penetrated with a new sensation—a strange sympathy with something apart from all the definable interests of her life' (ch. 27). The sensation Romola feels here is a sympathy for something that is outside of herself. It is a 'strange sympathy', by which the narrator might mean an altogether different kind of sympathy, a sympathy with what is strange or other rather than with what is fundamentally familiar and similar. Unlike the connective form of sympathy that Romola increasingly feels for the human beings with whom she comes into contact, it is not a sympathy that recognises an underlying commonality or bond with other persons. On the contrary, it intuits the essential otherness of someone or something from herself. It is a feeling of apartness, not of nearness.[19] And so Romola's moral attention is in this instance not directed at something that she fundamentally relates in one or another way back to herself, but rather is directed at 'something apart from all the definable interests of her life'. Eliot's phrasing here echoes realism's ethical imperative as she defines it in her important essay 'The Natural History of German Life' (1856), 'the extensions of our sympathies ... into that attention to what is apart from [us], which may be called the raw material of moral sentiment'. In that essay, Eliot's moral polemic is directed against human shallowness and egoism, against 'the trivial and the selfish'.[20] And here too, the narrator intimates Romola's transcendence of her earlier egoism by means of a newly gained feeling for something that is wholly separate from herself and her interests.

One specific form of otherness of which Romola becomes increasingly aware, and to which she increasingly opens herself, is the otherness of other persons, the separateness from herself and her mind of themselves and their minds, experience, and feelings. And once again, the narrator's word for her awareness and openness is sympathy. But here too, this sympathy is based less on a sense of fellowship or commonality with those persons, and more on her intuition of their essential alterity. As part of her sympathy with the minds and feelings of others, Romola recognises their separateness from her own mind and feelings. As she later recalls it, her first encounter with Savonarola gives her 'a glimpse of understanding into ... lives which had before lain utterly aloof from her sympathy' (ch. 36). Thinking back on her brother Dino's death, she directs herself to think 'less of what was in my own mind and more of what was in his', thus acknowledging and respecting the difference that exists between their two minds (ch. 17). And hastening her return to Florence after her rescue of the plague-stricken village, a 'compunction which is inseparable from a sympathetic nature keenly alive to the possible experience of others, began to stir in her with growing force' (ch. 69). The use of the adjective 'possible' here makes explicit the speculative nature of the sympathy that moves her. Her sympathy does not presume to know for certain what other persons experience, and thus respects the otherness of those persons and of their experience. In a conversation with Tito, Romola makes explicit that such a keen sensitivity to the 'possible' thoughts and feeling of others is both a source of strength and an ethical imperative, both a vitalising force and a moral compunction. 'That seems to me very great and noble', she tells him, 'that power of respecting a feeling which [one] does not share or understand' (ch. 17).[21]

The ethical imperative of respecting a feeling which one does not share or understand is a power that Romola progressively develops over the course of the novel. In her confrontation with Savonarola on the road outside Florence, when he insists that she return to Florence and her marriage, she reflects that 'he could not know what determined her', and tells him, 'My father, you cannot know the reasons which compel me to go. None can know them but myself. None can judge for me' (ch. 40).[22] In her implicit critique of the demand that he puts to her, Romola essentially articulates an ethical imperative of recognising and respecting the other as other. When later in the novel she breaks with him over his declining for political reasons to intervene on behalf of the unjustly condemned Bernardo del Nero, she makes a similar critique. She reproaches him for having lapsed into shallowness and narrowness, suggesting that he thereby compromises the moral responsibility to otherness that his earlier sublimity has exemplified and inspired within herself. In response to his assertion, 'The cause of my party *is* the cause of God's Kingdom', she retorts, 'God's Kingdom is something wider' (ch. 59). For her, the kingdom of God is not something that could be reduced to a politics or party or programme. Rather, it is something less narrow, something more ideal and elusive: a vague, messianic 'something' of which she intermittently gains sublime intuitions, but which she does not presume to comprehend or define. As the narrator puts her idea, 'the Kingdom of God … is not without us as a fact, it is within us as a great yearning' (ch. 67). In their final meeting, Romola confronts Savonarola with a 'flame of indignation' and 'her whole frame shaken with passionate repugnance' (ch. 59). Her indignation is due to Savonarola having earlier inspired her with widening intuitions of alterity, an inspiration that she finds has degraded into narrow political opportunism. In his presence now, she feels 'unfed by any wider faith' (ch. 52). Assessing the reasons for her rupture with him, she reflects how 'the grand curve of his orbit … seemed now to reduce itself to narrow devices' (ch. 61). These statements suggest that what Romola ultimately deplores in Savonarola is not only his growing authoritarianism and egoism, paternalism and moral absolutism, dogmatism and political ambition, to all of which critics have called attention. It is his lapsed sublimity, the very sublimity that originally helped unfold her embryonic wings, that elevated her into a moral awareness and awe of something unknown outside and beyond herself.[23]

Following her disillusionment and break with Savonarola, Romola leaves Florence for a second time. And in the chapter entitled 'Drifting Away', as she lies in a small boat at dusk and lets herself float out to sea, she turns, as if to compensate for what she has lost, towards a more negative, Burkean form of the sublime. This alternate sublime inheres in her inner experience of the vastness of the night-time universe that surrounds her, and her reading that vastness as a sign of the universe's absolute indifference to herself.

She interprets this indifference as a self-annihilation, a premonition of her own death:

> And so she lay, with the soft night air breathing on her while she glided on the waters and watched the deepening quiet of the sky. She was alone now: she had freed herself from all claims …
>
> … Romola felt orphaned in those wide spaces of sea and sky. She read no message of love for her in that far-off symbolic writing of the heavens, and with a great sob she wished that she might be gliding into death.
>
> She drew the cowl over her head again and covered her face, choosing darkness rather than the light of the stars, which seemed to her like the hard light of eyes that looked at her without seeing her. Presently she felt that she was in the grave.
>
> (ch. 61)

Romola submerging herself in the 'deepening quiet' and 'wide spaces' of the sea and the 'far-off' sky is an existential predicament: her intuition of death and absolute disconnection from the universe. But for the narrator, and for Romola herself when she later reflects back on this scene, these feelings also have ethical connotations. Those connotations are distinctly negative. Insofar as Romola feels herself liberated from 'all claims' on her, and insofar as she conversely intuits the universe's absolute indifference to her own claims on it, the scene represents an antipode, ethically speaking, to the moral awareness of alterity, the ethical responsibility to otherness, that Savonarola's sublimity had earlier invigorated in her. The narrator diagnoses Romola's feelings on the boat as a lapse into fruitless, lazy egoism, as a 'barren egoistic complaining' and a longing 'for that repose in mere sensation' (ch. 61). For her part, Romola similarly assesses her feelings while drifting on the boat as a 'selfish discontent which had come over her like a blighting wind' (ch. 71), and critically reflects that 'She had felt herself without bonds, without motive; sinking in mere egoistic complaining that life could bring her no content; feeling a right to say, "I am tired of life, I want to die"' (ch. 69). This egoism, which the passage frames as Romola feeling sublimely isolated from the world around her, effectively negates the moral transcendence of self, the moral awareness of otherness, that Savonarola's sublimity had earlier aroused within her. If Kant in the *Critique of Judgment* directly correlates the sublimities of the starry heavens and the moral law within us, Romola by contrast experiences them in this scene as radically disconnected from one another.

Romola's trip on the boat, however, does not culminate in her death, either figurative or literal. Instead, the boat overnight washes back up on shore, and on the next morning, Romola awakens into 'a new life' (ch. 68). Critics have generally interpreted this *vita nuova* as a reaffirmation, following her momentary lapse into egoism and moral apathy, of her—and Eliot's—ethics of human fellowship. Romola affirms such an ethics when she actively intervenes to rescue the scattered survivors of the plague-stricken village, reconnects them with one another, and works to restore them and their broken community to life:

> from the moment after her waking when the [surviving infant Benedetto's] cry had drawn her, she had not even reflected ... that she was glad to live because she could lighten sorrow—she had simply lived, with so energetic an impulse to share the life around her, to answer the call of need.
>
> (ch. 69)

The motive for her intervention is sympathy as a feeling of human solidarity, as an 'impulse to share the life around her'.

But Romola's awakening into a 'new life' does not only revive her ethics of human fellowship, the ethics to which the narrator refers in shorthand as her feeling 'the needs of the nearest' (ch. 69). Less noticeably, it also revives her ethics of alterity, what the narrator calls her 'feel[ing] the needs of others' (ch. 69). Following her reawakening in the boat from figurative death and moral paralysis, Romola offers aid and fellowship to the plague-stricken villagers. And more abstractly, she redirects her mind to something beyond herself, something of which she had her first sublime intuition on the road outside of Florence, something of which Savonarola's teaching has subsequently widened her awareness. '[T]he grounds on which Savonarola had once taken her back [to Florence]', she reflects, 'were truer, deeper than the grounds she had had for her second flight [from Florence]' (ch. 69). Here, she not only distinguishes between Savonarola's moral grounds and the comparative groundlessness of her transitory escape into moral irresponsibility. She also draws a distinction between, on one hand, Savonarola, the flawed human being and, on the other hand, the deep grounds of his moral intervention in her life, his larger ethics, the intuition of something unknowable beyond the self, the great yearning within us for a Kingdom of God. That ethics, she recognises, is something to which Savonarola can himself only imperfectly aspire, and to which he has inspired her to aspire:

> her sense of debt to Savonarola was recovering predominance. Nothing that had come, or was to come, could do away with the fact that there had been a great inspiration in him which had waked a new life in her.
>
> (ch. 69)

Romola's revived commitment to an ethics of alterity emerges particularly in the novel's 'Epilogue', in the Platonic lesson she teaches her adopted son Lillo:

> [Being both great and happy] is not easy, my Lillo. It is only a poor sort of happiness that could ever come by caring very much about our own narrow pleasures. We can only have the highest happiness, such as goes along with being a great man, by having wide thoughts, and much

feeling for the rest of the world, as well as ourselves; and this sort of happiness often brings so much pain with it, that we can only tell it from pain by its being what we would choose before everything else, because our souls see it is good.

('Epilogue')

Romola's lesson about a convergence of greatness and happiness, which in her conversation with Lillo she credits to Savonarola's example and influence, once more contrasts narrowness and poverty with breadth and plenitude, with 'wide thoughts, and much feeling'. And here again, narrowness and poverty designate the fallacy of human egoism, the 'poor sort of happiness' of 'caring very much about our own narrow pleasures'. But breadth and plenitude, for their part, do not designate here that 'great army' of human fellowship and solidarity with which Romola over the course of the novel comes increasingly to feel herself marching. Rather, they characterise the thoughts and feeling that we may have (or may arduously strive to attain) for what Romola refers to as 'the rest of the world'. The phrase 'rest of the world' is a shorthand for otherness, for that which is not part of ourselves, for the otherness from ourselves of other persons and the world. In what she says to Lillo, Romola does not posit 'the rest of the world' as being in any way coextensive with 'ourselves'. Instead, she pointedly, deliberately sets it apart. She sets it apart from herself, from Lillo, and from any one self or group of selves. And by setting it off as she does syntactically, she also sets it off ethically. A feeling for what is truly apart from us, she teaches Lillo, is difficult and even painful. But it also may raise us to great heights and reveal to us great depths. It may inspire within our souls the sublime highest happiness, the greatness that for Romola, and for her creator George Eliot, inheres in a feeling for alterity.[24]

Notes

1 *The George Eliot Letters*, 9 vols, ed. Gordon S. Haight (New Haven: Yale University Press, 1954–78), 4: 97.

2 Quoted in Andrew Brown, 'Introduction', in George Eliot, *Romola*, ed. Andrew Brown (Oxford: Oxford World's Classics, 1994), xi.

3 Eliot, *Romola*, ch. 5. All subsequent references to *Romola* will be to the Oxford World's Classics edition and give chapter numbers parenthetically in the text.

4 George Eliot, *Adam Bede*, ed. Carol A. Martin (Oxford: Oxford World's Classics, 2008), ch. 50.

5 On an ethics of sympathy in Romola and *Romola*, see Bernard J. Paris, *Experiments in Life: George Eliot's Quest for Values* (Detroit: Wayne State University Press, 1965), 214–22; Virgil A. Peterson, '*Romola*: A Victorian Quest for Values', *Philological Papers*, 16 (1967), 49–62, esp. 50–8; William J. Sullivan, 'Piero di Cosimo and the Higher Primitivism in *Romola*', *Nineteenth-Century Fiction*, 26 (1972), 390–405, esp. 399–405; J.B. Bullen, 'George Eliot's *Romola* as a Positivist Allegory', *The Review of English Studies*, 26 (1975), 425–35, and

The Myth of the Renaissance in Nineteenth-Century Writing (Oxford: Oxford University Press, 1994), 208–38; Elizabeth Ermarth, 'George Eliot's Conception of Sympathy', *Nineteenth-Century Fiction*, 40 (1985), 23–42, esp. 27–31; Pauline Nestor, *George Eliot* (Basingstoke: Palgrave, 2002), 96–104; Melissa Anne Raines, *George Eliot's Grammar of Being* (London: Anthem Press, 2011), 54–61; Ilana M. Blumberg, 'Sacrificial Value: Beyond the Cash Nexus in George Eliot's *Romola*', in *Economic Women: Essays on Desire and Dispossession in Nineteenth-Century British Culture*, ed. Lana L. Dalley and Jill Rappoport (Columbus: Ohio State University Press, 2013), 60–74; Ariana Reilly, 'Always Sympathize! Surface Reading, Affect, and George Eliot's *Romola*', *Victorian Studies*, 55 (2013), 629–46; Mary Beth Tegan, 'Strange Sympathies: George Eliot and the Literary Science of Sensation', *Women's Writing*, 20 (2013), 168–85; Jacob Jewusiak, 'Large-Scale Sympathy and Simultaneity in George Eliot's *Romola*', *Studies in English Literature*, 54 (2014), 853–74; and Meechal Hoffman, '"Her Soul Cried Out for Some Explanation": Knowledge and Acknowledgement in George Eliot's *Romola*', *George Eliot-George Henry Lewes Studies*, 68 (2016), 43–59. See also Sandra M. Gilbert and Susan Gubar, *The Madwoman in the Attic: The Woman Writer and the Nineteenth-Century Literary Imagination*, 2nd edn (New Haven: Yale University Press, 2000), 494–9; K.M. Newton, *George Eliot: Romantic Humanist: A Study of the Philosophical Structure of Her Novels* (London: Macmillan, 1981), 66–75; and Avrom Fleishman, *George Eliot's Intellectual Life* (Cambridge: Cambridge University Press, 2010), 126–9. The four latter critics do not use the actual word sympathy, but nevertheless define the novel's ethics in a fundamentally similar way. Ermarth frames Eliot's conception of sympathy in *Romola* in terms of the influence of Ludwig Feuerbach; Bullen and Fleishman frame it in terms of the influence of Auguste Comte; and Paris frames it in both Feuerbachian and Comtian terms. Some of these critics are, to varying degrees, sceptical of Eliot's ethics of sympathy in the novel, or alternately posit a scepticism on Eliot's own part vis-à-vis her ethics of sympathy. Gilbert and Gubar frame this scepticism in feminist terms; Fleishman frames it in tragic and Hegelian terms (128–9); Raines frames it in psychological and syntactical terms; Tegan frames it in generic, sensationalist terms; Jewusiak frames it in terms of sympathy's feasibility and expediency; and Hoffman frames it in epistemological terms. Contrary to Gilbert and Gubar's line of scepticism, Nestor (96–104); Susan E. Colón, *The Professional Ideal in the Victorian Novel: The Works of Disraeli, Trollope, Gaskell, and Eliot* (New York: Palgrave Macmillan, 2007), 97–120; and Blumberg define Eliot's ethical vision in *Romola* as deliberately feminist. A few critics have defined the ethics of *Romola* in terms other than sympathy. See Caroline Levine, *The Serious Pleasures of Suspense: Victorian Realism and Narrative Doubt* (Charlottesville: University of Virginia Press, 2003), 138–57; Colón, 97–120; Moira Gatens, 'George Eliot's "Incarnation of the Divine" in *Romola* and Benedict Spinoza's "Blessedness": A Double Reading', *George Eliot-George Henry Lewes Studies*, 52/53 (2007), 76–92; Fredric Jameson, *The Antinomies of Realism* (London: Verso, 2013), 123–33; and Dermot Coleman, *George Eliot and Money: Economics, Ethics and Literature* (Cambridge: Cambridge University Press, 2014), 128–38. Levine defines the novel's ethics in narratological, temporal, and epistemological terms; Colón defines it in terms of responsible mentorship and tutelage; Gatens defines it in Spinozist terms; Jameson defines it in terms of the Sartrean concept of bad faith and of undermining ethical binaries; and Coleman defines it in sociological, collective, and economic terms.

6 Haight, *GEL*, 4: 97.

7 Compare also:

> [Romola] felt that there could be no law for her but the law of her affections. That tenderness and keen fellow-feeling for the near and the loved which are the main outgrowth of the affections, had made the religion of her life.
>
> (ch. 36)

8 On the initial limitations and egoism of Romola's ethics, see Heather V. Armstrong, *Character and Ethical Development in Three Novels of George Eliot:* Middlemarch, Romola, Daniel Deronda (Lewiston: Edwin Mellen Press, 2001), 44–7.

9 George Eliot, *Middlemarch*, ed. David Carroll and David Russell (Oxford: Oxford World's Classics, 2019), ch. 76.

10 In *Romola*, the narrator makes reference to 'that large freedom of the soul which comes from the faith that the being who is nearest to us is greater than ourselves' (ch. 36), and later refers to Romola's 'trust in Savonarola's nature as greater than her own' (ch. 44).

11 On the dimensional expansion of Romola's initially narrow sympathy, see Jewusiak, 'Large-Scale Sympathy'. On Savonarola's positive, transformative influence on Romola's ethics and moral development, see Paris, *Experiments in Life*, 217–20; Peterson, '*Romola*', 51, 54–5; Newton, *George Eliot*, 74; Nestor, *George Eliot*, 96–7, 103–4; Colón, *The Professional Ideal*, 107–13; Fleishman, *George Eliot's Intellectual Life*, 126–9; Blumberg, 'Sacrificial Value', 68–71; and Reilly, 'Always Sympathize!', 635–42. Colón frames this influence in terms of mentorship, while Fleishman frames it in Comtian terms, as a 'full array of religion-of-humanity topoi' (127). And whereas Nestor and Blumberg define Savonarola's ethical example in terms of transcending egoism and self-interest, Reilly, following the work of John Kucich, conversely frames it as an 'egoism [presented] as the prerequisite for all meaningful and inspired action', as an 'obligatory narcissism of believing oneself right' (641). For readings that stress Savonarola's ultimately negative function within *Romola*'s moral or developmental scheme, see Peterson, 51, 55–6; Sullivan, 'Piero di Cosimo', 402; Bullen, 'George Eliot's *Romola*', 432; Newton, 68–70; Ermarth, 'George Eliot's Conception', 29–30; Nestor, 100–2; Colón, 107–13; Gatens, 'George Eliot's "Incarnation"', 86–90; Fleishman, 127–9; Raines, *George Eliot's Grammar of Being*, 56–8; and Jewusiak, 858–62. These latter readings variously associate Savonarola's person, teaching, or example in the novel with political opportunism and ambition; intellectual and spiritual sophistry; religious and political authoritarianism; religious and moral absolutism; dogmatism and ideology; egoism, self-interest, and personal ambition; militancy and coerciveness; paternalism; intellectual and spiritual hypocrisy; manipulativeness and deceptiveness; religiosity, monotheism, and Christianity; and intellectual and moral fixity, among other (actual or perceived) liabilities.

12 The sublimity of Romola's responses to Savonarola's preaching resembles Maggie Tulliver's sublime response in *The Mill on the Floss* to the writings of Thomas à Kempis: 'A strange thrill of awe passed through Maggie while she read, as if she had been wakened in the night by a strain of solemn music, telling of beings whose souls had been astir while hers was in stupor' (George Eliot, *The*

Mill on the Floss, ed. Gordon S. Haight and Juliette Atkinson [Oxford: Oxford World's Classics, 2015], bk. 4, ch. 3).

13 William Wordsworth, *The Prelude: 1799, 1805, 1850,* ed. Jonathan Wordsworth, M.H. Abrams, and Stephen Gill (New York: W.W. Norton, 1979), 214, 216.

14 George Eliot, *The Lifted Veil; Brother Jacob,* ed. Helen Small (Oxford: Oxford World's Classics, 2009), 2; and Haight, *GEL,* 4: 472.

15 On Eliot's evocation of the sublime in ethical terms, see Harold Bloom, *The Western Canon: The Books and School of the Ages* (New York: Riverhead Books, 1994), 298–309, and *Novelists and Novels: A Collection of Critical Essays* (New York: Checkmark Books, 2007), 137–50; Stephen Hancock, *The Romantic Sublime and Middle-Class Subjectivity in the Victorian Novel* (New York: Routledge, 2005), 81–111; and Victoria Shinbrot, '"The Risks That Lie Within": Beauty, Boredom, and the Sublime in *Daniel Deronda*', *Pacific Coast Philology,* 55 (2020), 68–82. On Eliot and the sublime, see also Neil Hertz, *George Eliot's Pulse* (Stanford: Stanford University Press, 2003); and Claire Thomas, 'From the Sublime to the Picturesque: Dorothea's Husbands, Embodied in Rome', *George Eliot-George Henry Lewes Studies,* 71 (2019), 1–17.

16 On the experience of the sublime as an encounter with, and relationship to, forms of otherness or alterity, see Barbara Claire Freeman, *The Feminine Sublime: Gender and Excess in Women's Fiction* (Berkeley: University of California Press, 1995).

17 Victoria Shinbrot makes a complementary ethical argument about Gwendolen Grandcourt's experience of the sublime in *Daniel Deronda,* arguing that 'The sublime … starts a gradual process of upending moral certainty … which ultimately leads to a reshaping of static models of selfhood and morality in the novel' ('"The Risks" ', 67). Shinbrot defines Gwendolen's sublime ethics in terms of risk-taking.

18 Nestor, *George Eliot,* 97.

19 On Eliot's conception of this form of sympathy in *Romola,* a sympathy that does not presume knowledge of, or identification with, the other, see Hoffman, '"Her Soul" '.

20 George Eliot, *Selected Critical Writings,* ed. Rosemary Ashton (Oxford: Oxford University Press, 2000), 270.

21 On Eliot's conception of sympathy not in terms of an identification or fellowship with the other, but rather in terms of recognising the other's distinctiveness and separateness from oneself, see Ermarth, 'George Eliot's Conception'; Rae Greiner, *Sympathetic Realism in Nineteenth-Century British Fiction* (Baltimore: The Johns Hopkins University Press, 2012), 122–40; Cara Weber, '"The Continuity of Married Companionship": Marriage, Sympathy, and the Self in *Middlemarch*', *Nineteenth-Century Literature,* 66 (2012), 494–530; and Caroline Levine, 'Surprising Realism', in *A Companion to George Eliot,* ed. Amanda Anderson and Harry E. Shaw (Chichester: Wiley-Blackwell, 2013), 62–75. On *Romola*'s moral development in terms of her increasing openness to, and relationship with, a human other, see Armstrong, *Character and Ethical Development,* 41–76.

22 In *The Mill on the Floss,* Maggie similarly challenges her brother Tom Tulliver, who is, like Savonarola, a spokesman for patriarchal authority: 'you can't quite judge for me—our natures are very different. You don't know how differently things affect me from what they do you' (*MF,* bk. 6, ch. 4). Like Romola's challenge to Savonarola, Maggie's challenge here is a fundamentally ethical

one, an ethics based on an awareness of, and respect for, differences. And like Romola's challenge, it is a distinctively feminist form of ethics.

23 The narrowness and shallowness to which Romola finds Savonarola's sublimity reduced is anticipated earlier in the novel by the narrowness and shallowness Romola diagnoses in his followers, for instance in Fra Silvestre, 'a shallow soul … sincerely composing its countenance to the utterance of sublime formulas' (ch. 41), and in the 'shallow excitability' of Camilla Rucellai (ch. 52).

24 For a different but complementary reading of Romola's lesson to Lillo in the 'Epilogue', see Colón, *The Professional Ideal*, 117–8. Colón interprets the ethics of Romola's lesson as a resistance to dogmatism and absolutism, and as recognising the contingency of all truth claims, interpretations, and moral principles.

7 Reading the Riot Act
The Case of *Felix Holt, the Radical*

Helen Groth

When Felix Holt, George Eliot's eponymous hero, runs towards an election-day riot, his story becomes part of literature's enduring and ongoing engagement with riotous activity. *Felix Holt, the Radical,* this chapter argues, does far more than merely register riotous practices. The riot both stimulates the novel's formal development—introducing contingent, chaotic, and unpredictable scenography and dramatis personae—and accelerates its critical responsiveness to the questions of just and ethical representation that drive the plot. Eliot draws on multiple senses of riotous activity, ranging from the archaic to the legal. To riot, in the archaic sense of riotous emotion, captures the shift of mood as an election-day crowd turns from anger to rage, but to riot is also a criminal offence in *Felix Holt,* literally defined by the Riot Act of 1714. When the Riot Act is read, the crowd is reified by a legal 'formula', as Eliot puts it, and chaos ensues.[1] Lives and property are destroyed, and scapegoats named. To riot, in this sense, is to be subject to a legal process that extends beyond a transient moment of violence and into the courtroom where questions of criminal intent, individual responsibility, and just consequences are argued. As these multiple senses indicate, the riot signifies far more than a momentary lapse in collective judgement in Eliot's novel. This chapter will maintain that even in moments of profound ambivalence, Eliot's novel aligns with E.P. Thompson's seminal contention that the nineteenth-century riot was anything but a spontaneous or 'spasmodic' event.[2] Instead, in *Felix Holt,* the riot is part of a complex political sequence that Eliot perceives as a threat to the intricate weblike structure of community—a web that links the local to the global and one particular lot to another, no matter how antipodally located.

Reading the novel through the lens of nineteenth-century conceptions of criminal responsibility, Lisa Rodensky proposes that Eliot's staging of an election-day riot—which results in Felix Holt being drawn into an altercation with a constable whom he unintentionally kills—sets up a 'simplistic conflict between legal and moral bases of judgment'.[3] In Rodensky's reading, the riot provides the backdrop for the more significant crime of manslaughter and the failure of the law to take adequate account of individual 'motive, desire, intention, and knowledge', ethical questions that the novel addresses

DOI: 10.4324/9781003362821-8

outside the courtroom.[4] Despite the exculpatory evidence of his future wife Esther, testifying to his state of mind and innocence of riotous intent, the law briefly prevails in the courtroom when Felix is convicted. And yet, while the charge of manslaughter is quickly resolved by the machinery of the plot, which turns on the romantic and ethical recuperation of Eliot's oratorical Radical, the riot as both legal construct and disintegrative affective force haunts this novel, its prehistory, its reception and fictional afterlives, in ways that have been critically underexplored.

Eliot's novel has much to say about rioting and the worst excesses of the political system that the riot manifests. While it may be true that, as the narrator informs us in the opening pages of the novel, the majority of rural Englishmen in 1832 no longer confuse reform with a 'combination of rick-burners, trades-unions, Nottingham riots, and in general whatever required the calling out of the yeomanry', reform is nevertheless rhetorically yoked here to rioting and the reading of the Riot Act required to 'call out the yeomanry' (*FH*, 'Introduction'). This associative sequence is, as the reader discovers, proleptic, infusing the riot, when it finally erupts, with a providential inevitability that the narrative diagnoses as the predictable outcome of artificially accelerated reform. As the narrator is at pains to clarify a few pages earlier, the individual lot of a shepherd 'with a slow and slouching walk, timed by the walk of grazing beasts' is as deeply connected and vulnerable to the actions of 'that mysterious distant system of things called "Gover'ment"' as a miner or factory worker in an industrial town (*FH*, 'Introduction'). 'Gover'ment' may seem to be as distant as 'the most-outlying nebula or the coal-sacks of the southern hemisphere', but as the noisy clatter of the stagecoach signals in this scene, the lots of country and city dwellers are inextricably and vitally connected to a precariously maintained collective (*FH*, 'Introduction'). These sage-like opening pronouncements link the field to the nation, to the world, and indeed to the galaxy. Distance is rhetorically traversable, at speed, a geographical elision that amplifies the temporal and geopolitical implications of the novel's critical elaboration of the violent consequences of unfettered market forces and political reform. Eliot's novel ultimately passes judgement on a political system predicated on the atomising protection and enrichment of individual property and private interests. It is the pursuit of mammon on a global scale that is ultimately to blame for the riot and the radical destruction of property it unleashes. While Felix may be judged for his egoism and naivete in trying to contain the riot, Eliot pardons (if not entirely absolves) him of his misguided contribution to this more pervasive criminality. In this reading, the riot becomes a test of Felix's character as a representative civic subject who challenges the atomistic chaos of private interests in defence of the ethos of community.[5]

This chapter is divided into two parts. The first positions *Felix Holt* within a nineteenth-century genre of writing about the legal and ethical implications of political violence and rioting, which includes the critical reception of the Riot Act. The second examines Eliot's fictional riot as an intentionally chaotic manifestation of collective political experience that evidences the severe limitations of both individual (protagonist-driven) responses to the complex needs of the many as well as those of formal legal structures, such as directive laws, the interpretation of evidence, court-orchestrated testimony, and advocacy. By placing the local community under threat of violent disintegration, this chapter argues, Eliot's novel ultimately asserts the value of the peaceful many and by so doing supplants the epistemological authority of the law with the evidential force of realist description. By rhetorically harnessing the violence of the riot, Eliot thus raises the stakes of the political argument her novel makes against centralised forms of government and for a radical turn to the moral education, as opposed to the material enrichment, of the general populace. Felix channels and embodies this ethos, which owes much to John Stuart Mill's concept of *homo civicus*, as Lauren Goodlad elucidates it: 'the contingent product of equalitarian social relations, liberal education, and participatory citizenship'.[6] Other voices also echo through Eliot's historical imagining of the violence of the riot. These voices emanate from her research for the novel, which included copious note-taking as she read both Samuel Bamford's popular account of his ill-fated role in Peterloo in *Passages in the Life of a Radical*, and the media coverage of the riotous passages of the 1832 and 1867 Reform Bills, the latter of which consumed the years when she was writing *Felix Holt*.[7]

Riotous Acts

Eliot's naming of the law that determines whether a crowd or a gathering of people has become a riot invites a particular kind of attention to the riot as an object of inquiry. Invoked in this way, the Riot Act functions as a resonant historical artefact that the novel transforms into a fictional construct to raise questions about the epistemological authority of the law as a technology of truth-telling and order, and, more implicitly, to accumulate evidence that substantiates the novel's larger argument for the necessity of democratised access to education as the foundation of a civil society. Collective ignorance, according to this governing ethos, begets violence and riot. Coming at the end of the second part of the novel, the riot and its consequences play out over its remaining third. Faced with a scuffling anarchic crowd threatening to overpower the constables in their midst, the Rector of Treby resorts to reading the Riot Act 'to get military aid within reach':

> The Rector wished to ride out again, and read the Riot Act from a point where he could be better heard than from the window of the Marquis; but Mr Crow, the high constable, who had returned from closer observation, insisted that the risk would be too great. New special constables had been sworn in, but Mr Crow said prophetically that if once mischief began, the mob was past caring for constables.

But the Rector's voice was ringing and penetrating, and when he appeared on the narrow balcony and read the formula, commanding all men to go to their homes or about their lawful business, there was a strong transient effect. Every one within hearing listened, and for a few moments after the final words, 'God save the King!' the comparative silence continued. Then the people began to move, the buzz rose again, and grew, and grew, till it turned to shouts and roaring as before. The movement was that of a flood hemmed in; it carried nobody away. Whether the crowd would obey the order to disperse themselves within an hour, was a doubt that approached nearer and nearer to a negative certainty.

(*FH*, ch. 33)

A failure of the law unfolds in these paragraphs, and when the Rector tries once again to read the Riot Act, the narrator informs us that 'all effect from the voice of the law had disappeared' (ch. 33). When the crowd pauses to listen, it is not to the voice of the law but to the 'ringing and penetrating' voice of the local Rector. When they respond with 'comparative silence' to the familiar repetition of 'God save the King!' they do so from habit, not out of any respect for the monarchic authority those words enshrine. Manipulated by the political ambitions of the landed gentry who have fallen well short of an Arnoldian ideal of a cultured elite, and by a state that focuses on policing and the protection of property at the expense of the needs of its people, the crowd responds to the violence of the law with violence. The narrative does not sanction this outcome, only dramatises and comments on its inevitability as the riot sweeps up all in its path.

Eliot's writing reveals a characteristically thorough understanding of the legal process and challenges of the reading of the Riot Act, so it is worth digressing for a moment to clarify what this historical intertext would have signified to readers in the mid-1860s. The Riot Act was a statute of English law initially passed in 1714 for the purpose of suppressing the Jacobite Rebellion. The Act specified that if 12 or more people behaving in a riotous manner were commanded to disperse 'with loud voice' by a Justice of the Peace or an equivalent magistrate and did not comply within one hour, then they would be guilty of a felony punishable by death.[8] It was vital that when the act was read that it was done so 'with loud voice'—indeed, this stipulation appears in the original legislation—and the relative audibility of the reading voice remained a subject of sustained controversy. In some cases, the 'feeble voice' of a local magistrate was blamed for the ensuing chaos.[9] In this legal context, Eliot's stress on the Rector's 'ringing and penetrating voice' and the subsequent inaudibility of 'the voice of the law' when the Act is read for a second time resonates with contemporary criticisms of the Act as causing more problems than it solved.

Failed readings of the act were common in both the eighteenth and nineteenth centuries and were particularly prevalent in large industrial towns where it was difficult to 'evoke deference by such means'.[10] There were numerous parliamentary submissions attesting to the logistical problems of being heard above the noise of an angry crowd, such as the following dramatic account provided by a Justice of the Peace from Middlesex:

> Being asked, whether their attempting to read the Riot Act, was not the occasion of the mob throwing stones?—he said, they threw stones before it was attempted to read—that he believes it was after the second volley of stones that the Act was attempted to be read, whereupon the mob threw more stones, and the magistrates went in—that he thinks the threatening to read the Riot Act, an unlikely method to quiet the people; and wishes it were otherwise.[11]

These reports convey a shambolic image of the power of the state and the local police. Likewise, the Riot Act was commonly represented as an inaudible text bereft of the necessary authority to quell crowds that refused its definitive force. Echoing these scenes, Eliot's mob is equally defiant in the face of the second reading of the Act. As the narrator observes: 'all effect from the voice of the law had disappeared' (*FH*, ch. 33). Eliot's ironic characterisation of Crow likewise sets the stage for the ensuing chaos:

> Mr Crow, like some other high constables more celebrated in history, 'enjoyed a bad reputation;' that is to say, he enjoyed many things which caused his reputation to be bad, and he was anything but popular in Treby. It is probable that a pleasant message would have lost something from his lips, and what he actually said was so unpleasant, that, instead of persuading the crowd, it appeared to enrage them.
>
> (ch. 33)

Eliot's demystifying prose unsettles both theological and secular legal authority in this scene in the guise of a carefully observed presentation of the facts. The Rector reads the act for the second time to little effect, while Crow's scandalous reputation undermines his tactical efforts to implement the law and only intensifies the crisis.

This pre-emptive apportioning of responsibility for the riot to such minor characters as the unnamed Rector and the incompetent policeman (a stock character of riot narratives of this period) is both true to the Act's intent to make local magistrates responsible for the keeping of the peace and to the novel's ultimate absolution of Felix's individual criminal offences. Both Rector and constable function in this sense as manifestations of the inherently unreliable voice of the criminal law, which stands in contrast to the epistemological authority the narrative grants to Felix through the elaboration of the dissonance between his interior motives and external actions as the riot unfolds. Eliot's prose does not give the reader access to the thoughts of either the Rector or Crow; we know nothing of the range of possible emotions they may have felt in the face of a riotous crowd pelting them with potatoes, while Felix's emotional state is anatomised in depth and in contrast to the unreflective melee that jostles for space on the page, to invoke Alex Woloch.[12]

Eliot's creative decision to have the Riot Act read not once but twice also suggests some awareness on her part of the common concerns raised about the logistics of reading the Riot Act multiple times. Not least of these concerns was the question of whether so-called rioters should time their dispersal with the first reading of the act or with subsequent ones. People typically misunderstood the meaning of the hour warning, assuming that their actions, including the destruction of property, would not be defined as felonious or riotous until the hour had passed. This was not the case, even in the unlikely situation that the timing of the riot was being accurately recorded. In fact, the cavalry was empowered to intervene from the moment the Riot Act was read, although the nature of that intervention became a subject of heated parliamentary debate, particularly following the St George's Field Massacre of 1768, which had initially been dubbed a riot and set a notable precedent for the criminal prosecution of magistrates and soldiers for the use of force.

Eliot herself witnessed an election riot that extended over two days in December 1832 when she was a schoolgirl in Nuneaton. True to the contested mediation of all riots, this riot generated conflicting accounts of the military's role and the effectiveness of the Riot Act in diffusing violence. John Cross, Eliot's widower and early biographer, quoted a lengthy extract from a local Tory-aligned newspaper as evidence of the influence of this event on the riot scene in *Felix Holt*. Reporting on the supporters of the radical candidate's disruption of both Tory and Whig supporters exercising their right 'to give an honest and conscientious vote', the journalist gives an account of the reading of the Riot Act that constructs both magistrates and the soldiers of the Scots Greys as victims of a murderous mob. The magistrates, in this version of events, had to be prevailed on 'at length' before they were prepared to resort to the military to resolve a civil matter, a caution that the journalist contends inflamed the situation further:

> The tumult increasing, as the detachment of the Scots Greys were called in, the Riot Act was read from the windows of the Newdigate Arms; and we regret to add that both W. P. Inge, Esq., and Colonel Newdigate, in the discharge of their magisterial duties, received personal injuries.
>
> On Saturday the mob presented an appalling appearance, and but for the forbearance of the soldiery, numerous lives would have fallen a sacrifice. Several of the officers of the Scots Greys were materially hurt in their attempt to quell the riotous proceedings of the mob. ... Two or three unlucky individuals, drawn from the files of the military on their approach to the poll, were cruelly beaten and stripped literally naked.

We regret to add that one life has been sacrificed during the contest, and that several misguided individuals have been seriously injured.[13]

Melodrama structures this account, in which dutiful magistrates and heroic soldiers confront a cruel inhuman mob and 'two or three unlucky individuals' are beaten and humiliated by 'several misguided individuals'. Whilst hardly sympathetic to the mob at large, Eliot's characterisation of the riot differs significantly from this account, allowing for the possibility that responsibility for the violence is more distributed and systemic.

Eliot's canonical twentieth-century biographer reverses this binary between virtuous law enforcement and felonious riotousness. Gordon Haight's reading of Eliot's fictional remediation of the Nuneaton riot in *Felix Holt* aligns with the Nuneaton Town Diarist's official record of events, which described the village's strong support for the radical candidate and registered 'surprise' when 'Horse soldiers' entered the town, charged 'upon the people, cutting and trampling down many', causing 'one or two' fatalities.[14] Haight's version of the riot notes Eliot's recollection of the plight of unemployed weavers and miners and the excitement surrounding the riots. He also stresses that the majority of the townspeople were 'strongly Radical' and supported the local Radical candidate, Dempster Heming, whom Haight compares to Eliot's fictional Radical candidate Harold Transome:

> In a fair election [Heming] would have won easily. But the Tories, seeing the tide going against them, suspended the poll, and called in a detachment of Scots Greys, which had been kept in readiness at Meriden: the Riot Act was read, and when the mob did not disperse, horse soldiers with drawn swords rode through the town, charging the people, cutting and trampling them down. One man died of his injuries. These events were events not to be forgotten.[15]

Haight notes the hefty price paid by the Tory candidate to achieve electoral success, including a tab for four hundred pounds at the Newdigate Arms. Compounding this electoral travesty, the Town Diarist records the subsequent charging of the Radical candidate under the Riot Act in January 1833 and the trial three months later of two of his supporters 'for continuing assembled with others to the number of twelve after the Riot Act had been read over an Hour'.[16] The trial lasted for 12 hours and resulted in acquittal, with the Diarist noting: 'The result was highly satisfactory to the People here and great mortification to the Dugdalites (Tory loyalists). There was an abundance of false swearing on the side of the Prosecution'.[17]

Eliot's research for *Felix Holt* included reading newspapers, pamphlets, and accounts of the violence surrounding the tumultuous passage of the 1832 Reform Bill, during which the precarious authority of the Riot Act was repeatedly enacted and critically observed from contesting political perspectives. A notable example of this nationally mediated ferment was a lengthy and querulous pamphlet on the Bristol Riots of October 1831 authored by a self-described citizen of Bristol, the conservative cleric and amateur artist, John Eagles. While anxiously describing his town's descent into chaos, Eagles repeatedly swipes at both sympathetic radicals and the Captain of the Dragoons—the latter empowered by the reading of the Act—both of whom saw a 'good natured mob' and excessive use of force, where he saw riotous 'ruffians' and a heroic constabulary in need of military reinforcement:

> About dusk, when the mob was greatly increased, the Mayor and three other Magistrates again came out of the Mansion-house, and were received with a volley of stones, brickbats, &c., with which they were severely struck. The Riot Act was then read three times by the Mayor. When standing on a chair for this purpose, a top rail was thrown at him, which, had it struck him, would probably have killed him.[18]

The scene described here was a climactic moment during three days of rioting sparked by local resistance to the anti-reform oligarchy that ran Bristol.[19] Writing in support of the status quo, Eagles' stylistic predilection for snarky asides and melodramatic polarisation imposes a precarious narrative order that oscillates between evidence-gathering and emotive testimonial bias. Like Eliot's rioters, Eagles' Bristolians hurl epithets and curse the readers of the Riot Act in a series of carefully orchestrated incendiary utterances and gestures that align with a trend Ivan Kreilkamp has observed in the work of middle-class authors in the 1830s and 1840s towards demonising 'certain speech acts—such as "curses" or "oaths", political oratory delivered before a crowd or whispered Chartist strategies delivered to conspirators— as emerging from and directed by irresponsible and irrational bodies rather than circulating within a rational public sphere'.[20]

Samuel Bamford's *Passages in the Life of a Radical* echoes Eagles' critical treatment of crowd violence, although not his conservative politics or abiding faith in the magistracy. Haight remarks on Eliot's copious notetaking from Bamford while she wrote *Felix Holt*, which may explain both the striking parallels between Bamford's autobiographical narration of his Bunyan-inspired passage from precocious, literate radical activist to reflective, mature working-class author, and the narrative arc of Felix Holt's *Bildung* from radical reformism to anti-revolutionary quiescence. Tracing the alignments between Bamford's memoir and middle-class industrial novels of the 1840s, such as Gaskell's *Mary Barton* and Disraeli's *Sybil*, Ivan Kreilkamp has suggested that the encoding of speech mediated 'between the two poles of violence and literacy' in the representation of working-class character in this period, whether fictional or non-fictional.[21] In this reading, education becomes central to the relative positioning of working-class speech between 'illiterate bodies and writing'.[22] When linked to 'rational education and conversation', working-class speech was legitimate and audible, but when linked to protest, it 'began to migrate from writing to physical violence' and illiteracy.[23] Following Kreilkamp's logic, Bamford's construction of the celebrated orator Henry Hunt as a demagogic conduit for violence contrasts with his own literate, reasoning narration and carefully chosen word, an effect that bolsters the ultimate positioning of *Passages in the Life of a Radical* as an antidote to the mob politics of Chartism and to what Bamford saw as the dangerous demagoguery that catalysed the declaration of the People's Charter in 1838.[24] What becomes more muted in this focus on protagonists duelling for attention against a backdrop of political violence, however, is the radical criticism of the law in Bamford's *Passages* and the assertion of realist description as the antidote to systemic injustice. This is where Eliot's novel and Bamford's memoir align most starkly in their challenge to the epistemological authority of the law and advocacy for the testimonial truth of interpretive description. The remaining section of this chapter expands on this alignment in the context of the larger claims both texts make for the failure of legal methodologies to represent the complexity of collective responsibility that the riot materialises, a failure typified by scapegoating individuals and the generation of false or biased narratives.

Radical Description

Passages in the Life of a Radical culminates in two climactic moments, the 'so-called riot' of Peterloo and Bamford's subsequent trial for riotous assembly, his 'attempt to alter the laws of the country by force' for which he was sentenced to 12 months imprisonment in Lincoln jail.[25] This trajectory is mirrored in Eliot's novel in the third phase of the arc of Felix Holt's character, which extends from the election-day riot at the end of the novel's second volume to his trial and short-lived imprisonment. Like Bamford's *Bildung*, this final stage in Felix's political education progresses through a series of scenes that magnify the fallibility of a judicial system that conspires against the audibility of working-class voices and diverts those same voices into forms of writing designed to reach the attentive ears of middle-class liberals. Arguing against the prevailing construction of Bamford as an exemplar of the waning of early nineteenth-century radicalism in the face of the economic recovery of the 1840s and 1850s, Martin Hewitt traces a sustained resistance to 'structures of tyranny' in *Passages,* which manifested in a deeply felt anti-clericalism directed at those who wielded dogma to limit access to education, as well as an equally passionate attack on the ritualised structures of a deeply flawed legal system.[26] It was in relation to the latter, Hewitt contends, that

> Bamford came closest to a purely class analysis of the ills of society, developing a picture of the legal system as the arena in which the power of the upper classes was bolstered and the working class denied the opportunity of improving their condition.[27]

Hewitt's reading evokes a less pliable image of Bamford than that conjured by Kreilkamp's emphasis on his subservient performance of working-class literary civility to a suitably impressed court in the trial scenes in *Passages*. In this version of Bamford's passage, a persistent radicalism remains, one that is exemplified by his reflections, published in *Early Days*, the first volume of his autobiography (*Passages* is the second), on the failure of the Reform Act of 1832:

> We have now been at peace during thirty years, and the multitude are still here, many-headed-loud-tongued, as of yore, but where is the loyalty? Here absolutely it is not ... Assuredly there has been a great deal of mismanagement somewhere.[28]

While Bamford's account of Peterloo, and the rioting of the years preceding it, diverges from Eliot's fictional riot in both scale and complexity, the resonance lies in their mutual exposure of the law's limited capacity to justly and accurately attribute intent and responsibility in the context of a legally defined riot. Rioting pervades Bamford's account of the life of a radical. Some riots are enumerated as evidence of the pervasive unrest of the years leading up to and beyond Peterloo, while others are invoked to exemplify conflicting truths generated by both the law and the media. The popular 'convulsions' sparked by the Corn Bill in 1815, for example, consume the opening pages of *Passages,* setting the scene for the ultimate 'convulsion' of Peterloo.[29] The medium for silencing this particular litany of national rioting, in Bamford's estimation, is not the reading of the Riot Act but rather the words of farmer turned pamphleteer, William Cobbett. Bamford paints a vivid picture of working-class families turning away from violence and towards reform as they read Cobbett by the fireside, a pacifying scene that Bamford implicitly aligns with his own reading and expert writing (2: 12). Contrasting with this quiet, democratising mediation of reforming ideals, Bamford portrays the seditious volubility of his fellow activists boasting of their riotous exploits as a risk to the ultimate goal of universal suffrage, just as the 'wild hubbub' and 'babel howl' of the House of Commons like 'a kennel of hounds at feeding time', threatens both the rule of law and the ethos of democratic representation: 'And are these, thought I, the beings whose laws we must obey?' (2: 28)

Bamford informs his readers that throughout these tests to the 'progress' of his character, he remained true to the maxim, 'Hold fast by the laws' (2: 33). One such test was the illegal assembly of his fellow reformers on St Peter's Field on 9 March 1817, two years prior to Peterloo. Bamford describes the magistrates coming onto the field to read the Riot Act, the dispersal of the crowd and arrest of 29 people, including two advocates of 'extreme measures', as a grim harbinger of things to come (2:33). In another, Bamford recalls his arrest on suspicion of high treason in a melodramatically staged scene in which he features as both pacifist and martyr, calming the angry crowd gathered to protest his arrest with heroic assurances that he was prepared to suffer for the cause (2: 43, 74). Bamford's eventual acquittal before the Privy Council serves as a dramatic prequel to his ultimate trial in the wake of Peterloo; in both instances, Bamford advocates for himself as a 'friend of peace and order' and for reform as the means of preserving 'the country from Revolution', whilst conveniently showcasing his literary reputation and oratorical skills (2: 109). The enumeration of all of these qualities builds a character profile of an 'honest enthusiast' 'craving for something for the nation' that would transcend violence, as well as the individualistic hubris that he attributes to many of his fellow reformers, including the famous orator and Peterloo co-conspirator, Henry Hunt (2: 133).

Bamford's exculpatory narrative intensifies in his account of Peterloo, a detailed reconstruction that extends the retrospective reach of his trial testimony and pre-emptively frames his critique of the fallibility of the jury system. Throughout Bamford's narration, as with Eliot's characterisation of Felix's struggle to bring the riot under control, the focus is on establishing virtuous intent through the mitigation of violence. Bamford assures his readers that the meeting was intended to be as 'morally effective as possible' to silence the taunts of a scurrilous press and the anxieties of their political opponents (2: 142). He also emphasises the meeting organisers' belief that their rights of legal assembly would be protected, quoting Hunt's attempt to assuage his fears of violent retribution:

> Were not the laws of the country to protect us? Would not their authority be upheld by those sworn to administer them? And then was it likely at all that magistrates would permit a peaceable and legal assemblage to be interfered with? If we were in the right, would they not be our guardians? If wrong, could they not send us home by reading the Riot Act? Assuredly, while we respected the law, all would be well on our side.
>
> (2: 146)

Betrayed by outside agents who misrepresented their intent and by a legal system that accepted false testimony as fact, Bamford and his fellow reformers are again let down when the Riot Act fails to protect them from both the ensuing massacre and the subsequent arrests, trials, and convictions. According to Bamford's account, the Riot Act was not read at Peterloo, or at least not in his hearing, or that of the majority of his fellow protesters. His shocked realisation that the cavalry was 'riding upon us' without the warning of the Riot Act vividly enacts the violent realities of the law's failure to protect people over property, as he details sabres cutting through flesh, blood-stained clothes, and maimed innocents (2: 156). This horror is amplified by Bamford's account of the conflicting views of the 'stunned' authorities, the 'wealthy classes' who recoiled from the violent excesses of the cavalry, 'the people' who thirsted for revenge, and a media who wilfully misrepresented him as a political opportunist and theatrical hack (2: 164, 174).

Bamford's not-guilty defence against the false charge of making 'great tumult, riot, and disturbance' parallels Eliot's dramatisation of Felix's criminal trial (Bamford, *Passages*, 2: 197). Bamford chose, against legal advice, to speak with sincere 'purpose and with common sense' in defence of his non-violent intent and against those who may have taken advantage of their peaceful assembly to 'create a riot' (2: 238, 242). He attributes his ultimate conviction to the incompetence of the jury and condemns their selective misinterpretation of evidence as an infamy that has 'seldom been surpassed' (2: 252). In what remains of *Passages* Bamford discourses at some length on the inequality built into a jury selection process that privileges property and class over moral character and disinterestedness, before returning to the ultimate purpose of the narration of 'his pilgrimage' in the concluding chapter, aptly entitled 'An Author and his book':

> Have I not led thee on a somewhat strange and painful, yet not altogether unpleasing pilgrimage? Whilst the consciousness that thou wast all this time treading the ground of reality, of this earthly world, must have rendered thy sojourn more strange. Even so it is; reality is always romantic, though the romantic is not always real.
>
> (2: 339)

With an eye on the market, Bamford cannily amplifies his book's 'romantic' features, the unexpectedly heroic appeal of a 'group of characters which otherwise would have passed into oblivion' but will now 'be useful to the future historian of the days recorded' (2: 309). Bamford's use of character here is striking, inviting a slippage between romance and realism to justify the anecdotal recursive structure of *Passages*. Bamford is keenly aware that his narrative is not an historical record, although it may be of some use to historians who seek to write one. His autobiographical persona is a 'character', a construct operating within and constrained by a complex network of competing social, political, and legal forces that his writing materialises through the sustained prosaic observation of everyday interactions alongside momentous historical events, deliberately entangling both as evidence of the literal impact of injustice in all its permutations on the lives of working class people.

Felix's exculpatory narrative diverges from Bamford's in form and style, but the two are aligned in their mutual enactment of the failure of the law to fairly or accurately attribute responsibility for what it defines, under the Riot Act, as an illegal riotous assembly. Bamford allows himself space to remediate his testimonial analysis of the false nomenclature applied to his actions and the consequent biased reconstruction of the events of 16 August 1819. Eliot chooses, by contrast, to limit Felix's self-advocacy to a blundering opening argument and an unsworn statement, both of which eschew the evidentiary weight of sworn testimony in favour of a staging of the 'sublime delight of truthful speech' (*FH*, ch. 46). As Jan-Melissa Schramm has argued, Eliot was well versed in both criminal trial procedure and the Prisoners' Counsel Act. Eliot corresponded with the respected radical advocate, Frederic Harrison, on the topic of the latter, and her understanding of the history of legal representation in criminal cases is revealed in a series of narratorial observations that address the inequity of the law current in 1832, but mercifully obsolete by the 1860s:

> Even if pleading of counsel had been permitted (and at that time it was not) on behalf of a prisoner on trial for felony, Felix would have declined it: he would in any case have spoken in his own defence. He had a perfectly simple account to give, and needed not to avail himself of any legal adroitness.
>
> (*FH*, ch. 37)

Felix's lack of legal adroitness, as Schramm argues, makes him oblivious to the definitional complexity of a system in which the reality of his 'behaviour during the riot' is constructed by the 'mediating mind of a lawyer', a mind that 'shapes the narratives of the witnesses without their acknowledgement, allowing for both the prosecutorial arrangement of the allegedly self-evident facts and the more deliberate operation of personal prejudices'.[30]

Moving quickly and dismissively through the trial, the narrator observes that the 'case for the prosecution 'was nothing more than a reproduction, with irrelevancies added by witnesses, of the facts already known to us' (*FH*, ch. 46). The 'us' invoked in this context unites the epistemological authority of the 'literary intellectual'—to use Fredric Jameson's characterisation of Eliot's authorial persona—with her readers and against the interpretive limitations of the law and the coercive ministrations of its agents.[31] The novelist and her readers can see what the law and her protagonist cannot. The 'tangled business' of the riot and the 'mass of wild chaotic desires and impulses' it materialises exposes the tenuous hold all those present had and have over the facts of the case: 'How numerous the mob was, no one ever knew: many inhabitants afterwards were ready to swear that there must have been at least two thousand rioters' (*FH*, ch. 33). This collective confusion includes Felix who, Eliot suggests, may have been under the sway of the kind of 'passionate enthusiasm' that 'makes world-famous deeds' (ch. 33). The riot and subsequent trial signal the demise of such epic individualism. The 'tangled business' of the riot extends into the courtroom where Felix repeats the same mistake he had committed as he rushed towards the mob, accidentally killing a policeman, a naïve exceptionalism that Eliot punishes using the representational limitations of the law and ultimately absolves through the tonic of love.

When Felix addresses the court, he assumes that others will share his passion for 'the sublime delight of truthful speech', that they will attend to his reasoning and that his words will break through the political sophistries and distortions that have led them all to this culminating moment, a romantic hope that Eliot briefly allows the reader to share by giving Felix narrative space and a lengthy swathe of direct speech to defend his innocence:

> I'm not prepared to say I never would assault a constable where I had more chance of deliberation. I certainly should assault him if I saw him doing anything that made my blood boil: I reverence the law, but not where it is a pretext for wrong, which it should be the very object of law to hinder. I consider that I should be making an unworthy defence, if I let the Court infer from what I say myself, or from what is said by my witnesses, that because I am a man who hates drunken motiveless disorder, or any wanton harm, therefore I am a man who would never fight against authority. I hold it blasphemy to say that a man ought not to fight against authority: there is no great religion and no great freedom that has not done it, in the beginning. It would be impertinent for me to speak of this now, if I did not need to say in my own defence, that I should hold myself the worst sort of traitor if I put my hand either to fighting or disorder—which must mean injury to somebody—if I were not urged to it by what I hold to be sacred feelings, making a sacred duty either to my own manhood or to my fellow-man.
>
> (ch. 46)

The tactical error of uttering these words in court in defence of a charge of rioting and manslaughter is blatantly clear and reinforced by Harold Transome's aside to Esther, who bemoans the 'whole peroration' as better 'left unsaid': 'It has done him harm with the jury—they won't understand it, or rather will misunderstand it' (ch. 46). Eliot may have hoped that the reader, by contrast, would understand the need for revolutionary action in defence of a 'sacred' cause and the ethical imperative to act when a wrong is being done even when the perpetrator is the law itself.

To riot, for Eliot, is thus ultimately to fail to achieve the promise of revolutionary transformation that Felix's testimony offers the reader. It is to open up the possibility of misinterpretation and confusion. In this conceptual construction, the inchoate emotion and noise generated by the riot is antipodally positioned against the heroic passion and ethical clarity required of those who act selflessly in the interest of their fellow humans. *Felix Holt* consequently materialises the untimeliness of both riot and revolution in the 1830s and the 1860s, enlisting the novel to elaborate the prospect of a future utopian collectivity in which the voices of the many may find alternative forms of resistance and meaning outside the official spheres of law and professional politics. This is also the promise that haunts Bamford's account of his political disillusionment in the wake of Peterloo. While he remains critical of Chartism, he never relinquishes his belief that he was part of a struggle for 'a great freedom', a freedom of the kind Felix Holt gestures towards in his testimony, and Eliot offers as one of many possibilities open to both her hero and her readers.

Notes

1 George Eliot, *Felix Holt, the Radical*, ed. Fred C. Thomson (1866; Oxford: Oxford World's Classics, 1998), ch. 33. All subsequent references are to this edition and will be made in text.

2 E.P. Thompson's seminal criticism of the 'spasmodic view' of popular history is in 'The Moral Economy of the English Crowd in the Eighteenth Century', *Past and Present*, 50 (1971), 76.

3 Lisa Rodensky, *The Crime in Mind: Criminal Responsibility and the Victorian Novel* (New York: Oxford University Press, 2003), 89.

4 Rodensky, *Crime in Mind*, 89.

5 John Kucich discusses the alignment of Eliot's collectivism with traditions of Organicism in 'The "Organic Appeal" in *Felix Holt*: Social Problem Fiction, Paternalism and the Welfare State', *Victorian Studies*, 59 (2017), 609–35.

6 Lauren Goodlad, 'Moral Character', in *Historicism and the Human Sciences in Victorian Britain*, ed. Mark Bevir (Cambridge: Cambridge University Press, 2017), 134.

7 George Eliot, *The Journals of George Eliot*, ed. Margaret Harris and Judith Johnston (Cambridge: Cambridge University Press, 1998), 124.

8 Cited in W. Nippel, 'Reading the Riot Act: The Discourse of Law-Enforcement in 18th Century England', *History and Anthropology*, 1.2 (1985), 404.

9 R. Quinault, 'The Warwickshire County Magistracy and Public Order, c.1830–1870', in *Popular Protests and Public Order: Six Studies in British History 1790-1920*, ed. R. Quinault and J. Stevenson (London: George Allen and Unwin, 1974), 181–21: cited in Nippel, 'Reading', 404.

10 J. Stevenson, 'Social Control and the Prevention of Riots in England, 1789-1829', in *Social Control in Nineteenth-Century Britain*, ed. A.P. Donajgrodzki (London: Croom Helm, 1979), 27–50: cited in Nippel, 'Reading', 404.

11 *Cobbett's Parliamentary History of England*, 36 vols, ed. J. Wright (London, 1813), 17: 228, cited in Nippel, 'Reading', 404.

12 Alex Woloch, *The One vs. The Many: Minor Characters and the Space of the Protagonist in the Novel* (Princeton: Princeton University Press, 2003), 13.

13 Cited in J.W. Cross, *George Eliot's Life, as Related in her Letters and Journals*, 3 vols (Edinburgh: William Blackwood, 1884), 1: 28–9.

14 John Astley, *The Nuneaton Town Diary*, vol. 2, May 1825 to 27 November 1845, entry for 21 December 1832, Nuneaton Library and Information Centre, MS.

15 Gordon S. Haight, *George Eliot: A Biography* (Oxford: Oxford University Press, 1968), 382.

16 John Astley, 'Occurrences at Nuneaton', *The Nuneaton Town Diary*, vol. 2, May 1825 to 27 November 1845, entry for January 1833.

17 John Astley, 'Occurrences at Nuneaton,' *The Nuneaton Town Diary*, vol. 2, May 1825 to 27 November 1845, entry for April 1833.

18 John Eagles, *The Bristol Riots: Their Causes, Progress, and Consequences* (Bristol: Gutch and Martin, 1832), 73–4.
19 Eagles, *Bristol Riots*, 57.
20 Ivan Kreilkamp, *Voice and the Victorian Storyteller* (Cambridge: Cambridge University Press, 2005), 37.
21 Kreilkamp, *Voice*, 40.
22 Kreilkamp, *Voice*, 40.
23 Kreilkamp, *Voice*, 40.
24 Kreilkamp, *Voice*, 47, 43.
25 Martin Hewitt, 'Radicalism and the Victorian Working Class', *The Historical Journal*, 34 (1991), 876.
26 Hewitt, 'Radicalism', 881.
27 Hewitt, 'Radicalism', 881.
28 Samuel Bamford, *Early Days* (1849), cited in Hewitt, 884.
29 Samuel Bamford, *Passages in the Life of a Radical, and Early Days*, ed. Henry Dunckley, 2 vols (London: T. Fisher Unwin, 1893), 2: 11.
30 Jan-Melissa Schramm, *Testimony and Advocacy in Victorian Law, Literature, and Theology* (Cambridge: Cambridge University Press, 2000), 131. Haight details Eliot's correspondence with Harrison on legal matters (*George Eliot*, 383); Schramm cites and discusses Eliot's letters to Harrison on the subject of the Prisoner's Counsel Act.
31 Fredric Jameson, *The Antinomies of Realism* (London and New York: Verso, 2013), 110.

8 *Middlemarch* and Reform

Looking Back versus 'The Thick of It'

Joanne Wilkes

'Every limit is a beginning as well as an ending', begins the 'Finale' of George Eliot's *Middlemarch* (1872). This chapter takes the novel's ending as its beginning. Since *Middlemarch* is set about 40 years before the time of publication—between September 1829 and May 1832—the 'Finale' lets readers know what happened to the novel's central characters in the ensuing period.

The 'Finale', fittingly, ends with Dorothea, née Brooke, the figure evoked in the 'Prelude', and frames her fate in terms of the presentation of her there as a contemporary Saint Theresa living in an era inimical to transformative action by women. 'A new Theresa will hardly have the opportunity of reforming a conventual life', the narrator comments, 'any more than a new Antigone will spend her heroic piety in daring all for the sake of a brother's burial', since 'the medium in which their ardent deeds took shape has forever gone'.[1] So what Dorothea has elected to do is to marry Will Ladislaw and offer him 'wifely help'. Will, we are told, goes on to become 'an ardent public man' who struggles against 'wrongs' and eventually becomes an MP; Dorothea, meanwhile, welcomes the fact that her husband is 'in the thick of' these struggles ('Finale'). But the narrator laments that, in the early 1870s, there are still barriers to the ambitions of idealistic young women: 'we insignificant people with our daily words and acts are preparing the lives of many Dorotheas, some of which may present a far sadder sacrifice than that of the Dorothea whose story we know'.

Thus the novel is obviously enjoining the reader not to engage in the social 'medium' in ways that thwart the aspirations of contemporary Dorotheas. But the outcome of Dorothea's story has been a source of critical debate. One line of thinking emerged as early as 1873, expressed by a woman very much linked with transformative achievement in mid-Victorian Britain. Florence Nightingale regretted in *Fraser's Magazine* that George Eliot could 'find no better outlet for the heroine' than to marry what Nightingale saw as two unsatisfactory husbands in quick succession. Dorothea might instead have become, for example, a fictional version of slum-housing reformer Octavia Hill, an actual connection of George Eliot's, who 'brought sympathy and education to bear from individual to individual … by personal

DOI: 10.4324/9781003362821-9

acquaintance'.[2] (Octavia's sister Gertrude Hill had married George Henry Lewes' son Charles.)

Nightingale also found Will Ladislaw an unconvincing political activist, seeing him as a fairy or a faun more than a human being. Strictures against the characterisation of Will also have a long history, and Mark Allison has reminded us that the Dorothea-Ladislaw couple may seem a poor substitute for the pairing that never happens in the novel, that of Dorothea and Lydgate. (Allison, discussing the novel in connection with Utopian socialist movements of the period of its setting, draws attention to the male-female 'priest-couple' whom early nineteenth-century socialists believed necessary for triggering social transformation.[3]) Certainly, Ladislaw for much of the novel lacks direction, and his involvement in Mr Brooke's abortive political campaign is initially motivated by his yearning to stay near Dorothea. Lydgate, on the other hand, comes to Middlemarch with concrete research plans, plans that he hopes to further partly through practical activity that will benefit his patients as well. Dorothea is enthusiastic about Lydgate's aspirations when she finds herself, belatedly, in a position to help him—but by that time, it is too late for any assistance of hers to turn his career around.

A counter-argument here might be that Dorothea makes of Will Ladislaw the man that he might not have become otherwise—as is the case with Mary Garth's impact on Fred Vincy. Nonetheless, the novel does leave open the question as to what Will's parliamentary activity achieves in practice; it hints too that his success, whatever it consists in, will be short-lived, for he worked 'well in those times when reforms were begun with a young hopefulness of immediate good which has been much checked in our days' ('Finale'). *Middlemarch*'s retrospective view of the Reform era and its aftermath means that it can contrast the characters' past and the reader's present, as here. Not only has Dorothea failed to fulfil her own potential, acting instead in a subordinate role in her husband's political career—but even once that husband gained the motivation to pursue specific goals, his endeavours ended up having limited impact on the reader's present.

Christian Isobel Johnstone and Political Journalism

This chapter will return to the lives of Will and Dorothea Ladislaw, and in addition will canvass the vexed issue of how George Eliot envisaged beneficial progress coming about. In this context, a woman who did intervene in the political world in the aftermath of the 1832 Reform Bill offers an illuminating comparison. This was the Scottish journalist and editor Christian Isobel Johnstone (1781–1857). Together with her husband John, in the early 1830s, she managed two magazines, until the pair's *Johnstone's Edinburgh Magazine* merged in June 1834 with the radical monthly *Tait's Edinburgh Magazine*. Christian Johnstone took a leading role in editing and writing for *Johnstone's* and then *Tait's*, up to her retirement in 1846. Her husband seems to have concentrated on the business side of things.

Information about Christian Johnstone, especially of a personal kind, remains scanty. But her writing for *Tait's* has been analysed by Alexis Easley in her *First-Person Anonymous* (2004).[4] Subsequently, Pam Perkins has studied Johnstone's career, giving particular attention to her earlier work as a novelist, and as author of her *Cook and Housewife's Manual* from 1825, a cookbook with political overtones that went into many editions.[5] But neither the *Manual* nor Johnstone's journalism was published under her name: the former was attributed to 'Meg Dods' (a housekeeper character from Walter Scott's *St Ronan's Well*), while the latter followed the convention of anonymous publication that governed most journalism of the time. Johnstone published fiction, before and during her journalistic career, including serials that appeared anonymously in *Tait's*, before coming out under her own name in the mid-1840s as part of a multi-volume, multi-author collection called *Edinburgh Tales*. Thus she gained some profile as a writer of fiction.[6] As regards Johnstone's journalism, Easley has shown how journalistic anonymity obscured her authorship of her many contributions to *Tait's*—but also enabled her to adopt a voice, or voices, not hampered by conventional and essentialist assumptions about women, their knowledge, and their intellectual capacities. Her journalism was very various: political writing proper, plus reviews which covered a wide range of fields and often had a political inflection. Unlike Eliot the novelist, Johnstone was responding to events as they happened and publications as they appeared.

This chapter concentrates on Johnstone's work in the year from mid-1834, just after *Johnstone's* merged with *Tait's*, and she became not just a writer for *Tait's*, but also *de facto* co-editor (in tandem with William Tait). This was part of a very turbulent period in national politics for everyone, so challenging too for those in Will and Dorothea's putative situation. After the passing of the Reform Bill in June 1832, there was much internal dissension among those in the dominant group in Parliament, a mixture of Whigs and Radicals, as well as among the Tories in the Opposition, creating conditions of political instability. Johnstone's writing and editing responded to this situation in a variety of ways, and one of these—my focus here—was to create a series where characters of different political persuasions reacted to and debated events as they happened, as well as speculating about prominent personalities. Johnstone published five such articles from July 1834 through to March 1835. They are likely responding not just to political events and the merging of magazines, but also to a move on the part of the rival, Edinburgh-based Tory monthly, *Blackwood's Edinburgh Magazine*, namely the revival, in May 1834, of *Blackwood's*' famous series, the *Noctes Ambrosianae*, inaugurated in 1822, after a hiatus of 18 months. This rival series came to an end (this time for good) in February 1835, while Johnstone's series had its final instalment in the following month. The last episodes of the *Blackwood's* series were written by the magazine's (and the series') longstanding contributor John Wilson (1785–1854), and featured a variety of figures, notably his own alter ego, 'Christopher North', and the 'Shepherd', based on writer/ shepherd James Hogg.

That Johnstone's series has not been recognised as a reply to the *Noctes* would be due in part to the irregular titles it was given. The first episodes of the five were called 'What Is Going On. No. 1.—Scenes in Edinburgh' (July 1834) and 'What Is Going On. No. II.—Scenes in Edinburgh' (August 1834). But the third episode (October 1834) had the title 'Scenes in Edinburgh.—No. III. I The Pry Bureau. II.—The Fiddlers' Gallery, at the Grey Dinner', while the fourth (February 1835) was 'Scenes in Edinburgh.—No. IV. The Pry Bureau', and the last (March 1835) is 'The Pry Bureau.—No. V. Branch Establishment, Birmingham'. Although the format is rather loose, there are many continuities. There is an important figure who, like the Shepherd in the *Noctes*, uses Scots rather than standard English, and in an outspoken and vivid way: John of the Girnel. He is a small-holder dispossessed by the Highland clearances, and a sympathiser with the working classes. There are, however, no female characters in Johnstone's series, just as there are very few in the *Noctes*. The world of political discussion in the *Tait's* series is unquestionably masculine, but one in which a female editor/contributor, because of the convention of anonymity, can intervene.

Both series echo the doctrinaire politics found in their respective magazines' more overtly political articles, yet they also treat this politics in more nuanced ways. In addition, both magazines canvass politics in other kinds of contributions, such as satirical poetry and fiction. Robert Morrison has observed of *Blackwood's* that its 'hard political line emerged through a welter of wit, liberality, mirth, contradiction, and squibbery',[7] and I would argue that the same was true of *Tait's* in its Radicalism. Johnstone, too, since she functioned as both contributor and co-editor, had some say in what went into the magazine. Above all, the two series highlighted the ever-changing and often-puzzling nature of political happenings and personalities: what it might have been like to be in 'the thick of it'.

The focus here, then, is a comparison between, on one hand, the writings of a real-life female political journalist of the 1830s, and on the other, the putative activities of George Eliot's fictional political activists, plus the storylines in *Middlemarch* that culminate in their eventual careers. These storylines entail, of course, the lives and destinies of many other figures: one of my concerns will be the intertwined stories of Tertius Lydgate and Nicholas Bulstrode. In addition, I set a journalist responding to events as they occur against characters whose lives are presented retrospectively from 40 years later. Investigating Christian Johnstone's endeavours in this way highlights how *Middlemarch* treats both causality and the potential for meaningful change.

It is worth recalling too that, like Johnstone, Eliot herself practised both fiction-writing and journalism. She also wrote (in the 1850s) for a radical publication, the *Westminster Review*, and, as Johnstone had done, took on a *de facto* editorial role in relation to a male editor (John Chapman, in Eliot's case). Eliot's radicalism was, however, intellectual rather than political. Indeed, one of her most frequently-cited *Westminster* essays, 'The Natural History of German Life' (July 1856), which reviews books dealing with the German peasantry, argues against both the practicability and the desirability of radical change. Change best happens organically, Eliot avers, and in any case, one significant barrier to it is human beings' egoism. When Eliot embarked on writing fiction not long after this essay, it was through the medium of Johnstone's old Tory adversary, *Blackwood's Edinburgh Magazine*, where the three stories of *Scenes of Clerical Life* were serialised in 1857. Most of Eliot's engagement with the Blackwood firm thereafter concerned the publication of her fiction outside the magazine, while novels would largely supplant journalism in her output. Yet she would publish in January 1868, at John Blackwood's request, a political speech in the voice of the hero of her then most recent novel, *Felix Holt, the Radical* (1866). 'Address to Working Men, by Felix Holt' was directed to the men lately enfranchised by the 1867 Reform Bill, and echoed the message of the *Westminster* article, that change should be slow and organic.

National Politics, 1829–35

The political events evoked in *Middlemarch* before the 'Finale' begin with Catholic Emancipation (March 1829, recalled in September), and end with the House of Lords' rejection of the 1832 Reform Bill in May of that year. The Reform Bill was, however, passed the following month.

Catholic Emancipation, which granted the franchise to Catholic males for the first time, was a highly controversial move, not least because it was unexpectedly enacted by a Tory government led by Sir Robert Peel and the Duke of Wellington. The main impact was felt in largely Catholic Ireland, and there resulted an influx of Irish Catholic MPs, the most prominent being the charismatic Daniel O'Connell. Emancipation was a move aimed at curbing unrest in Ireland, but from the perspective of governments on the mainland, both Tory and later Whig, Irish policy continued to be a major source of difficulty and disagreement. In Eliot's novel, Emancipation is also a source of concern and distrust for some of the characters.

The Whig Government in power after the passing of the 1832 Reform Bill—the Government still in office when Johnstone's 'Pry' series began in July 1834—was led by Earl Grey in the House of Lords and Lord Althorp in the House of Commons. Notable measures over the 1832–34 period included the Factory Act of 1833, which restricted the employment of children in factories, the Poor Law Amendment Act, and, not least, the abolition of slavery in Britain's colonies. But the Government's majority, although large, was diverse and therefore unwieldy. Not only were there the new Irish

MPs, but Radical figures were also prominent, including Grey's son-in-law Lord Durham. Hence, it was difficult to get agreement on legislation.

The most complex matter relating to Ireland concerned the Church, since the Church of Ireland, an extension of the Established Church in England, was entitled to impose tithes on the Irish population, despite the fact that the vast majority of the Irish were Catholic and had their own priests. Moreover, most of the landlords of this Catholic population were Protestant, many of them non-resident. Unsurprisingly, there was much resentment on the part of the Catholics directed at both Protestant clergy and Protestant landlords, and thus much support for repeal of the union between Ireland and the rest of Britain. So the Government proposed that some of the money due in tithes would be appropriated for the benefit of the Irish population—but the precise conditions were not agreed on. Some Government MPs (and many Tories) believed that allowing the State to appropriate Church revenues represented a dangerous precedent, so that four ministers resigned, including Edward Lord Stanley and Sir John Graham. Complicating matters in 1834 were negotiations over the proposed renewal of the 1833 Irish Coercion Bill, so as to give the authorities wide powers to curb dissension and violence. These dealings, involving apparently clandestine negotiations with O'Connell, served to expose the Government's divisions, including a disagreement between Grey and Althorp. In July 1834, Grey resigned. Another Whig Government was then put together by Lord Melbourne.

Melbourne's administration was short-lived as well, since disagreement over the Irish Church continued, and the sovereign, William IV, was concerned over the State's potential interference in Church matters. There had also been dissension among Ministers evident during the Parliamentary summer recess of 1834, when—in moves which were of particular interest for periodicals based in Edinburgh—there were various public gatherings in Scotland centred on Earl Grey himself, the Radical Lord Durham, and the brilliant but volatile Lord Chancellor, Henry, Lord Brougham. In particular, the hostility between the latter two became obvious, with Durham the advocate of further reform, whereas Brougham, like Grey, wanted to hold back.

On 15 November 1834, William IV removed Melbourne's administration in what turned out to be the last such intervention in British politics by a monarch. William sent for veteran Tory, the Duke of Wellington, but as he was a controversial anti-Reformer, the Government was centred on the more moderate Tory leader in the Commons, Sir Robert Peel. An election ensued, which increased the Tories' numbers, but did not give them a majority. This administration was also unstable, and in April 1835, just after the end of Johnstone's 'Pry' series, the King was obliged to send again for Lord Melbourne. This new administration lasted till 1841 (into Victoria's reign), though with difficulty. Such then was the complex political world with which Christian Johnstone engaged, and which people like Will and Dorothea Ladislaw would have had to confront.

Christian Johnstone's 'Pry' Series, 1834–35

That Johnstone's series focuses on the contingent and unstable world of political rumour is signalled by the prominence given to a fictional figure called Paul Pry, Jun., whose arrival at the *Tait's* premises gets the series going. He is the son of the Paul Pry whom readers would have recalled as the protagonist of John Poole's popular 1825 comedy, *Paul Pry*, played for many years by prominent comic actor John Liston. Poole's Pry is an inveterate busybody, unable to stop himself from interfering in others' affairs, and Johnstone's version of his son is of similar ilk. He has come to Edinburgh to set up another branch of his family's centre for coordinating gossip, a 'Pry Bureau' collecting and disseminating information on 'What Is Going On' (hence the title of the first two instalments of the series). Pry Jun. has already been to 'No. 45'—that is, 45 George St., the headquarters of Blackwood's—where, he says, 'our friend there:– makes no strangers of our family'.[8] The Bureau will be a '*General Register of Politics, History, Births, Marriages, Deaths, Wooings and Quarrellings, Flirtations and Breakings-off*'.[9] As the *Tait's* series develops, the focus comes to be primarily on politics, with 'Quarrellings' of the political world looming large. Interestingly, although it was to feature no women characters, Pry does point to female involvement in the magazine itself, mentioning 'Mrs. Gore, Miss Martineau, and ever so many ladies'.[10] (Under Johnstone's editorship, the proportion of *Tait's* contributions from women would increase from 19% to 37%).[11]

The inception of the Pry Bureau highlights both the public's thirst for gossip and the crucial role of the periodical press in retailing it. 'Disguise it as we will', declares Pry, 'there is no denying that … nothing under the sun, or within the sphere of the gas-lamps is half so interesting as WHAT IS GOING ON'. Interest in gossip, Pry Jun. avers, is

> that universal passion with makes men daily *pry* so eagerly into the *speculum* of the *Times*, and peer into the *Mirror* which the *Chronicle*, in the 311 lawful days of the year, boasts of holding up to nature, showing the very age and body of the time, its form and pressure,— watch over the spots in the *Sun*, examine with the *Examiner*, observe with the many *Observers*, review with all the *Reviews,* and with the *Spectator* become spectators.[12]

As the series develops, Pry Jun. and the activities of his Bureau *per se* become less salient, but the first instalment has established the premise that the characters' discussions are based partly on gossip, and that truth-claims are difficult to sustain. Much rumour swirled around the circumstances of Earl Grey's retirement from office, including the motives and behaviour of various ministers, and then later around the fall of the Melbourne Ministry. Johnstone knows that what is really 'going on' is hard to fathom, and so a discussion format which canvasses views and possibilities is apposite.

Tait's' Radical agenda means that for it, the Grey administration ended in July 1834 because of the Whigs' lack of commitment to thoroughgoing change and the betrayal of the cause of Reform by Stanley and Graham. Hence, a revitalised and radicalised ministry would flourish free of Grey, according to a *Tait's* editorial in August, since he had been 'the *incubus* which smothered its energies, or reduced them to a feeble, ineffectual struggle'.[13] But when the Melbourne administration was dismissed by the King, it became essential that Reformers of all stripes unite against the Tories, embracing the Radicals' programme, and taking the lead from Lord Durham: as Johnstone herself wrote in a political article in the December 1834 issue, 'He is either an imbecile or a traitor to the cause of Reform, who does not, at the present crisis, adopt the sentiments of Lord Durham, and proclaim, that in UNION lies the strength of the Reformers'.[14] The Radical programme included the removal of taxes on newspapers, triennial parliaments, further extension of the suffrage, and the introduction of secret ballot to stamp out intimidation of voters. Moreover, neither Catholics nor Protestant Dissenters should have to pay any money to a Church they did not belong to, and admission to Oxbridge should not be confined to members of the Church of England. *Tait's* further maintained that the dismissal of Melbourne's Ministry was suspicious, Peel was a devious character, and the supposedly 'honest' Whig Lord Althorp was not honest at all. Lord Brougham, meanwhile, was frustratingly unpredictable.

Johnstone's series is heterogeneous, comprising conversations that feature well-differentiated characters, while the conversational format in itself fosters gossip that focuses on individuals. To convey some idea of its character, I will consider the visit to Scotland of Whig politicians in the summer of 1834—and especially the dinner held for Earl Grey in Edinburgh on 15 September—together with the representation of Lord Brougham. These elements are related, but Brougham warrants separate consideration because he loomed so large in events of the period. More specifically, he comes across as a subject of genuine puzzlement in the *Tait's* series (as indeed in the *Noctes*). Although now a member of the House of Lords, Brougham had been known to the Scottish political and literary world for many years, partly as one of the founders of the *Edinburgh Review* back in 1802. Brougham was also a friend of William Tait, while he and his ideas had been canvassed before in the Johnstones' previous periodicals, *The Schoolmaster* and *Johnstone's Edinburgh Magazine*.[15]

The third episode of Johnstone's series (October 1834) is called 'Scenes in Edinburgh' and comprises two scenes, one at the Pry Bureau, and the other in 'The Fiddlers' Gallery at the Grey Dinner'. Just before this, however, is the magazine's official report of the dinner, 'The Edinburgh Gathering', by Sir Thomas Dick Lauder, a popular local figure. Dick Lauder writes as a Scotsman and takes the usual *Tait's* line that Earl Grey's Whig government had not gone far enough in Reform. Doing honour to Grey was only the 'ostensible' purpose of the gathering, he says, but people did not come to Edinburgh from all over Scotland 'to approve the *juste-milieu* system of Whig placemen, nor to uphold the Whigs in power, that they might *do* less'. For praise, he singles out speeches by the Radicals Lord Durham and John Cam Hobhouse.[16]

Johnstone, on the other hand, uses the event partly for comedy, but also to suggest how fluid political allegiances might be when faced with the exigencies and temptations of the here and now. John of the Girnel is the focal point of these scenes. He starts off in the Pry Bureau, saying that he had made a point of joining the welcome to Earl Grey earlier in the day, since he respected the Earl personally as a fellow 'staunch, consistent, forty-year Reformer', but he had expected to meet his regular friends at the Bureau. As a Radical, he had not intended to go to the dinner himself.[17] But young fellow-Radical Sydney Tucker rushes in to tell John that the gallery at the dinner is the only place to be, especially now that the speech from Lord Durham has 'struck the true chord'. Of the Bureau regulars, scholar Dr Erasmus Lingo 'forms the rosy centre of a knot of Conservative Whigs and quondam Tories'—that is 'occupying a *juste-milieu* position' (compare Dick Lauder's comments) (638). Moreover, the Tory Counsellor Blarney has been so keen to be in on the action that he has posed as a butler to Lord Chancellor Brougham—not wanting to betray himself by appearing overtly 'in such an assembly of idol and Mammon worshippers' (639).

Eventually, John joins the assembly by repairing to the fiddlers' gallery and is overwhelmed by the numbers of people in the hall (a building specially constructed on Calton Hill for the occasion). But he is not overawed, describing them as 'that immensity of heads, jointed and compact thegither, [who] remind [him] of nothing sae muckle as a pen covered wi' turnips' (640). Eventually furnished with Blarney's telescope, John examines the assembled dignitaries, trying to figure out who they all are. His experience at the dinner conveys to the reader a sense of movement, drama, uncertainty, and even incipient chaos, an ever-changing scene, with various others commenting on proceedings—notably Blarney offering the Tories' cynical take on the Whigs. Meanwhile 'Sir Thammas' (Dick Lauder), says John, 'jinks up and down to keep the peace, like a flea in a blanket' (642). John holds fast to his preoccupation with Radicals, welcoming the Radical speeches and championing Lord Durham in particular. Yet, he does end up compromising, just as the Tory Blarney had done in posing as Brougham's butler, since he eventually accepts wine from his namesake John Campbell. This is the Attorney-General, who, despite always representing himself electorally as 'Plain John Campbell', was really Sir John, and a moderate Whig rather than a Radical like John of the Girnel. So when the latter says that the Radicals like himself who did turn up to the dinner 'were sounder politicians who came boldly forward and converted what was intended for a packed whig meeting into a liberal meeting, than those that stood sullenly aloof to let the *Clique* carry the day' (644), there is an element of rationalisation, not to mention tipsiness. Whereas Dick Lauder himself represented the gathering in *Tait's* as a straightforward political triumph, Johnstone dramatises the question of how much truck a Radical, or indeed a Tory, might have with those who may not be his real allies, without compromising himself.

Meanwhile, as far as Brougham was concerned, there were widespread rumours that he had conspired against Earl Grey, and then tried to upstage him by touring Scotland and giving speeches. At the actual dinner, Brougham had not targeted Grey directly, but had spoken scathingly about colleagues who wished to go 'faster or further than sound reflection, calm deliberation and statesman-like prudence enable them to go'—comments that were construed as directed at Lord Durham.

The first episode of the *Tait's* series in July 1834 had puzzled over Brougham's behaviour. Erasmus Lingo quotes from a (fictional) guide to Edinburgh which implies that the politics of Brougham have lately shifted from those of the magazine.[18] This presumably relates to Brougham's backtracking on legislation dealing with tithes and church-rates imposed on Catholics and Dissenters. In the dinner episode in October, where Brougham's relations with Grey and Lord Durham are in question, *Tait's* acknowledges the tension: John of the Girnel asks Blarney about the demeanour of Grey and Brougham, since '[a]fter what has been surmeesed, the twa would be watched by many eyes, as close as cats do mice, or courtiers Kings'. Blarney is non-committal, responding that Brougham (a famously prolix speaker) 'was judiciously chary of his blarney upon this occasion', but also claiming that he had lavished it all upon his gracious master'—that is, the King. Meanwhile, the Earl himself was 'pokerly' (639).

Yet John bridles at any criticism of Brougham from others. Brougham has admittedly 'rendered but a lame account of his stewardship', but John struggles to believe that he is a 'Judas loon—traitor and flatterer of a' sides', out only for himself. If Brougham could only repent and change, John would forgive him, 'for he is the man for the darg [day] before us' (640). John of the Girnel, then, is the *Tait's* common man, emotionally invested in Brougham. Dick Lauder, in his political article, on the other hand, is more direct about Brougham: he laments his flattery of the King, his general kowtowing to those in power, and his newfound preference for the '*juste-milieu*', and declares that 'Lord Brougham is the only enemy of Lord Brougham's reputation'.[19]

Events continued to be extremely unpredictable in the political world. Melbourne returned to power in April 1835, but he turned out to want neither Durham nor Brougham in his administration. He got his way, and the careers in high office of both were over—not an outcome that Johnstone (or her Tory rivals) saw coming. So Johnstone's 'hopefulness of immediate good', to recall *Middlemarch*, would have been checked. However volatile Brougham may have been, the rapid eclipse of his influence had not been foreseen.

Tait's and *Middlemarch*

For all the differences in their priorities and perspectives, both Johnstone's 'Pry' series and Eliot's *Middlemarch* demonstrate the complex ways events can play out, including the unpredictable impact of gossip. In the novel, these phenomena are illustrated especially in the Lydgate–Bulstrode plot. The first Middlemarcher to learn of Bulstrode's ignominious past, for example, is Caleb Garth. As a result of hearing about it from Raffles, Garth refuses to work any longer for Bulstrode, but being above scurrilous gossip, he also undertakes not to spread the news. Mr Hawley, however, learns that Garth has met Raffles and then swiftly declined employment from Bulstrode, and he broadcasts this suggestive information. The result is that everyone assumes that Garth, the man least likely to communicate damaging rumours, had been 'the chief publisher of Bulstrode's misdemeanours' (ch. 71).

It has already emerged, too, by half-way through the novel, how much Lydgate is becoming the victim of misunderstanding, hostility, and gossip, and it is interesting that local politics here are expressed in terms of national politics, suggesting a parallel between the microcosm and the macrocosm. Bulstrode's 'views' that the hostility arises from 'medical jealousy' as well as 'a determination to thwart' his religious mission are characterised as 'ministerial', whereas the narrator points out that 'oppositions have the illimitable range of objections at command, which need never stop short at the boundary of knowledge, but can draw forever on the vasts of ignorance' (ch. 45). Bulstrode does indeed arouse enmity due to his arrogance and sanctimony, so that Lydgate's association with the domineering banker damages him from the outset of his career. Meanwhile, the 'vasts of ignorance' are powerful, and ultimately more responsible than Lydgate's actual behaviour for both his popularity and the strong suspicions about him. That is, both the 'ministerial views' and those of the 'opposition' injure Lydgate's reputation.

Moreover, Lydgate's story features a crucial instance of his responding in 'the thick of it', with damaging consequences. Lydgate has to cast his vote in the matter of the chaplain for the Infirmary, choosing between his friend Farebrother and Bulstrode's protégé Tyke. This is a complex choice for him, but he arrives late at the relevant meeting and ends up with the casting vote. Dr Wrench then announces that Lydgate is 'expected to vote with Mr Bulstrode'; bridling, Lydgate declares that he will indeed vote with Bulstrode, and so promptly writes down Tyke's name (ch. 18). The community's impression that Lydgate has firmly aligned himself with the unpopular banker is thus reinforced.

Both Johnstone in her 'Pry' series and Eliot in *Middlemarch*, then, foreground the power of rumour and the strongly contingent nature of events. But the 'Pry' series gives the impression of embracing and being energised by these circumstances, even if things do not always work out how the speakers (and the writer behind them) would have preferred. This is what being in 'the thick of' events means, and commentators on the general periodical culture of the first half of the nineteenth century often remark on how these potentially ephemeral products relish their own ephemerality, not to mention the speed of developments and the unpredictable personality clashes which foster this very transience.[20] Thus, the temporising of Johnstone's characters with their political opponents at the Edinburgh dinner is not shown as having consequences—they can just move on to the next episode. By contrast, in a novel looking back to the early 1830s, the revelations about Bulstrode, the gossip and rumour swirling around Lydgate, and the latter's own impulsive choices, mean that the pair are exiled from Middlemarch and effectively blighted forever. So how then might Ladislaw's career of being in 'the thick of' struggles against 'wrong' have played out in practice? Can we imagine him, as he faces the vicissitudes of political life, making impulsive choices—as would be consistent with his personality—but potentially then confronting their negative consequences? Or might Dorothea's influence have guarded against such outcomes? The novel does not offer answers to these questions.

George Eliot and Progressive Change

Carolyn Steedman, echoing earlier strictures from Terry Eagleton and Daniel Cottom, points to what she calls 'George Eliot's difficulty in actually describing change, the move of Old Corruption into new corruption', such that the novelist expresses this only 'through the lens of "culture"'.[21] As Eagleton and Cottom had suggested, Steedman argues that the mid-century middle-class cultural discourse which Eliot exemplifies tends to elide actual class differences. As far as the representation of politics in *Middlemarch* is concerned, according to this view, there is little attention given to the working classes, or to the Political Unions which were very active in the campaign for Reform. It is interesting that John Morley, a friend of Eliot's and a literary man who took to practical politics from 1883, commented—shortly after his own career change—on what he saw as Eliot's difficulty in representing progressive change. 'That the nobler emotions roused by her writings tend "to make mankind desire the social right" is not to be doubted', he says. But he is uncertain whether 'she imparts particular energy to the desire'—for he finds that '[w]hat she kindles is not a very strenuous, aggressive, and operative desire'. Moreover, Morley believes that Eliot identifies 'inexorable forces of the past' and that her sense of these is stronger than her 'resolution to press on'. Considering too what he knows of Eliot's political views from her letters as well (he is reviewing Cross' *George Eliot's Life*), Morley concludes that after 1848, a year of great impetus for political change in Britain and Europe, Eliot had much less of the 'energy of sympathy'.[22]

I concur that *Middlemarch* plays down the role of the working classes and Political Unions, and indeed reading journalism of the 1830s—that of Christian Johnstone and others—reinforces this impression. Recalling too the novels published on either side of *Middlemarch*, *Felix Holt* and *Daniel Deronda* (1876), serves to deepen the quandary about how Eliot believes meaningful and beneficial change can eventuate. What precisely did Felix Holt do in the 30 years following the end of the novel? What can Gwendolen Grandcourt, née Harleth, actually achieve back in Britain, once Daniel and Mirah Deronda have disappeared on their international mission? And as regards *Middlemarch* itself, the evocation in the 'Finale' of 'those times when reforms were begun with a young hopefulness of immediate good which has been much checked in our days' backs up Morley's argument. In addition, Lydgate's choices (the links with Bulstrode, not to mention his marriage to Rosamond Vincy) arguably come to function as what Morley calls 'inexorable forces of the past'. He cannot escape them, and his later career is in fact represented as a gradual depletion of desire and energy: Lydgate feels like a failure, comes to counter Rosamond 'less and less', and dies at fifty ('Finale').

Nonetheless, *Middlemarch* does imply through a couple of notable plotlines that events can move in a progressive direction, at least at the level of individuals or families. For example, the novel gives much attention to the ways both Edward Casaubon and Peter Featherstone strive to control the future—Casaubon by depriving Dorothea of his fortune if she marries Will Ladislaw, and Featherstone by leaving Stone Court to his illegitimate son Joshua Rigg rather than to his nephew Fred Vincy. But Dorothea is prepared to forego fortune for love and a future, and Bulstrode's disgrace has as one outcome Fred's gaining Stone Court and living a happy life there with his beloved Mary. The novel points as well to the more general historical development of greater contact between classes. The narrator observes of '[o]ld provincial society':

> Municipal town and rural parish gradually made fresh threads of connexion—gradually, as the old stocking gave way to the savings-bank, and the worship of the solar guinea became extinct; while squires and baronets, and even lords who had once lived blamelessly afar from the civic mind, gathered the faultiness of closer acquaintanceship.
>
> (ch. 11)

Dorothea is one who welcomes this kind of development. As she watches Featherstone's funeral, we are told that '[t]he country gentry of old time lived in a rarefied social air: dotted apart on their stations up the mountain they looked down with imperfect discrimination on the belts of thicker life below'—but that 'Dorothea was not at ease in the perspective and chillness of that height' (ch. 34). This mingling of classes had in fact been foreshadowed when Mr Brooke's electoral ambitions had induced him to invite to an evening party a much greater variety of Middlemarch men than usual. Here, Dorothea first encountered Lydgate. By this time, she was already engaged to Casaubon, but perhaps when such mingling of social groups became more frequent in later decades, there would be greater potential for fruitful encounters between like-minded people of different classes?

What emerges, however, if we follow the trajectory of how national politics is registered in the novel, is a rather melancholy sense that the prejudice and self-interest that contribute to Lydgate's treatment by the Middlemarch community inflect politics proper as well. There are plenty of references to national politics—and these include glancing allusions to some of the men who figured largely in the political journalism of the 1830s (Peel, Wellington, Stanley, Brougham, Althorp). Politics naturally moves to the fore in the treatment of the 1831 election that Brooke almost contests. Brooke's behaviour obviously highlights the potential gap between aspirations and ideals, on one hand, and human pusillanimity and incompetence on the other. In addition, many of the allusions to Middlemarch in a political context offer a discouraging picture of the town. There is disquiet about Catholic Emancipation, as championed by Robert Peel: the local Whig newspaper the *Pioneer* had lost subscribers for supporting Peel 'about the Papists' and thus tolerating 'Jesuitry and Baal' (ch. 37), and later, one of the crowd at the Tankard discussing the Bulstrode-Lydgate scandal refers to the Duke of Wellington going 'over to the Romans' (ch. 71). Characters also comment on the prevalence of bribery in Middlemarch elections (ch. 37, ch. 38). In any case, the characters' private concerns soon overshadow interest in national politics. Bulstrode and Lydgate, riding back from Stone Court after Raffles' death, do indeed discuss 'the chances of the Reform Bill in the House of Lords, and the firm resolve of the Political Unions' (one place where the Unions are mentioned)—but it is clear that they do this so as to avoid discussing what has just happened at Stone Court. Most obviously, the Bulstrode–Lydgate scandal becomes the focus of a meeting initially called to discuss a feared cholera epidemic. The narrator highlights that from this local preoccupation, 'all public conviviality … gathered a zest which could not be won from the question whether the Lords would throw out the Reform Bill' (ch. 71).

The 'Finale' then reinforces this bleak view of the town. Fred and Mary Vincy may lead happy lives, but because of its preconceptions about the pair, Middlemarch refuses to believe that Fred has written a book on *Cultivation of Green Crops and the Economy of Cattle-Feeding*, while Mary has produced *Stories of Great Men, taken from Plutarch*. Middlemarch is sure that it 'had never been deceived, and that there was no need to praise anybody for writing a book, since it was always done by somebody else' ('Finale'). And while Will Ladislaw fights against 'wrongs' and makes it into Parliament, his and Dorothea's son declines the opportunity to represent Middlemarch because he thinks 'that his opinions had less chance of being stifled if he remained out of doors' ('Finale'). Whatever Will and Dorothea have achieved politically, confidence in political endeavour—at least political endeavour based in Middlemarch—has not lasted till the next generation. 'Old Corruption' has presumably been succeeded by 'new corruption'.

The final lines of *Middlemarch* do turn to acknowledge the contributions of people like Dorothea:

> the growing good of the world is partly dependent on unhistoric acts; and that things are not so ill with you and me as they might have been, is half owing to the number who lived faithfully a hidden life, and rest in unvisited tombs ('Finale').

There is an assertion here of a certain kind of progressive development, although it is expressed in rather tentative terms ('not so ill', 'half owing').

Conclusion

Christian Johnstone died in July 1857, her husband John a few months later. Their joint tomb in Edinburgh, erected the following year, is impressive. Christian is not named; the part of the inscription relevant to her reads simply, 'A memorial of literary excellence and private worth'. 'Literary excellence' most obviously refers to her fiction, which was known as hers, while 'private worth' is a conventional tribute for a woman of her period. Unluckily, although Christian Johnstone included much of her own output in the novels and stories she brought out in 1845–46 as *Edinburgh Tales*, her fiction earned her no lasting fame, while her work as an editor and a journalist was obscured for decades.

Nonetheless, Christian Johnstone's journalism produced sharp and energetic writing, and manifested independent initiative, rather than just 'wifely help', and hers has not remained a completely 'hidden life'. From 1835, too, Johnstone powered on for several more years with her ever-varied output, often politically inflected. And to further her political agenda, she soon produced a two-part story which actually foreshadowed some of the concerns of *Middlemarch*.

The eponymous hero of 'Frankland the Barrister' (March–April 1835, set in the present)[23] goes into Parliament on the Radical side, but his career is blighted by marriage to a woman who has been brought up to value only wealth and social prominence. Ultimately, in order to survive financially, Frankland sells out his principles to the Tories; then, as he is consequently attacked in the House, he is so overwhelmed by guilt that he collapses and dies. Of *Middlemarch* calibre this story is not—but like the Lydgate–Rosamond plotline in Eliot's novel, it points to the potentially damaging results of contemporary notions about women's upbringing. Did George Eliot once read Johnstone's effort? Or rather, was it that the two women writers shared an awareness, both of the potential risks of trying to translate ideals into action, and of how narrow conceptions of women's potential might contribute to thwarting such aspirations—narrow conceptions that Johnstone and Eliot themselves had both overcome, but which for women and men alike, they knew, had led to many a 'sad[der] sacrifice' ('Finale')?

Notes

1 George Eliot, *Middlemarch: A Study of Provincial Life*, ed. David R. Carroll (1872; Oxford: Clarendon Press, 1992), 'Finale'. Further references to this edition appear parenthetically in text.

2 Florence Nightingale, 'A Note of Interrogation', *Fraser's Magazine*, n.s. 7.41 (May 1873), 567.

3 Mark Allison, 'Utopian Socialism, Women's Emancipation and the Origins of *Middlemarch*', *English Literary History*, 78.3 (Fall 2011), 715–39.

4 Alexis Easley, *First-Person Anonymous: Women Writers and Victorian Print Media, 1830-1870* (Burlington, VT: Ashgate, 2004), ch. 3.

5 Pam Perkins, *Women Writers and the Edinburgh Enlightenment* (Amsterdam: Rodopi, 2010), ch. 3.

6 I have discussed some of Johnstone's fiction in my 'Confronting the 1840s: Christian Johnstone in Criticism and Fiction', in *British Women's Writing from Brontë to Bloomsbury, Volume 1: 1840s and 1850s*, ed. Adrienne E. Gavin and Carolyn W. de la L. Oulton (Cham, Switzerland: Palgrave Macmillan, 2018), 67–80.

7 Robert Morrison, 'William Blackwood and the Dynamics of Success', in *Print Culture and the Blackwood Tradition, 1805-1930*, ed. David Finkelstein (Toronto: University of Toronto Press, 2006), 36.

8 [Christian Johnstone], 'What Is Going On. No. 1. Scenes in Edinburgh', *Tait's Edinburgh Magazine*, n.s. 1.6 (July 1834), 419.

9 [Johnstone], 'What Is Going On', 420.

10 [Johnstone], 'What Is Going On', 420.

11 Easley, *First-Person Anonymous*, 69.

12 [Johnstone], 'What Is Going On', 420.

13 Anon, 'The Improved Character of the Government', *Tait's Edinburgh Magazine*, n.s. 1.7 (August 1834), 437.

14 [Christian Johnstone], 'Political Register', *Tait's Edinburgh Magazine*, n.s. 1.11 (December 1834), 780.

15 Pam Perkins, *Women Writers and the Edinburgh Enlightenment*, 259ff.

16 [Thomas Dick Lauder], 'The Edinburgh Gathering', *Tait's Edinburgh Magazine*, n.s. 1.9 (October 1834), 633–6 (emphasis in original).

17 [Christian Johnstone], 'Scenes in Edinburgh—No. III', *Tait's Edinburgh Magazine*, n.s. 1.9 (October 1834), 637. Further quotations from this article will be inserted parenthetically into the text.

18 [Johnstone], 'What Is Going On', 427.

19 [Dick Lauder], 'The Edinburgh Gathering', 633–4.

20 See, for example, David Stewart's *Romantic Magazines and Metropolitan Literary Culture* (Basingstoke: Palgrave Macmillan, 2011).

21 Carolyn Steedman, 'Going to *Middlemarch*: History and the Novel', *Michigan Quarterly Review*, 40.3 (Summer 2001), 547. See also Terry Eagleton, *Criticism and Ideology: A Study in Marxist Literary Theory* (London: Verso, 1978), 120ff; Daniel Cottom, *Social Figures: George Eliot, Social History and Literary*

Representation (Minneapolis: University of Minnesota Press, 1987), *passim*, and Stefanie Markovits, 'George Eliot's Problem with Action', *Studies in English Literature*, 41.4 (Autumn 2001), 785–803.

22 John Morley, 'Life of George Eliot' [1885], reprinted in his *Critical Miscellanies*, 3 (London: Macmillan, 1909), 127.

23 [Christian Johnstone], 'Frankland the Barrister', *Tait's Edinburgh Magazine* (March–April 1835), reprinted in *Edinburgh Tales*, ed. Christian Johnstone, 3 vols (Edinburgh: William Tait; London: Chapman and Hall, 1845–46), 1: 111–52.

9   The Grounds of Exception

Liberal Sympathy and Its Limits in *Daniel Deronda* and C.H. Pearson's *National Life and Character*

Tim Dolin

At the beginning of Volume Two of *Daniel Deronda* (1876), the story pauses a little to defend its titular hero and the pleasure he is allowing himself as the rescuer of a vulnerable, traumatised young woman. We must think of Daniel, the narrator pleads, as we think of the heroes of old-time poetry and romance, who are 'as plentiful as ever' in the modern world and 'exist very easily in the same room with the microscope and even in railway carriages'. Their heart-stirring gallantry and fervour has only been banished from contemporary life because there is a 'vacuum in gentleman and lady passengers', for whom 'all the apparatus of heaven and earth' could not 'make poetry'. For they are people whose minds have 'no movements of awe and tenderness, no sense of fellowship which thrills from the near to the distant, and back again from the distant to the near'.[1] In this passage, Eliot characteristically deploys the language of the physical sciences to draw a likeness between the dynamics of human emotion and moral sensibility and the action of electromagnetism.[2] Here, as elsewhere in *Deronda* (and in the parallel work of G.H. Lewes culminating in *Problems of Life and Mind* [1874–80]), interpersonal, social, and cross-cultural communications and failures of communication are likened to the vibration of electric charges travelling through a vacuum producing signals to be deciphered: signals between and among men and women, Gentile or Jew, in the narrow and the wider worlds of the novel.[3] With his highly developed sympathetic imagination, Daniel finds himself increasingly called upon to be a kind of repeating station for receiving, decoding, and relaying these signals, which are 'dispersed across separate but interconnected nodes of perception and control',[4] along narrative threads described by Henry James as 'long electric wires capable of transmitting messages from mysterious regions'.[5]

By the time Eliot began work on the novel in the mid-1870s, the apparatus suggested by her scientific terminology and by James' metaphor, the telegraph, had reached as far as the Australian continent. Communications that still took eight weeks to arrive by sea could now reach Britain's most distant and isolated colonies almost instantaneously. The first telegraphic news from London was published in the Melbourne daily *Argus*, which had

DOI: 10.4324/9781003362821-10

sole rights of distribution in the colonies, in July 1872.[6] Within weeks, the 'Latest English Intelligence [By Submarine Telegraph]' was a regular feature of newspapers across the country. Overseas cable services were extremely expensive, however (press charges were ten shillings a word[7]), and news had to be abbreviated into elliptical telegraphese to be decoded back into a coherent report at its destination. The service was also plagued by delays, broken lines, and the garbling of messages as they were passed on by operators (not all of them English-speaking) in countless remote telegraph stations along the 10,000 miles of line, a problem that led the *Argus* to complain to the Colonial Cable Conference in 1877 that 'we find different interpretations of the same message given in all the Colonies, owing, in great measure, to so much being left to guess work'.[8]

Literary works may also be said to transmit and receive messages to and from mysterious regions: places and times that are not always self-evidently, conventionally, or legitimately part of the historical context of their production or reception, but are nevertheless part of their history. This is because, as John Frow contends, works 'exist only in their readings': their ongoing uses. Their historicity 'is not a matter of the *singular* moment of their relation to a history that precedes them, because that moment is in its turn endowed with meaning in a succession of later moments, as well as in the lateral movement of texts across cultural boundaries'.[9] They 'have not one history but many', precipitated by the increasing 'temporal or cultural distance from [their] first moment of reception'.[10]

Whether such later readings of literary works survive, however, can depend more on the strictly local and transitory uses to which those works were once put in any of the numberless succession of later moments to which Frow refers—their value to a particular local matter at hand rather than any innate value the work may possess. The continuing intelligibility or usefulness of such readings to subsequent readers is also open to question, moreover, since to recover a past reading properly obliges us to recover the historical meaning it had for those past readers, and to map in some crude way the long and complex routes by which the work must have arrived at the reading, identifying in the process some of the now vanished or derelict relay stations through which it had to pass. And what constitutes a 'reading' in the past? It is not always a professional interpretation—a review, public lecture, essay, or academic article, an adaptation or other rewriting. It is often little more than a passing reference in a personal communication such as a letter or diary, or in a public work of a genre or subject otherwise completely unrelated to literature. Such readings can be so coloured by concerns of their own as to distort their object—to scramble its message, as it were. We could think of them as 'extraneous' readings or perhaps, in light of the word's double meaning, 'partial' readings: readings that can nevertheless throw a sudden, revealing new light across an older work by their very distance or obliqueness from it.

Just such a reading of *Daniel Deronda* occurs in *National Life and Character: A Forecast*, the last work of Charles Henry Pearson, a British-born

Australian politician and historian who returned home in poor health to complete and publish it in 1893. An international bestseller in its time, it 'won immense critical acclaim' in the English-speaking world[11] and is now notorious as an ethnological justification and plea for immigration restriction, and a classic work of *fin de siècle* degenerationist scaremongering. It was a bible to the founders of Australian federation, especially Pearson's younger Australian-born fellow-Victorian, Alfred Deakin, who enshrined its principles in the statutes enacted as the White Australia Policy in 1901. Yet Pearson also 'posed a radical challenge to conventional race thinking', as Marilyn Lake and Henry Reynolds show.[12] His book 'forecast the emergence of a post-colonial world and the parallel decline of the white man' and 'anticipated the progressive asianisation of Europe' in the twentieth century.[13]

Two interlocked sets of ideas lay at the heart of Pearson's book, which predicted a world order transformed by the geopolitics of race and race migration. The first was racial environmentalism or climatic determinism, the idea that (in David Walker's words) 'each race, being the accumulated, historically-formed expression of a distinctive set of energies and capacities, functioned best within its own climatic zone and would degenerate outside this region.'[14] On one hand, racial homogeneity was a prerequisite for a democratic state (hence, immigration restriction). On the other, there was a geographical limit to European civilisation and for Pearson that limit had been reached. The British settler empire could not go on expanding: British settlers would not and could not survive in the tropics. Pearson's second idea was a version of the soon-to-be-familiar 'decline of the West' thesis. Here, he applied eugenic ways of thinking. Eugenics was defined 'officially' in 1908 as 'the study of agencies under social control that may improve or impair the racial qualities of future generations, either physically or mentally.'[15] In Pearson's study, well-meaning state agencies misdirect liberal ideology and social policy, exacerbating the problem of hereditary genius (as explained by Francis Galton in 1869):

> Owing to ... several causes, there is a steady check in an old civilization upon the fertility of the abler classes; the improvident and unambitious are those who chiefly keep up the breed. So the race gradually deteriorates, becoming in each successive generation less fitted for a high civilization, although it retains the external appearances of one, until the time comes when the whole political and social fabric caves in, and a greater or less relapse to barbarism takes place, during the reign of which the race is perhaps able to recover its tone.[16]

The gradual deterioration of the British people was a cause of special alarm for Pearson when considered alongside the undeniable advancement of the 'lower races', who were becoming autonomous, taking control of their naturalised domains, and forming civilised, self-governing states of their own: a hair-raising prospect for the economic welfare of free-trade Britain. Both the deterioration of the one and the advancement of the other were, in Pearson's view, produced by liberalism and its ideals—the first by the metamorphosis of the liberal state into the social democratic state, and the second by liberal internationalism. Liberal values, practices, and institutions had been successfully exported with empire to non-white societies, creating the conditions for self-determination and economic independence. At the same time, as Stuart Macintyre claims,

> the historical forces he saw transforming the world [would lead to] a disappearance of the energy and creative vitality of European civilization as the temperate zones of America, south Africa and Australasia were fully occupied. This in turn would hasten a transition to the State socialism that settler societies had pioneered. Vigorous independence would give way to reliance on the State, originality to conformity, poetry and drama to journalism and ephemeral criticism, heroism to a secure comfort without deep convictions or enthusiasm.[17]

The race thesis in *National Life and Character* now overshadows its associated thesis of the liberal double-bind: the idea that liberalism itself created the conditions for the demise of the liberal subject. The 'decay of character' was for Pearson a catch-phrase for the leftward drift of progressive liberalism away from what we would now call libertarianism—free markets uninhibited by state interference, and radical individualism as well as civil liberty, religious tolerance, and protection of minority rights—and towards social democracy. Among its direst consequences were systems of state support that drained the energy of individuals and fostered indifference to and incapacity for 'independence of thought'.[18] If that phrase sounds uncannily like a slogan of social conservativism a century later, *National Life and Character* reads uncannily like a foundational document of the culture wars, in which democratic levelling is deplored, family values are imperilled, Western civilisation is assailed from within, high culture is doomed to debasement, and moral relativism holds sway:

> the classes which have been the depositary of refinement and breeding will be submerged below the level of democracy, ... distinctions of rank and fortune, of character and intellect, will become unimportant, ... the family with its consecrated memories and duties will be transformed into a genial partnership of independent wills, ... fancy and imagination will find no expression in literature, and ... the faiths for which men have lived and died in times past will only survive as topics of meditation or as the discipline of ethical practice.

(363)

As evidence of what had happened both to independent thought and imaginative literature Pearson singles out the decline of George Eliot. 'At this distance of time', he remarks, 'few would dispute that [her] works after *Middlemarch* exhibit distinct and lamentable falling off in power, but *Daniel Deronda* at least was as vociferously praised as the author's best work had been' (327).[19] This is all that he has to say about Eliot, whose fate is, in the context of his argument, simply the fate of liberalism itself played out in the waning of the pre-eminent English liberal novelist of the century. Pearson was not alone in being baffled and unconvinced by the directions Eliot's art took after *Middlemarch*. What is revealing, however, is that this novel should be cited as evidence of an empire-wide deterioration in creative imagination and forfeiting of critical integrity under conditions in which the vigour of 'the lower races' was beginning to assert itself. After all, an incipient form of the same conditions, the same anxieties, and something very much like the same solutions, can be found in Eliot's last novel. Undeniably, there are a great many differences between *Daniel Deronda* and *National Life and Character*; but as Theophrastus Such remarks, 'amid all differences there will be a certain correspondence; just as there is more or less correspondence in the natural history even of continents widely apart, and of islands in opposite zones'.[20]

National Life and Character cannot be explained as the product of a progressive liberal's late-life slide into social conservatism (it wasn't; he didn't). Its anti-Asian xenophobia is of a piece with Australian progressive politics and cultural life in the 1890s. 'Geographically, Australia was a frontier of European capitalism in Asia', as Humphrey McQueen argued in 1970. 'The first of these circumstances gave rise to the optimism that illuminated our radicalism; the second produced the fear that tarnishes our nationalism'.[21] Yet it departs significantly from the more familiar story of the nationalist nineties, captured in the Sydney *Bulletin*'s infamous manifesto for a virulent racism serving radical labour politics: 'The cheap Chinaman, the cheap nigger, and the cheap European pauper to be absolutely excluded'.[22] But *Bulletin* republicanism was to be safeguarded not just by controlled borders but by the colonial liberal innovations that for Pearson posed a threat to the welfare and security of advanced nations: free state education, a state bank, compulsory life insurance, and the abolition of private property.

Pearson's foreboding is all the more remarkable because of who he was. Far from being an educated metropolitan liberal observing from his colonial outpost how State socialism was weakening settler democracies even as they emerged, making them vulnerable to their more vigorous near neighbours, he was the very architect of State socialism in the colony of Victoria. What he discovered at his great distance from the centres of liberal social thought and practice in Britain was a surprising and disturbing paradox: that liberalism's greatest achievements, its most cherished ideals, would eventually undo those achievements and undermine those ideals. The paradox was neatly captured in the conservative *Saturday Review*'s notice of *National Life and Character* in 1893, which described the book as

> a laboured, and to a great extent a successful, attempt to prove that the substitution of the State for the Church, the decay of the family, the equalization of rights and privileges, the dominance of industrial organizations, the great increase of population, and so forth, will destroy character, weaken the interest of life, kill genius, favour only the lower races and individuals, obliterate by degrees all that is noblest, most precious, rarest, best worth living for; yet [Pearson] is imperturbably sure that it was quite the right thing to enlarge the suffrage, to allow a legal status, and practically a free hand to Trade Unions, to impair the authority of husband and fathers, to abolish class distinctions, to vulgarize education. His paradox is quite different from the old one; he abhors the end, but delights in the means. He views with horror the roof about to fall in, but he feels a glow of honest joy and pride when he thinks how he helped to pull down the pillars.[23]

The *Saturday* was curious to know how so 'grim and wretched' a view of the world could have originated in a man who 'lived, and lived with distinction, in a world which has long shaken off caste and tradition, and has attained … the purest expression of democracy'.[24]

Pearson was indeed the epitome of the 'cultured radical'.[25] At King's College, London, he was taught by F.D. Maurice and studied with A.V. Dicey, Leslie Stephen, Frederic Harrison, and many other liberals. Later, he moved in progressive circles with Dilke and Chamberlain, Grant Duff, George Goschen, and Goldwin Smith, as well as the Cambridge liberals Henry Sidgwick and Henry Fawcett. Profoundly influenced by Mill, he coedited the *National Review* briefly with Bagehot in the 1860s, and later published in the *Fortnightly*.[26] As one of the leading sixties 'University Liberals', Pearson was prominent among those making the case for democratic extension and countering the arguments of the anti-reform faction (arguments like those made by George Eliot in *Felix Holt*) and the influence of Robert Lowe, a liberal who had emigrated to Australia in 1841, was an MP in the NSW upper house, and returned to England in 1850.[27] Lowe gained a formidable reputation as the fiercest and most articulate opponent of reform. He used the cautionary example of the Australian colonies, which he and his fellow anti-reformers accused of being (in Pearson's characterisation of their argument) severely 'retarded by their self-government under institutions that may be called Democratic,' suffering from 'unstable government, a low standard of parliamentary representatives, timid, venal or indifferent voters, judges of poor character, licentious press, neglect of religion and education, increasing crime, lack of legislative progress and social cohesion'.[28]

Pearson had already visited Australia by then, and his impressions of the colonies, he wrote in response to Lowe, contradicted those of disaffected 'old colonists' who claimed that 'society has been inverted in the Antipodes … so that what is low here is high there'.[29] And when he finally settled in Victoria a decade later, 'an Oxford don flung into the burly-burly of Victorian politics', Pearson found a liberal paradise.[30] The tens of thousands of British emigrants attracted to Victoria by gold were, he wrote, 'commonly men sufficiently below the upper classes to leave no valuable prospects behind them, and sufficiently above the lowest to be able to pay their own passages'.[31] They 'carried with them the ideas of the English middle classes at home; a strong feeling for an extended suffrage, a desire for cheap land on a simple tenure',[32] and—because they included 'an unusually high proportion of earnest, improving Dissenters'—'a determination not to repeat the experiment of a State Church'.[33]

But Pearson also found a political culture with many of the problems his old opponents had identified. It was riven with factionalism, there was no stable party system, and an undemocratic upper house constantly vetoed popular legislation. As John Tregenza puts it, the land,

> within a few decades of discovery, seemed destined to fall into the hands of an even smaller number of great proprietors than England's; full equality of educational opportunity seemed quite Utopian; while the popular party was quite in danger of falling into what [Pearson] once described as 'the conservative apathy of men partially shut out from the world'.[34]

Pearson faced these challenges head on, laying special stress on the double meaning of self-government, as his great colleague George Higginbotham had done: 'in proportion to a man's self-control is observed to be his capacity to be entrusted with political power'.[35]

Like Higginbotham and the *Age* proprietor David Syme—and like George Eliot—Pearson had grown up under the shadow of strict evangelicalism. When the three Australians broke away from it, they placed 'an awesome trust in the capacity of human reason', but in Macintyre's view, 'remained prisoners of a secularized Protestant conscience'.[36] Their versions of a religion of humanity preserved all the evangelical hallmarks of 'a highly developed conscience and an elevated moral tone', and 'the traits of constant internal scrutiny, absolute candour, self-conscious rectitude, industry and good works'.[37] And Pearson (again like Eliot) 'used the language and values of an enlightened Protestantism to make the transition from a society unified by faith to one joined in citizenship'.[38] For colonial liberals as for liberals everywhere, the extension of the franchise 'rested heavily on a vision of educational enlightenment in which intellectuals such as [Pearson] were to play a central role in upholding morality and imbuing a self-governing people with responsibility and purpose'.[39] Education was 'first and foremost a means of instilling the vital capacity of self-regulation', and over the following decades, Pearson struggled for and achieved 'a complete system of free state education ... equal university rights for both sexes; entrance to the civil service by competitive examination' as well as

> national insurance and pension schemes; a state system of arbitration; progressive taxation on large estates; use of the referendum to resolve constitutional deadlocks; reform or abolition of undemocratically elected upper houses; the abolition of 'barrack-like' state orphanages and the boarding out of children; [and] state banks able to provide loans on low rates of interest for small settlers.[40]

Because taxation and export earnings were insufficient to build the necessary infrastructure and finance these initiatives, the Victorian economy depended on the investment of British capital, most of it loaned to successive governments to build public railways and telegraph lines, as well as roads, bridges, and schools, and water supplies and sewers; to pay for the migrant assistance schemes essential to growth and the teachers in the state education system; to annex land for small-holders; and to protect local industries. These were the conditions that brought about the 'strange and unaccountable transformation of the word [liberalism] in the Antipodes': a liberalism characterised by 'a willingness to interfere with the liberty of the individual'.[41] Pearson was by conviction a free-trader compelled by circumstance to advocate for protection. His primary object was to achieve land reform, but he soon realised that under the dominant influence of Syme and the *Age* support for land reform would only succeed if coupled to support for protection.[42] He also soon discovered that laissez-fairism was not going to work in Victoria: that beneficial forms of state action were essential in a young country.

The experience of the 1890s awoke Pearson violently to the problems his own State socialism had created. By then Victoria's three-decade boom was busting spectacularly, as hyper-accelerated post-goldrush economic growth drifted into rampant land speculation in Melbourne, and government debt reached unsustainable levels until the bubble burst, sending the colony spiralling into depression. What had happened to the ideal liberal subject—that 'autonomous, self-sufficient individual [with] the capacities of reason and moral responsibility, both to guide desire and emancipate the bearer from the tyranny of impulse'?[43] What did it mean for liberal assumptions about progress?

Colonial liberals had imagined themselves marching triumphantly into a future of limitless human capacities, but suddenly a new liberalism was called for, one which recognised that 'the social impulses had become far more problematic'.[44] In particular, Macintyre argues, these dire conditions brought 'a heightened awareness of the complexity of behaviour and the persistence of atavistic impulses', forces that 'threatened the notion of the rational individual and his conscience'.[45] The only antidote to these ills in colonial Victoria was intentional nation-building for the new century: a nation for a continent; Australia for Australians; Australia for the white man.

Settler colonialism had proceeded on the assumption that primitive races would 'perish on contact with civilization'.[46] Yet, as the century progressed, it became evident 'that many of the supposedly feeble races—the Australians, for instance—were not dying out as rapidly and completely as had often been predicted'.[47] In addition, non-white populations elsewhere in the world were growing. It was one thing to dispense an easy liberality to them (those outside the grip of the subject empire at least): to support them in setting up democratic and representative institutions, and in pursuing national self-determination; to model the virtues of tolerance, the right to individual liberty and human dignity, freedom of expression and association; and to recognise their property rights. But it was a horror for readers of *National Life and Character* to think that the world would shortly be overrun not by 'lower' races but by people just like themselves—except they were not white-skinned. 'The day will come', Pearson forecast, 'when the European observer will look round to see the globe girdled with a continuous zone of the black and yellow races, no longer too weak for aggression or under tutelage, but independent, or practically so, in government, monopolising the trade of their own regions, and circumscribing the industry of the European' (*National* 89); when they are 'represented by fleets in the European seas, invited to international conferences, and welcomed as allies in the quarrels of the civilised world' (90):

> [They] will then be taken up into the social relations of the white races, will throng the English turf, or the salons of Paris, and will be admitted to intermarriage. … We shall wake to find ourselves elbowed and hustled, and perhaps even thrust aside by peoples whom we looked down upon as servile, and thought of as bound always to minister to our needs. The solitary consolation will be, that the changes have been inevitable. It has been our work to organise and create, to carry peace and law and order over the world, that others may enter in and enjoy. Yet in some of us the feeling of caste is so strong that we are not sorry to think we shall have passed away before that day arrives.
>
> (90)

Pearson wrote *National Life and Character* under 'sentence of death',[48] and died long before the coming of the postcolonial world fulfilled his fearful prophecy. In this impassioned, revealing passage, he tries to keep to the measured, dignified language of the rational liberal. But he cannot resist the rhetoric of the invasion scare or hide his bitterness at the thought that Britain had brought it all on itself by its compassion and tolerance, and the success of its enlightened institutions. In the end, no amount of compassion or reason can suppress the anger and disgust with which his own 'feeling of caste' surges up off the page like an atavistic impulse at this vision of a cosmopolitan hell.

Pearson was able to instance *Daniel Deronda* and deal with it so summarily and inattentively in *National Life and Character* because Eliot's novel had by then settled into its place in the widely accepted narrative of her artistic career. Its title alone conjured a history of critical failure. That history was captured succinctly in Oscar Browning's 1888 description of *Deronda's* unhappy fortunes. Browning, a close friend of the Leweses, took pride in being, as he styled himself, its solitary long-time defender:

> I know well, only too well, the criticisms which have been levelled at the book from its first appearance to the present day. I have become tired and sick of hearing that the characters are unreal, that there is not a man or woman in the story whom you can take away with you and live with. I know that Daniel is thought to be a prig, and the Jew Mordecai a bore; that Gwendolen is thought impossible, and Grandcourt a stage villain; that the language is held to be strained and uncouth, full of far-fetched tropes and metaphors drawn from unfamiliar science. It is said there is no motive power in the action, no reason for the characters behaving as they behave. What rational person can care for the return of the Jews to Palestine? Is a young man who stakes his life on such an issue worthy of five minutes' consideration? Would a handsome young Englishman, brought up as a Christian at a public school or university, be suddenly overjoyed to find that he was a Jew? No, in *Daniel Deronda* thought and learning have usurped the place of art. It belongs to the worst type of all novels, a novel with a tendency. ... George Eliot has passed her prime. As in the 'Transfiguration' of Raphael, we see in *Deronda* the downward movement of a great mind, a movement which, if followed, would have disastrous effect upon the national literature.[49]

Pearson was in all likelihood familiar with this passage.[50] Browning's rhetoric of 'the downward movement of a great mind' and its likely 'disastrous effect upon the national literature' echoes in Pearson's remarks on Eliot's 'distinct and lamentable falling off in power', and in the surrounding argument about the consequences of derivative thought on national life and character. It may even have been Browning, whose heterodox view reignited the debate about *Deronda* in the early nineties,[51] that Pearson had in mind when he alleged the novel to have been 'vociferously praised' (*National*, 327). For although *Deronda* was by no means universally condemned in the 1870s, the majority of its first reviewers were dismayed and irritated by it, and many wondered aloud who among Eliot's readers would identify with its extravagant world-historical romance: what rational person cares about the return of the Jews to Palestine? They also complained that Eliot in enlarging her canvas had developed an insidious tendency towards cant and

obfuscation: a 'lavish profusion of sententious utterance' and 'obtrusive …
moralising' spoiled for the 'want of simplicity'.[52]

Art, Eliot had declared at the very beginning of her career, was the nearest
thing to life.[53] As she wrote to Charles Bray in 1859,

> the only effect I ardently long to produce by my writings is that those
> who read them should be better able to *imagine* and to *feel* the pains
> and joys of those who differ from themselves in everything but the
> broad fact of being struggling erring human creatures.[54]

Realism's truthfulness lies in the work it does to introduce its readers to those
they might otherwise avoid, awakening their social sympathies by helping
them to *feel with* others, and so recognise their commonality with them. And
to the last, art remained for her as it was when she began: a 'mode of amplifying experience and extending our contact with our fellow-men'.[55] *Daniel
Deronda* offers as a counterpoint to the familiar 'home epic'—the narrative
of unexceptional, erring, unhistoric individuals—a genuine epic of an arch-
historic people in exile from their homeland. But even readers well-disposed
to Eliot's project of thinking themselves 'imaginatively into the experience of
others' (*DD*, ch. 41) found it difficult to 'adjust their sympathies' to include
the tragic experience of the Jews.[56] Such sympathies were 'not, as in the case
of *Adam Bede*, the common sympathies of all the world'.[57] In departing
from 'the usual speech of [her] day and generation', moreover, Eliot was
'instantly in danger of being led away into affectations which separate [her]
from a wide sympathy with the heart and life of the people'.[58] Her constantly evolving art eventually carries its unsuspecting contemporary readers
so far 'beyond the bounds of [their] personal lot' that it comes to seem to
them no longer universal.[59] Captured by a cause, Eliot's sympathy is at once
excessive and remote. In thrall of ultramodern ideas and aesthetics—'the
eccentric and the passing … the mere fads of "culture" and "advancement,"
and all the rest of it'—she alienates her admirers and forfeits the fellow
feeling of all the world.[60] The cosmopolitan plot goes along with cosmopolitan ideas, as though the novelist has abandoned the solid homeliness of her
domestic realism for something alien, faddish, and continentally recondite,
like Klesmer's modern music ricocheting around the sedate drawing-rooms
of the old aristocracy and newly-minted gentry.)

Nothing if not liberal, Eliot braces herself to bear unpopularity for the
sake of championing an unpopular minority, defending the rights of others to
religious freedom, freedom of speech, and national self-determination, and
promoting universal tolerance and respect. Ironically, the terms of *Daniel
Deronda*'s critical failure only confirm the fears the novel raises about the
limits of those liberal values. (The sympathetic imagination, revered for its
power of quickening the lives of a miscellaneous, self-interested, unthinking,
unhistorical populace into national life, is called into the service of a great
national movement from which that populace is necessarily to be excluded.

Gwendolen Grandcourt is the novel's representative figure for this exclusion. She ends up feeling as Eliot's bereft readers would: left behind. Her only consolation is that there is to be no consolation. She must face the worst about herself and her kind, achieving, as Nancy Paxton diagnoses it, 'the tragic consciousness of time and loss which, Eliot suggests, all her compatriots—male and female—must achieve if they are to avert the "national tragedy" that seems to be threatening English society'.[61] This interpretation of Gwendolen's lonely, penitential fate as a reaffirmation of the old doctrine of self-fulfilment through suffering does not quite square with the tremendous challenges the novel confronts when it sets out to export Eliot's worldview to the world. Deronda's gain is Gwendolen's loss (whether we suppose that Gwendolen is no mere victim of chance in this regard, but only gets what is coming to her). The heroine in Eliot is once again the victim of an impartially exclusionary logic—in this case, ethnic nationalism; and once again a novel of Eliot's contradicts its own 'project of creating a cohesive national identity'.[62]

Struggling to communicate his newfound passion to Gwendolen, Deronda casts about for some common ground between them, effusing that since discovering his Judaism he has become 'possessed' with the idea of 'restoring a political existence to my people, making them a nation again, giving them a national centre, such as the English have, though they too are scattered over the face of the globe' (*DD*, ch. 69). He falls short of calling England a *great* national centre, but the comparison with the Promised Land is obvious, and obviously disingenuous given Deronda's otherwise clear-eyed critical observations of an England characterised chiefly by Grandcourt's 'ebbing energy' (ch. 28) and 'diseased numbness' (ch. 14), Sir Hugo's affable, born-to-rule complacency, and Gwendolen's own 'puerile state of culture' (ch. 5).

Such a stirring outbreak is all the more perplexing—or perhaps all the more explicable—because Eliot, if she, like Deronda, has lost faith in England, never loses faith in the Englishness that endows Deronda with the Ivanhoe-like power to found a nation by fusing the best of the ancient and the best of the modern, the vigour of the one and the refinement of the other. The partiality that Deronda craves and finds at last in his ethnic heritage is not meant to cancel out the impartiality his liberal upbringing had engendered in him but to complement and enhance it. As he tells his mother:

> I think it would have been right that I should have been brought up with the consciousness that I was a Jew, but it must always have been a good to me to have as wide an instruction and sympathy as possible.
>
> (ch. 53)

As the nation 'which has been scoffed at for its separateness' but which 'has given a binding theory to the whole human race' (ch. 61), Judaism becomes the ideal vehicle for the enlargement of the Eliotean religion of humanity beyond England. Hers is, as one reviewer acutely noted, 'a purified Judaism

... a devout Theism, purged of Jewish narrowness, while retaining the intense patriotism which pervades Judaism'.[63] In keeping with Eliot's liberal humanism, however, the 'universal instinct of Christendom' attaches itself to a 'mystical enthusiasm for race and nation' in the person of the always reasonable, morally responsible, autonomous, self-sufficient individual, who is rewarded for rectitude, right conduct, and unflagging adherence to duty.[64] We never feel that Deronda's reason and conscience are likely to be impaired by the atavistic impulses he finds himself mysteriously experiencing in his developing relations with Mordecai—quite the opposite. But that is only because the novel displaces the worst consequences of this crisis of the liberal subject onto other characters. Deronda's paralysing superabundance of sympathy is, from this perspective, just another form of the 'world-nausea' that afflicts our faulty heroine. For all her 'young energy' (ch. 14), Gwendolen is throughout in tormented uncertainty about her own mind. So oppressed is she by the obligation to decide for herself (ch. 14) that she is addicted to basing every important decision on a roll of the dice. Like other Eliot heroines before her, she is made sick by the 'struggle of opposite feelings' (ch. 48) that meet and press against each other, and drain her strength: 'pride, longing for rebellion, dreams of freedom, remorseful conscience, dread of fresh visitation' (ch. 48). She is 'governed by many shadowy powers' (ch. 44) and 'divided impulses' (ch. 13). In the end, her desperate and unconvincing self-affirmations—'I am going to live ... I mean to live ... I shall live' (ch. 69)—do not augur well for her regeneration or for the regeneration of her like. Eliot efficiently mobilises a familiar meliorism at this late stage ('it shall be better with me because I have known you', she tells Deronda [ch. 70]), but readers leave the novel with little or no faith in Gwendolen's vague mission to 'make herself less ignorant, ... be kindest to everybody, and make amends for her selfishness and try to be rid of it' (ch. 69). Much more plausible is her fearful 'vision of possible degradation' (ch. 65). As in Eliot's earlier novels, self-redemption begins at home and must be suffered at home, in the silence of unhistoric space.

By contrast, Deronda, the paradox as well as the paragon of the ethical liberal, is lucky that his mother's anguished, reluctant revelation of his birthright rescues him from his younger self. Beset by a 'large imaginative lenience toward others' (ch. 59) that causes him to waste his energy 'wandering in the mazes of impartial sympathy' (ch. 63), he is prone to 'a meditative numbness' that holds him 'from that life of practically energetic sentiment' (ch. 32) for which he vaguely yearns. His problem, he finds, is that his 'plenteous, flexible sympathy' always ends 'by falling into one current with that reflective analysis which tends to neutralize sympathy' (ch. 32). He is compelled to do justice to all sides of a question, which hinders him from finding a course of action, a course of life, equal to his morality. He desperately wants to be *partial* to something, which means, ultimately, confining his sympathies to 'the closer fellowship that makes sympathy practical' (ch. 63). He finds that fellowship only when his 'meditative yearning after wide knowledge' (ch. 16) is converted into feeling by his newly-discovered ethnic identity: when he can at last exchange 'that bird's eye reasonableness which soars to avoid preference and loses all sense of quality for the generous reasonableness of drawing shoulder to shoulder with men of like inheritance' (ch. 63).

In recent critical work on the novel, this paralysing 'many-sided sympathy' (ch. 32) of Deronda's, and Eliot's ethnonationalist remedy for it, have been the focus of much debate about the virtues of liberal cosmopolitanism. The question here is not whether *Daniel Deronda*, in Aleksandar Stevic's words, 'decisively upholds the value of narrow—let us say it explicitly: nationalist—loyalties against the threat of uprootedness' or whether it embraces 'a cosmopolitanism understood as a commitment to open exchange between nations and races, rather than as the erasure of all cultural difference'.[65] Eliot was cosmopolitan to the extent that her fiction set out 'to achieve a larger, more comprehensive view of matters that might seem petty, domestic, or provincial'.[66] Her characters are judged according to whether they can be 'penetrated by a feeling of wider relations' (ch. 14). But it is not merely affections rooted in the personal past that make it so difficult to fulfil the moral obligation of taking 'in the world's neglected subjectivities'.[67] The 'task of making space in one's feelings for the inhabitants of distant countries'[68] is simply too great because the feeling that motivates virtue in Eliot is not predominantly the 'awe and tenderness' that brings a 'sense of fellowship which thrills from the near to the distant, and back again from the distant to the near' (ch. 19). It is pain. Eliot's ethics of alterity is necessarily localised because suffering is necessarily 'close to home': it exists within a circumscribed affective economy. It is not a happy inclination to widespread kindliness and liberality but must be earned by a gruelling rite of passage through unpleasant, uncharitable emotions in the here and now: hardheartedness, pride, anger, grief, humiliation.

The 'larger order' (ch. 48) of the world being created by and for freetrade liberalism therefore necessarily puts pressure on the ideals of liberals accustomed to engaging in what Theophrastus Such calls the constant 'discerning and adjustment of opposite claims' and the 'distribution of sympathy or pity for sufferers of different blood or votaries of differing religions' (*TS*, ch. 18). We cannot feel a sense of fellowship with *everything* near and distant, and indeed, awe and tenderness are not what we are likely to feel when peoples once safely distant have become worryingly near. As ever in Eliot, 'the effective bond of human action is feeling' (*TS*, ch. 18), but disgust is a feeling, too, and one as powerful as 'affectionate joy' or 'tender attachment' (*TS*, ch. 2). When in *Daniel Deronda* the narrator observes that there is 'a great deal of unmapped country within us', we remember Gwendolen's 'gusts and storms' (ch. 24): the 'shadowy powers' (ch. 44) of desire and revulsion by which she is governed.[69] But others are equally subject to impulses they cannot control or hide, and motives they cannot articulate, most notably involuntary 'physical antipathies' (ch. 11). In late

1876, Eliot recorded in her journal that she had been 'made aware of much repugnance or else indifference towards the Jewish part of *Deronda*'.[70] She cannot have been surprised. The words 'repugnance', 'disgust', and 'repulsion' recur frequently in the novel,[71] and not always directly in connection with racial difference and anti-Semitism. We think immediately of Deronda's alarm at the 'vulgar Jews' (ch. 32) and even the narrator's unconcealed distaste for the 'glistening' faces of the Cohens (ch. 33, ch. 42) and their 'oily cheerfulness' (ch. 40). With 'a strongly resistant feeling' Deronda shakes off Kalonymos' touch on his arm, saying frigidly: 'I am an Englishman' (ch. 32). But one thinks, too, of his 'first repulsion from Gwendolen' (ch. 45), the initial repugnance he feels towards his mother, and his fear that Mirah finds him repugnant (ch. 63), as well as Mirah's own feelings of 'strong repugnance toward certain objects that surrounded her', from which she walks 'inwardly aloof while they touched her sense' (ch. 61).[72]

Were we 'not enlightened by experience', Theophrastus Such reflects, we 'might believe in the all-embracing breadth of "sympathy with the injured and oppressed."' But

> [w]hat mind can exhaust the grounds of exception which lie in each particular case? There is understood to be a peculiar odour from the negro body, and we know that some persons, too rationalistic to feel bound by the curse on Ham, used to hint very strongly that this odour determined the question on the side of negro slavery.[73]

This is the revulsion that rises involuntarily in the nostrils (as it were) of Charles Henry Pearson as he assembles historical evidence for the end of free-trade imperial Britain and the world it created for itself. Pearson's mission was to warn fellow metropolitan liberals that Australian colonial experiments to create an enlightened State founded on an 'all-embracing breadth of "sympathy with the injured and oppressed"' posed a double risk. They were breeding in colonial Britons a desire for self-enslavement that would prove to be fatal to British national life and character were it to take hold at home. Were Australia's borders opened to its northern neighbours, those Britons would be 'thrust aside by peoples whom [they] looked down upon as servile, and thought of as bound always to minister to [their] needs'; peoples 'independent, or practically so, in government, monopolising the trade of their own regions, and circumscribing the industry of the European' (*National*, 89).

Pearson's book touches directly on *Daniel Deronda* only in passing, as we have seen. But its anxiety about the imminent rise of Asian power and the spectre of an interracial liberal world order in which non-white races were equal and fully assimilated (*National*, 90) inevitably draws a comparison with the Jews in Europe. To demonstrate how easy it would be for an advanced European power to be overrun by a 'lower race', Pearson cites the case of the Jews in Russia.[74] Here is an object lesson for the British Empire in what can happen when a relatively civilised lower race is freely admitted to a liberal polity, and given controlled access to the rights and privileges of citizenship, especially 'the protection of the law' (85). The 'exceptional privileges' (81) accorded the Jews in Russia have led to a disproportionate increase in their numbers, Pearson warns. As a result, they have become 'a nation in themselves, herding together, too numerous, and, it may be feared, too detested to be absorbed into the general population' (84–5).

Because, as Pearson feared, liberal-democratic civic nation states governed by inclusive, rationalistic principles created conditions for embedded minority nationalisms to survive, he believed that there were strong grounds for exception on the basis of ethnicity. Although *Daniel Deronda* inverts that scenario, its endgame is the same: the Jews cannot be kept out of England as the Chinese can be kept out of Australia, but they can be led out. This novel 'offers no ... vision of interracial coexistence', as Daniel Hack bluntly observes. 'Instead, [it] insists on the starkness of Deronda's choice between Jewish and English identities'.[75] At a stroke Eliot renounces the totalising ambitions of her English novels, with their metonymic upscaling of provincial to national to universal. Although as in those earlier novels 'there is no private life' in *Deronda* 'which has not been determined by a wider public life',[76] a rift opens up between an insular, backward-looking, feminine English private life—'a small social drama almost as little penetrated by a feeling of wider relations as if it had been a puppet-show' (*DD*, ch. 14)—and the great Zionist national epic. In the midst of 'that mighty drama', the girls back home still have their sacred purpose: to bear 'onward through the ages the treasure of human affections' (ch. 11). But it means something quite new in a novel described in the *Gentleman's Magazine* in 1876 as the 'first romance' of a great realist, which moves on from natural histories of provincial English life to a 'natural history of exceptions and intensities ... as true as reality, and more true than much that seems real'.[77] 'Every nation of forcible character—i.e. of strongly marked characteristics, is so far exceptional' (*TS*, ch. 18), and in *Daniel Deronda*, the liberal hero is called to a life of exceptionalism, as the liberal novel finds its new calling in a form of what Deronda's grandfather called 'separateness with communication' (*DD*, ch. 60).[78] Deronda tries to explain what this principle means in practice when he assures Gwendolen that even if they 'never see each other again' their 'minds may get nearer' than they would if they had not parted (ch. 69). His is a utopian faith in a future in which the sympathetic imagination can be internationalised, and the transmission and exchange of information, knowledge, and ideas between individuals far apart can create new networks and communities of understanding. The Spencerian character of this conception of communication systems and networks as the nerves and arteries of a greater social body is perhaps appropriate for the age of the telegraph, with its long electric wires capable of transmitting messages from mysterious regions.

Notes

1 George Eliot, *Daniel Deronda*, ed. Graham Handley (Oxford: Oxford World's Classics, 2014), ch. 19. Further references to this edition appear parenthetically in text.

2 See Richard Menke, *Telegraphic Realism: Victorian Fiction and Other Information Systems* (Stanford: Stanford University Press, 2008), 159–62: 'the novel's representation of the dynamic, fluctuating consciousness of Gwendolen Harleth closely follows the language and outlook of physiological experimentation' (159).

3 See Laura Otis, *Networking: Communicating with Bodies and Machines in the Nineteenth Century* (Ann Arbor: University of Michigan Press, 2001), 69–78.

4 Menke, *Telegraphic*, 136.

5 Henry James, unsigned notice in *The Nation*, in *George Eliot: The Critical Heritage*, ed. David Carroll (London: Routledge and Kegan Paul, 1971), 363.

6 Ann Moyal, *Clear across Australia: A History of Telecommunications* (Melbourne: Nelson, 1984), 65.

7 Dropping to 2s 6d per word in 1885 and 1s in 1902 (Moyal, *Clear*, 65).

8 Quoted in Moyal, *Clear*, 66.

9 John Frow, 'On Midlevel Concepts', *New Literary History*, 41 (2010), 244.

10 Frow, 'On Midlevel Concepts', 244, 247.

11 'It is doubtful that any book with an Australian inspiration has ever had a greater impact among intellectuals in Britain or the United States than Pearson's' (David Walker, *Anxious Nation: Australia and the Rise of Asia, 1850–1939* [St Lucia: University of Queensland Press, 1999], 2).

12 Marilyn Lake and Henry Reynolds, *Drawing the Global Colour Line: White Men's Countries and the International Challenge of Racial Equality* (Cambridge: Cambridge University Press, 2008), 88.

13 Lake and Reynolds, *Colour Line*, 75–6; Walker, *Anxious Nation*, 2.

14 Walker, *Anxious Nation*, 142. Climatic determinism was popularised by Robert Knox in *The Races of Men: A Fragment* (London: H. Renshaw, 1850).

15 Francis Galton, *Memories of My Life* (London: Methuen, 1908), 321.

16 Francis Galton, *Hereditary Genius: An Inquiry into Its Laws and Consequences* (London: Macmillan, 1869), 362.

17 Stuart Macintyre, *A Colonial Liberalism: The Lost World of Three Victorian Visionaries* (South Melbourne: Oxford University Press, 1991), 167. Already many 'forms of literature, such as the epic, the drama, the pastoral, and the satire appear to be ... exhausted', Pearson argued, and '[c]ertain kinds of poetry have become impossible' (Charles Henry Pearson, *National Life and Character: A Forecast* [London: Macmillan, 1894], 275). The novel, he added, was 'not likely to replace poetry for work of the highest kind', and in any case, its 'topics are being exhausted', and the 'less varied and emotional life we are approaching will not lend itself to energy and colour in description' (275).

18 Pearson, *National*, 277. Further references to this edition appear parenthetically in text.

19 But see p. 154, below.

20 George Eliot, *Impressions of Theophrastus Such*, ed. Nancy Henry (1879; Iowa: University of Iowa Press, 1994), ch. 13. Further references to this edition will be made parenthetically in text.

21 Humphrey McQueen, *A New Britannia: An Argument Concerning the Social Origins of Australian Radicalism and Nationalism*, 4th edn (St Lucia: University of Queensland Press, 2004), 3.

22 'The *Bulletin* Favours—'. *Sydney Bulletin* (17 November 1894), 2.

23 Anon, 'National Life and Character', *Saturday Review*, 75 (1894), 210.

24 Anon, *Saturday Review*, 209.

25 John Tregenza, *Professor of Democracy: The Life of Charles Henry Pearson, 1830-1894, Oxford Don and Australian Radical* (Carlton: Melbourne University Press, 1968), 3.

26 Tregenza, *Professor*, 64.

27 Lowe's radicalism was Felix Holt's radicalism. The working classes,

> under the modest claim to share in electoral power, are really asking for the whole of it. Their claim is to pass from the position of non-electors to the position of sovereign arbiters in the last resort of the destinies of the nation. They who set up such a claim must show that they are masters of themselves before they can hope to be masters of others.
>
> (Robert Lowe, *Speeches and Letters on Reform; with a Preface*, 2nd edn [London: Robert John Bush, 1867], 15)

28 Pearson, 'On the Working of Australian Institutions', *Essays on Reform* (London: Macmillan, 1867), 190, 192–3.

29 Pearson, 'Institutions', 192.

30 Macintyre, *Colonial Liberalism*, 3.

31 Charles Henry Pearson, 'Democracy in Victoria', *Fortnightly Review*, 25 (1879), 689.

32 Macintyre, *Colonial Liberalism*, 119.

33 Pearson, 'Institutions', 193. 'Practising Wesleyans outnumbered both Anglicans and Roman Catholics by 1861; Presbyterians, of a pronounced Free Church bent, were not far behind; and there were substantial contingents of Congregationalists and Baptists' (Macintyre, *Colonial Liberalism*, 115).

34 Tregenza, *Professor*, 2.

35 Macintyre, *Colonial Liberalism*, 27.

36 Macintyre, *Colonial Liberalism*, 5.

37 Macintyre, *Colonial Liberalism*, 118, 142–3.

38 Macintyre, *Colonial Liberalism*, 154.

39 Macintyre, *Colonial Liberalism*, 143.

40 Macintyre, *Colonial Liberalism*, 157; Tregenza, *Professor*, 3.

41 Macintyre, *Colonial Liberalism*, 10, 195.

42 Tregenza, *Professor*, 118.

43 Macintyre, *Colonial Liberalism*, 143.

44 Macintyre, *Colonial Liberalism*, 187.

45 Macintyre, *Colonial Liberalism*, 193.

46 Patrick Brantlinger, *Dark Vanishings: Discourse on the Extinction of Primitive Races, 1800–1930* (Ithaca NY: Cornell University Press, 2003), 194.

47 Brantlinger, *Dark Vanishings*, 197; raising the 'troubling idea that the white race [was] "passing"': 'extinction discourse comes full circle' (191).

48 W. Stebbing, ed., *Charles Henry Pearson, Fellow of Oriel and Education Minister in Victoria* (London: Longmans, Green, and Co., 1900), 290.

49 Oscar Browning, 'The Art of George Eliot', *Fortnightly Review*, 43 (1888), 539–40.

50 He was a contributor to the *Fortnightly* in the 80s and 90s and the London *Speaker* in 1890 and 1891, where criticism of Browning's unorthodox view appeared in Augustine Birrell, 'The Bona-Fide Traveller', *Speaker* (26 April 1890), 452–3.

51 As an anonymous reviewer wrote, 'Mr. Browning goes ... hopelessly and deplorably wrong ... in his preference for *Daniel Deronda*' ('George Eliot', *Saturday Review* 69 [15 February 1890], 205).

52 From reviews by George Saintsbury (*Academy*, 9 September 1876) and A.V. Dicey (unsigned, *Nation*, 19 October 1876), respectively, quoted in *Critical Heritage*, ed. Carroll, 371, 400, 401. When discussed at all in the 1890s, the view persisted that in *Deronda* Eliot 'sacrificed art to philosophical enthusiasm' ('Review of *Marcella*', *Edinburgh Review*, [July 1894], 113). See also D.F. Hannigan, 'Prospective Transformation of the Novel', *Westminster Review* (July 1893), 256–60.

53 Eliot, 'The Natural History of German Life', in *Essays of George Eliot*, ed. Thomas Pinney (London: Routledge and Kegan Paul, 1968), 171.

54 *The George Eliot Letters*, 9 vols, ed. Gordon S. Haight (New Haven and London: Yale University Press, 1954–78), 3: 111.

55 Eliot, 'Natural History', in *Essays*, ed. Pinney, 171.

56 Unsigned review, *Saturday Review* (16 September 1876), in *Critical Heritage*, ed. Carroll, 376.

57 R.E. Francillon, review of *Daniel Deronda*, *Gentleman's Magazine* (October 1876), in *Critical Heritage*, ed. Carroll, 382.

58 Unsigned review [R.R. Bowker], *International Review* (January 1877), in *Critical Heritage*, ed. Carroll, 438.

59 Eliot, 'Natural History', in *Essays*, ed. Pinney, 171.

60 Anon, 'George Eliot', *Saturday Review*, 205.

61 Nancy L. Paxton, *George Eliot and Herbert Spencer: Feminism, Evolutionism, and the Reconstruction of Gender* (Princeton: Princeton University Press, 1991), 225.

62 Elizabeth K. Helsinger, *Rural Scenes and National Representation: Britain, 1815–1850* (Princeton: Princeton University Press, 1997), 236.

63 Unsigned review [R.H. Hutton], *Spectator* (9 September 1876), in *Critical Heritage*, ed. Carroll, 366.

64 Unsigned review, *Saturday Review* (16 September 1876), in *Critical Heritage*, ed. Carroll, 377, and George Saintsbury, review, *Academy* (9 September 1876), also *Critical Heritage*, 374.

65 Aleksandar Stević, 'Convenient Cosmopolitanism: *Daniel Deronda*, Nationalism, and the Critics', *Victorian Literature and Culture*, 45 (2017), 595, 593.

66 Bruce Robbins, 'The Cosmopolitan Eliot', in *A Companion to George Eliot*, ed. Amanda Anderson and Harry E. Shaw (Chichester: Wiley-Blackwell, 2013), 400.

67 Robbins, 'Cosmopolitan', 401.

68 Robbins, 'Cosmopolitan', 401.

69 For example, the repugnance she feels for Rex (ch. 58), her 'dumb repugnance' in the face of her husband's animal domination (ch. 48), and 'her repulsion for Lush' (ch. 54).

70 *GEL*, 6: 314.

71 Eliot uses the word 'repugnance' 28 times in the novel, 'disgust' 27 times, and 'repulsion' 19 times.

72 Compare the novel's interest in animal instincts, and particularly in the pack-animal behaviours that establish and maintain hierarchies of power, status, and exclusivity—evidenced most starkly in Grandcourt's 'empire of fear' (ch. 35).

73 Eliot, *TS*, ch. 18.

74 In the 'global power struggle between the "higher and lower races"', Pearson is 'always careful to point out ... that these were relative terms, signifying not innate difference, but relative historical advancement' (discussed by Lake and Reynolds, *Colour Line*, 44). Cf. James Bryce, *The Relations of the Advanced and the Backward Races of Mankind* (Oxford: Clarendon Press, 1903), the 'Anglo-Saxon triumphalism and complacent assumptions about the never-ending expansion of Greater Britain' of Dilke and Seeley, and the chauvinism of E.A. Freeman's brand of 'extravagant Saxonism' (Lake and Reynolds, *Colour Line*, 45, 51).

75 Daniel Hack, 'Transatlantic Eliot: African American Connections', in *A Companion to George Eliot*, ed. Anderson and Shaw, 265.

76 George Eliot, *Felix Holt, the Radical*, ed. Fred C. Thomson (Oxford: Oxford World's Classics, 1988), ch. 3.

77 Francillon, review of *Daniel Deronda*, in *Critical Heritage*, ed. Carroll, 391.

78 As his mother warns him, this romance with separateness is attractive to him 'because I saved you from it' (ch. 51). From the inside, exclusiveness breeds exclusion and discrimination. As we might expect from Eliot, the novel is uncomfortably candid about the coercive narrowing and constraining that its big idea involves, especially for women. For Mordecai, it is an idea that unites the world, but for Alcharisi, her

> father's endless discoursing about our people ... was a thunder without meaning in my ears. I was to care forever about what Israel had been; and I did not care at all. I cared for the wide world, and all that I could represent in it.
>
> (ch. 51)

10 Counter Impressions

Ambiguous Habits in *Impressions of Theophrastus Such*

Penny Horsley

Interrogating aspects of habit in three chapters of *Impressions* ('A Too Deferential Man', 'Diseases of Small Authorship', and 'Shadows of the Coming Race') reveals patterns of habitual process in both form and content, including the relationship between habit and character, gender, and consciousness in the work—questions that pervade George Eliot's writing throughout her career. This discussion of the author's articulation of notions of habit in *Impressions* demonstrates George Eliot's entangled intimacy with the ambiguous nature of habit and its psychological, behavioural, and ethical consequences.

Habit is a deeply ambiguous concept. Its implications are antipodean: it can be a positive force for desirable change or it can form calcifications of a passive, disabling nature. It can sensitise us to new ways of thinking and feeling, or it can anesthetise us to violence and fear. As Claire Carlisle notes in *On Habit*, there is a distinction between active and passive habituation, 'between acquiring the habit of acting in a certain way, and becoming accustomed to familiar sensations and experiences'.[1] Philosophical arguments regarding the definition of habit and its positive or negative nature have been waged since the Ancients, with Aristotle's legacy on the matter being taken up by Spinoza, Hume, Hegel, and Nietzsche amongst others.[2]

Those who argue that Pavlovian habituation should be the dominant paradigm, wherein the subject becomes an insensitive automaton, obeying triggers with a more and more determined adherence to a single-minded response (regardless of the fallout) exclude an important, alternative aspect of habit reproduction.[3] According to Pater, the specific relevance of habit and habituation to art—and to literature in particular—involves the reader's pleasure in recognising anew aspects of the world that have been mossed over with familiarity, or in being struck by the pertinence of a sentiment or idea, composed before the reader's life began, to their experience in the here-and-now. 'The service of philosophy', he writes in the Conclusion to *The Renaissance*, 'and of religion and culture as well, to the human spirit, is to startle it into a sharp and eager observation'.[4] He continues:

DOI: 10.4324/9781003362821-11

> To burn always with this hard gem-like flame, to maintain this ecstasy, is success in life. Failure is to form habits; for habit is relative to a stereotyped world; meantime it is only the roughness of the eye that makes any two persons, things, situations, seem alike. While all melts under our feet, we may well catch at any exquisite passion, or any contribution to knowledge that seems, by a lifted horizon, to set the spirit free for a moment, or any stirring of the senses, strange dyes, strange flowers, and curious odours, or work of the artist's hands, or the face of one's friend.[5]

Pater's positioning of habit as a failure of existence emphasises the crucial role of art in disrupting the calcification of our perceptions and perspectives. Yet this very process of growing alert to our sensations, desires, and memories through interacting with art is also dependent on habituation. The former is a breaking of habits; the latter, a confirmation that one's habits of mind are not isolated from a broader community of humanity.

George Eliot depicts both the deadening and enlivening capacities of habit in her fiction. From *Scenes of Clerical Life* (1858), we hear about 'ladies of rank and of luxurious habits', Mr Pittman's display of 'a certain toothless pomposity habitual to him', and Caterina's 'old sweet habit of love' which sweeps aside her jealousy and hatred in a moment.[6] *Adam Bede* (1859) acknowledges symmetry in the establishment of physical and psychological habit: the narrator remarks,

> we get accustomed to mental as well as bodily pain, without, for all that, losing our sensibility to it: it becomes a habit of our lives, and we cease to imagine a condition of perfect ease as possible for us.[7]

Latimer, the condemned visionary of 'The Lifted Veil' (1859), refers to the statues of Prague as 'the fathers of ancient faded children ... who ... live on in the rigidity of habit, as they live on in perpetual mid-day, without the repose of night or the new birth of morning'.[8] This denunciation of habituation makes vivid the monotonous exhaustion that comes of *not* incorporating unfamiliar ideas and fresh experiences into our habitual practices. For example, Romola's habitual rejection of her own will seems counter-intuitive: 'it had become so thoroughly her habit to reject her impulsive choice, and to obey passively the guidance of outward claims'.[9] Yet, in *Middlemarch* (1871–72), Dorothea merges her ideal of sympathy with habit: 'All her eagerness for acquirement [of learning] lay within that full current of sympathetic motive in which her ideas and impulses were habitually swept along'.[10]

When George Eliot arrives at her final work, *Impressions of Theophrastus Such* (1879), the complexities of habit are elevated to a central element of the discourse. *Impressions* understands habit as both the problem with, and solution to, sympathetic human fellowship. It is in this work, more so than

in George Eliot's preceding novels, that the author tests the role of literature as an agent in the disruption and fortification of habits of thought and
feeling. *Impressions* is a self-conscious reflection on literary habit-making.
Literature, George Eliot understands, is the perfect artistic medium for the
transmission of habits due to the fact that, as Carlisle notes, 'language is
deeply habitual—learned by imitation and repetition, and entrenched by
common usage—it often becomes a transparent, inconspicuous medium that
simultaneously carries and conceals meaning'.[11] Considering, as Nicholas
Dames has done, the function of literary motifs and repetition of language
as 'motivic' practices, I too seek to understand George Eliot's writing 'as a
communicative act aimed at a nonfictional world of readers—as, in other
words, a political/ethical act shaped by attention to habits of cognition'.[12]
Ultimately, as is customary in George Eliot's generous scope and scale of
philosophical and psychological insight, *Impressions of Theophrastus Such*
refuses to distil general maxims from particularities, or to press dogmatic
perspectives upon its readers, but rather explores the shifting applications
of the ambiguous qualities of habit for ethical understanding and social
progress.

Human habit as a key to psychological enquiry is the subject of the
opening motto of *Impressions*, taken from Plato's *Phaedrus*: the purpose
of the text is 'truly to show life itself and the habits of men'.[13] However,
in his opening remark, 'It is my habit to give an account to myself of the
characters I meet with: can I give any true account of my own?' (*TS*, ch. 1),
Theophrastus aligns habit with the definition of the character of the Other
while doubting the possibility of defining his own. Habit is the source of
social cohesion and the scourge of human progress in 'A Too Deferential
Man', just as it is the excuse for violent behaviour and the product of 'a
growing harmony between perception, conviction, and impulse' in 'Only
Temper' (ch. 6). Habit sustains depression on one hand, and encourages fra-
ternity on the other, in 'A Political Molecule'. Mixtus and Scintilla underesti-
mate the rigid power of habitual beliefs and values in 'A Half-Breed', breezily
imagining they will be able to change each other once married life sets in,
while in the same sketch, moral habit is characterised as yielding and susceptible to material desire. 'Debasing the Moral Currency' is the expression of
Theophrastus' frustration with the disjunction between the accepted wisdom
that habits are formed from an early age and make a great impression upon
the development of a child's character, and the insistence, despite this, that
children will know instinctively when to override the habits into which their
parents push them. The gendered rendering of masculine and feminine qualities comes under the microscope in 'Diseases of Small Authorship', where
Theophrastus interrogates the socially and culturally constructed nature of
gender performance—a product of time-worn habit that presents itself as
'truth'. Even the penultimate chapter, 'Shadows of the Coming Race', weighs
habit in the material form of machine automata against the habitually inco-
herent 'screaming consciousness' of humanity (ch. 17).

The reviews of *Impressions* on publication expressed disappointment and criticised the intellectual demands it made on its readers. *The Atlantic Monthly* mourned the disappearance of the author of *Middlemarch* in the wake of a George Eliot whose 'eyes are bent on lower things'.[14] So confounded was he by *Impressions*, the author of the review supposed that '[t]o all thoughtful admirers of George Eliot the reading of *Theophrastus Such* must be a prolonged shock,—the after-effect a dull, stunned amazement' (619). Although the reviewer accurately predicted that this work would not elicit the same level of popularity as the novels, parts of the review demonstrate the very point of George Eliot's social criticism and satire in *Impressions*. For example, in commenting on the final chapter 'The Modern Hep! Hep! Hep!', the reviewer states:

> It is a plea for tolerance in behalf of the Jews ... The wrongs belong to the past; ghettos and Jewish disability laws have ceased to exist, and to put one's self into a passion of sympathy over the present condition of the race in civilized Christendom is as much an anachronism as to preach a crusade against Austrian tyranny in Italy or Negro slavery in America.
>
> (ch. 18)

George Eliot proves to be visionary in light of events in the twentieth century; the revocation of a law does not alter the deep-seated prejudices of 'civilized Christendom'. The reviewer's metaphorical hand-washing of any need to disturb himself further with the plight of the Jews (or that of the African-Americans, or the idea that tyranny could again dominate a European nation) marks him as the simplistically ignorant Briton against whom the polemical 'Modern Hep!' is directed. The reviewer is convinced that 'the recent great Jewish and Gentile intermarriages in England and France prove conclusively that she is fighting a dead ogre' (ch. 18); the irony of this deduction effectively nullifies his criticism of George Eliot's subjects in *Impressions* and is a pertinent demonstration of the deadening effect of time-worn habits of perspective regarding culture, race, and power.

Impressions has received relatively little critical attention—the dense prose, the fractured form, and the obscure allusions to individuals and works, make this the least accessible of George Eliot's literary productions. Few critics agree on the identity of the narrator: Robert Macfarlane is clear that 'Theophrastus is not George Eliot, nor was he meant to be';[15] Rosemarie Bodenheimer comes at it from the same angle but with a finer discrimination between the fictional and the real: 'Theophrastus Such is no different from George Eliot. Both are fictional male names for narrators who display a variety of styles, roles and attitudes'.[16] There are, however, enough clear links between some of the material in *Impressions* and a philosophical consistency across the George Eliot canon that includes letters, essays, novels, and notebooks, to suggest that Theophrastus is less a study in the impressions of a nineteenth-century bachelor than a vessel through which his creator refracts her concerns, pulling the strings to make him dance 'a hornpipe' to her music (*TS*, ch. 1).

Several critics have investigated the satirical engagement of *Impressions* with the notion of 'character types'. Richard Mallen understands the central purpose of the text as questioning 'both the assumption that a person's character can be read ... and the assumption that character types can be neatly classified'.[17] This reading intersects with Nancy Henry's observation in her introduction to *Impressions* that the name 'Theophrastus Such' is a pun on the phrase 'Such a Type Who ...' which was 'the formula used by the Greek Theophrastus as a way of introducing each of his characters'.[18] For the ancient Theophrastus, 'such' indicates the beginning of a generalisation about character types; the name 'Theophrastus Such' rescues the word 'such' and reserves it as a particular example—an individual name; a complete person rather than a category. The pattern of reasoning in *Impressions* flows from generalisations towards instances that are particular, and this name-game reinforces that premise.

Helen Small acknowledges the work's lack of appeal, but also claims that the acerbic tones and untranslated passages are intentional characteristics: 'it is not a work that expects or welcomes readerly affection. It is, on the contrary, rebarbative from the outset'.[19] S. Pearl Brilmyer, Small, and Sarah Allison all note *Impressions*' concern with hermeneutics: it investigates 'the limits of human perception',[20] the problem of the 'ineradicable presence of one's own self in one's ethical philosophy',[21] and, as opposed to offering an energising 'optimism about the moral power of fiction ... [it registers] a deep pessimism about how much people can ever know about each other's experience'.[22] These assessments help to show that the work poses more questions than it answers; it allows the reader to 'obtain not *results* but *powers*'.[23] Bodenheimer allows for more ambiguity in the tone of the work. In her view, the restrictions that play upon human awareness create a bittersweet effect, illuminating both 'the dangers and consolations of human illusion'.[24] Bodenheimer's nod to the satirical solace in *Middlemarch*—'the quickest of us walk about well wadded with stupidity' (*M*, ch. 20)—points to *Impressions*' interest in the ambivalences: the blessing and curse of the ego and of our limited capacity for empathy, and the equivocal nature of habit as both deadening and enlivening.

I now turn to consider habit in three chapters of *Impressions*: 'A Too Deferential Man', 'Diseases of Small Authorship', and 'Shadows of the Coming Race'. This selection offers insights into the relationship between habit and character, gender, and consciousness in the work, questions which pervade George Eliot's writing career. While there is clearly scope for a more in-depth study of the author's articulation of notions of habit in *Impressions*, this exploration will demonstrate George Eliot's entangled intimacy with the puzzle of the ambiguous nature of habit and its psychological consequences.

Habit as Character: 'A Too Deferential Man'

'A Too Deferential Man' follows the same discursive path that the majority of the chapters in *Impressions* carve out. As Brilmyer notes, 'Eliot's sketches often start with a meditation on a behavior, situation, or emotion and turn after a paragraph or so to a human instantiation of the phenomenon she is describing'.[25] This movement from the 'general to the special' upon which George Eliot had been writing in relation to the social sciences since her *Westminster Review* period in the 1850s offers an example of her theoretical consistency over three decades of active publication.[26] Sarah Allison's *Reductive Reading: A Syntax of Victorian Moralizing* considers the construction of literature at the level of syntax and its capacity to promote habits of judgement and empathic perspectives in the reader:

> Much contemporary criticism around the ethical work novels do considers reading as a relation between the reader and either the characters or narrator; I propose that there is also an ethics of syntax operating at the level of the clause. Instead of promoting specific values, these clauses inscribe a process of making judgments and aim to educate the reader in methods of assuming the perspective of other people.[27]

George Eliot's desire to develop in her reader habits of perception that follow the 'general-to-special' trajectory is expressed (in reverse) in chapter 11 of *Impressions*, 'The Wasp Credited with the Honeycomb', with a satirical jeer at phrenological theory:

> Looked into closely, the conclusion from a man's profile, voice, and fluency to his certainty in multiplication beyond the twelves, seems to show a confused notion of the way in which very common things are connected; but it is on such false correlations that men found half their inferences about each other.

Advising the reservation of judgement until the facts of a personality can be ascertained, 'A Too Deferential Man' calls for patience in the realm of communal life. In this instance, the narrator pleads a general case for a 'little unpremeditated insincerity' which should 'be indulged under the stress of social intercourse' (*TS*, ch. 5). On the scale of dishonesty, mouthing platitudes and borrowed opinions to new acquaintances before the party gets under way is considered entirely forgivable by Theophrastus. In fact, as the drinks circulate, this behaviour plays an important part in the incipient development of an atmosphere amenable to more forthright discussion, avoids causing offence too early, and allows those who have not yet formulated comprehensive thoughts in response to the politics of the day a chance to warm their vocal cords. The trepidation and anxiety that comes with new social interactions are 'the winds and currents we have all to steer amongst, and they are often too strong for our truthfulness or our wit' (*TS,* ch. 5). This nautical metaphor describes social alienation and the individual's inability to predict or control the broader social current. In this case, the habit of small-talk and the recirculation of common opinion is deemed useful for the greater good.

Shifting into specifics, we are introduced to Heinze—the star of this study in deference, and a figure who is subject to some of the most caustic barbs in the entire work (e.g. 'his mind is furnished as hotels are, with everything for occasional and transient use' [ch. 5]). Theophrastus immediately disrupts what he assumes will be the reader's tendency to generalise about Heinze: 'From his name you might suppose him to be German: in fact, his family is Alsatian, but has been settled in England for more than one generation' (ch. 5). Ironically, after this reminder to enquire into the particulars, Theophrastus reverts to the conventions of his ancient namesake, casting Heinze as an archetype: 'He is the superlatively deferential man, and walks about with murmured wonder at the wisdom and discernment of everybody who talks to him' (ch. 5).[28] George Eliot blends the framework of the Theophrastan character sketch with a more modern application of the genre; each 'type' is rendered the epitome of the general, and yet is delivered with the unique details that belong to her nineteenth-century realist aesthetic as we see him mixing with his peers and conducting specific instances of deference within his social circle. Heinze is a pure (though inverted) version of the Aristotelian concept of habit as character. Unlike the original version of 'The Flatterer' from the late fourth century BC who plays the sycophant for personal gain, Heinze has no motive for his flattery; his flattery simply defines him through his lifelong repetition of the trait. Heinze is drawn in opposition to the opening remarks of the chapter. He personifies the extremity of deference in social intercourse, delighting in regurgitating opinions:

> The 'Iliad,' one sees, would impress him little if it were not for what Mr Fugleman has lately said about it; and if you mention an image or sentiment in Chaucer he seems not to heed the bearing of your reference, but immediately tells you that Mr Hautboy, too, regards Chaucer as a poet of the first order, and he is delighted to find that two such judges as you and Hautboy are at one.
>
> (ch. 5)

Heinze is incapable of, and indifferent to, any primary investigation into art or science of his own—he 'would hardly remark that the sun shone without an air of respectful appeal or fervid adhesion' (ch. 5). George Eliot considers this trait in her notebooks in a manner that suggests Theophrastus is here a direct mouthpiece for the author's philosophical musings:

The habit of expressing borrowed judgements stupefies the sensibilities, which are the only foundation of genuine judgements, just as the constant reading and retailing of results from other men's observations through the microscope, without ever looking through the lens oneself, is an instruction in some truths and some prejudices, but is no instruction in observant susceptibility; on the contrary, it breeds a habit of inward seeing according to verbal statement, which dulls the power of outward seeing according to visual evidence.[29]

George Eliot's consideration of this particular disposition is directly concerned with the discrimination between active and passive habit formation. 'Inward seeing' is developed at the expense of 'outward seeing' in George Eliot's work; personality becomes, as George Levine points out, 'an obstruction to perception'.[30] George Eliot's notebook also expresses the difficulty inherent in teasing out the ambiguous nature of habit:

On this subject [social deference], as on so many others, it is difficult to strike the balance between the educational needs of passivity or receptivity, and independent selection. We should learn nothing without the tendency to implicit acceptance; but there must clearly be a limit to such mental submission, else we should come to a stand-still. The human mind would be no better than a dried specimen, representing an unchangeable type. When the assimilation of new matter ceases, decay must begin. In a reasoned self-restraining deference there is as much energy as in rebellion; but among the less capable, one must admit that the superior energy is on the side of the rebels.[31]

Unfortunately for Heinze, George Eliot portrays him to represent a 'dried specimen … an unchangeable type' rather than an example of the rebellion of 'reasoned self-restraining deference'.[32] He draws the ire of Theophrastus, not only for his habit of gushing and boot-licking, but for not even having a decent motive—self-interest or otherwise—for the performance which has 'no deep hunger to excuse it' (ch. 5).

Gender as Habit: 'Diseases of Small Authorship'

Gillian Beer reconsiders George Eliot's attitudes to gender in her revised edition of *George Eliot*, where she points to responses from critics such as F.R. Leavis and Lord David Cecil regarding George Eliot's depiction of 'attractive male characters', critiques which now seem 'loaded with outworn sexual stereotypes: neither Will Ladislaw in *Middlemarch* nor Daniel Deronda in the novel of that name conform to the expectations of much nineteenth or even twentieth century manhood'.[33] George Eliot's rendering of gender in her works urges a consideration of the culturally ingrained constraints of gender roles and dispositions, and refuses to accept inherent

differences in the capabilities of individuals on the basis of sex. Her incorp-
oration of material that points to male superiority and female inferiority
tends to be placed in ironic proximity to instances that show the fallacy
of these notions. The epigraph to *Middlemarch*, chapter 1, from Beaumont
and Fletcher's *The Maid's Tragedy*—'Since I can do no good because a
woman, / Reach constantly at something that is near it'—gives shape to
Dorothea's beliefs and desires, indicating her simultaneous inheritance of,
and frustration with, gender-based expectations. This epigraph is summoned
again to close the 'Finale': the 'growing good of the world' is a direct result
of the choices made and lives led by women like Dorothea. George Eliot's
work promotes the idea that gender enactment is a form of habit: subject
to inherited bias and the plague of custom while also malleable, fluid, and
adaptable. Looking particularly at the late novels, Beer notes 'the prescience
with which [Eliot] foresaw less rigid gender roles and began the withdrawal
from binary hierarchy'.[34]

Impressions offers a running commentary on gender, most often presented
through a satirical account of women's weaknesses in the eyes of men. Until
his obsession with a particular historical argument consumes him, Merman,
the tragic figure in 'How We Encourage Research', has the genial ability
to reserve the expression of complex scholarly arguments in company;
'Such flexibility was naturally much helped by his amiable feeling towards
woman, whose nervous system, he was convinced, would not bear the continuous strain of difficult topics' (ch. 3). 'How We Come to Give Ourselves
False Testimonials, and Believe in Them' offers a moment of amusement at
male generalisations regarding women's shortcomings:

> 'Twenty-six large lumps every day of your life, Mr Bovis,' says his wife.
> 'No such thing!' exclaims Bovis.
> 'You drop them into your tea, coffee, and whisky yourself, my dear,
> and I count them.'
> 'Nonsense!' laughs Bovis, turning to Pilulus, that they may exchange
> a glance of mutual amusement at a woman's inaccuracy.
> But she happened to be right. Bovis had never said inwardly that he
> would take a large allowance of sugar, and he had the tradition about
> himself that he was a man of the most moderate habits; hence, with
> this conviction, he was naturally disgusted at the saccharine excesses
> of Avis.
>
> (ch. 13)

The main target of Theophrastus' criticism here is the fictions we create
and believe about our identity and character—Bovis' hypocrisy is a product
of the distance between his creed and his reality. The 'glance of mutual
amusement at a woman's inaccuracy' broadens the argument, satirising
smug misogynistic generalisations about women's failings. The satire
deepens with Theophrastus' mock-earnestness—'But she happened to be

right'—which implies that Bovis' wife is an exceptional case in which a woman has managed to offer an accurate mathematical account, sure to stun the reader. George Eliot writes elsewhere about the culturally ascribed limits of women's intelligence and agency in an effort to demonstrate to her readers their fallaciousness:

> [I]f there were one level of feminine incompetence as strict as the ability to count three and no more, the social lot of women might be treated with scientific certitude. Meanwhile the indefiniteness remains, and the limits of variation are really much wider than anyone would imagine from the sameness of women's coiffure and the favourite love-stories in prose and verse.
>
> (*M*, 'Prelude')

Jennifer Judge offers a connection between this passage from the 'Prelude' to *Middlemarch* and the author's interest in dissecting the accepted wisdom of gendered habits:

> The examples of women's hairstyles and novel preferences create a powerful anticlimax to the momentous question of women's evolutionary potential. Invoking the catchwords of Darwinism ('indefiniteness' and 'variation'), the narrator asserts that despotic custom must not be confused with biological truth. The tendency to conflate science and custom in evaluations of female 'nature' is soundly satirized. George Eliot's ethology, 'step by step' evolutionary gradualism, and feminism are grounded in the 'logic of habit.'[35]

Furthermore, the extract from the 'Prelude' suggests that the inability to perceive difference amongst seeming likeness in women's 'social lot' is a failure of discernment that stunts social progress. The villain in the equation is the 'meanness of opportunity' available to women—a direct result of a distrust in female agency, in combination with fear, ignorance, and the desired continuance of patriarchal power systems.

The thrust of Ganymede's story in chapter 12 of *Impressions*, 'So Young!', is a broader sketch of Bovis' predicament: Ganymede clings to an account of his character long past its efficacy, and when it is patently contradictory to factual evidence. The summarising sentence (and moral) of this chapter skews what seems to be a story about the unreliability of self-perception into a gender-based argument: 'But let us be just enough to admit that there may be old-young coxcombs as well as old-young coquettes' (ch. 12). The double standards in the attribution of character flaws according to gender is Theophrastus' punchline and to acknowledge it is to be just. Here, the reader is offered insight into George Eliot's desire for the reformation of habitual social belief in male superiority.

The most comprehensive attack on simplistic categories of gendered dispositions is offered in chapter 15 of *Impressions*, 'Diseases of Small Authorship'. Theophrastus presents an acquaintance, Vorticella, who harasses everyone with her single published volume, 'The Channel Islands'. Vorticella's vanity recalls George Eliot's 1856 essay in the *Westminster Review*, 'Silly Novels by Lady Novelists', and seems for the first half of the chapter to be another rant against women writers who overestimate their talents and muddy the literary waters with drivel. Instead, the argument turns into a satirical attack on the culture of male dominance:

> My experience with Vorticella led me for a time into the false supposition that this sort of fungous disfiguration, which makes Self disagreeably larger, was most common to the female sex; but I presently found that here too the male could assert his superiority and show a more vigorous boredom.
>
> (ch. 15)

Theophrastus demonstrates again that general conclusions formed on the basis of specific instances are faulty, looping back on his habitual theme of reasoning from the macro to the micro. Not only is the quality of vanity applied to both sexes, but the way in which it is exhibited in men and women depends on the opportunities that are available to them:

> Depend upon it, vanity is human, native alike to men and women; only in the male it is of denser texture, less volatile, so that it less immediately informs you of its presence, but is more massive and capable of knocking you down if you come into collision with it; while in women vanity lays by its small revenges as in a needle-case always at hand. The difference is in muscle and finger-tips, in traditional habits and mental perspective, rather than in the original appetite of vanity.
>
> (ch. 15)

The reader is offered a chance to consider the ways in which attitudes to gender are culturally conditioned, and how they feed in to stereotypes that allow the maintenance of the power imbalance between the genders to continue. Theophrastus concludes with the assertion that he has debunked the myth of feminine vanity: 'there is no need to admit that women would carry away the prize of vanity in a competition where differences of custom were fairly considered' (ch. 15). The recognition of gender performance as a product of time-worn cultural habits opens a new realm for considering the positive possibilities of both women's and men's potential. It involves shifting from an unquestioning acceptance of custom to a belief in the human capacity to create dynamic new habits that serve not only the individual but the progress of society.

Consciousness and Habit: 'Shadows of the Coming Race'

'Shadows of the Coming Race', originally slated as the final chapter of *Impressions*, but switched at the last minute with 'The Modern Hep! Hep! Hep!' for reasons that are not known, is a kind of Socratic dialogue between Theophrastus and his friend Trost, laced with satire and irony, that considers the future of humanity's relationship with machines. Brilmyer suggests that '"Shadows" might be interpreted as a reaction to the "conscious automaton" debates of the 1870s among Thomas Henry Huxley, Herbert Spencer, William James, and John Elliott Cairnes', debates with which Lewes engaged in *Problems of Life and Mind*.[36] Theophrastus admires Trost for his optimistic belief that the 'extremely unpleasant and disfiguring work by which many of our fellow-creatures have to get their bread ... "will soon be done by machinery"' (ch. 17). The appeal to Theophrastus lies in the idea that the suffering he witnesses in the labouring classes might be appeased with technology that takes up the yoke; yet Trost's elaborated account of future robotic 'wonder-workers [who] are the slaves of our race' (ch. 17) inspires Theophrastus to imagine the end of human productivity, and, subsequently, the extinction of the species. As the narrator spirals into deeper dystopian tones, his 'fearful vision' becomes a meta-criticism of the Theophrastan genre, an element that Richard Mallen has argued is one of the defining features of the text:

> Eliot calls into question the central premise of the genre: the assumption that character 'types' can be known and classified. Eliot suggests that we can fully know neither our own character nor that of others, and that accordingly any classification of character 'types' reflects not so much the fixity of human nature as the fictions of human culture.[37]

At the Bank of England, Theophrastus has seen

> a wondrously delicate machine for testing sovereigns, a shrewd implacable little steel Rhadamanthus that, once the coins are delivered up to it, lifts and balances each in turn for the fraction of an instant, finds it wanting or sufficient, and dismisses it to right or left with rigorous justice.
>
> (ch. 17)

The implication here is that the value of an individual can become subsumed by the practice of typology; judgements made about the inadequacy or acceptability of character are necessarily fragmentary and skewed by circumstance—any superficial deformity can mark them unfit for purpose in the eyes of the critic. Additionally, the 'shrewd implacable ... Rhadamanthus'—one of the three Greek gods who judge the dead in Hades—summons the topic of legacy. Theophrastus' (and perhaps George

Eliot's) desire to 'keep the pleasing, inspiring illusion of being listened to' (*TS*, ch. 1) suggests an anxiety about posthumous reputation that is bound up with the erasure of human individuality and spontaneity.

Just as 'The Lifted Veil' tests the limits of sympathy, interrogates what constitutes true vision, and questions the basis of George Eliot's literary creed—that an authentic, intricate knowledge of those with whom we share the planet will extend our sympathetic capacity—so 'Shadows of the Coming Race' resists the automatic dismissal of the interfering, 'screaming consciousness' that precludes us from forming fair and rational judgements of others. As Helen Small argues, 'the problem Theophrastus seeks to resolve [is] … what to do with the ineradicable presence of one's own self in one's ethical philosophy'.[38] Theophrastus shares with Daniel Deronda a belief in the desirability of a diminishing sense of selfhood: Theophrastus is 'at the point of finding that this world would be worth living in without any lot of one's own' (*TS*, ch. 1), and Daniel, immediately before he rescues the suicidal Mirah from drowning,

> was forgetting everything else in a half-speculative, half-involuntary identification of himself with the objects he was looking at, thinking how far it might be possible habitually to shift his centre till his own personality would be no less outside him than the landscape.[39]

George Eliot refuses to leave untested her philosophical notions; this particular concept seems to have grown in appeal to Eliot as the years wore on:

> I try to delight in the sunshine that will be when I shall never see it any more. And I think it is possible for this sort of impersonal life to attain great intensity,—possible us to gain much more independence, than is usually believed, of the small bundle of facts that make our own personality.[40]

'Shadows of the Coming Race' explores the consequences of vanquishing our centre of self through the phases of machine evolution. In the satirical tradition of Swift, Theophrastus first floats a world of complete objectivity, imagining humanity being governed by

> a parliament of machines … which would act not the less infallibly for being free from the fussy accompaniment of that consciousness to which our prejudice gives a supreme governing rank, when in truth it is an idle parasite on the grand sequence of things.
>
> (ch. 17)

While disturbing, this new system of government needs only to be weighed for a moment against the parasitic prejudices that shape the path to power and subsequent rule of so many political leaders, before the rationality of the machines, and Theophrastus' argument, win out.

The formality and intellectual rigour of the Socratic process come in for a jibe as Trost's next response to Theophrastus along with the mock-serious parenthetical defence of his friend's crude language—'"Pooh!" says Trost (We are on very intimate terms.)' (ch. 17)—is designed to show the conditions of a specific relationship that allow for language to be understood and accepted on an emotional level. This purpose lies outside the convention of the cooperative-argumentative dialogue, emphasising the crucial bearing that specific circumstances and particular personalities will have on the interpretation of any philosophical or ethical conundrum (a return to the impossibility of escaping one's consciousness). As Theophrastus rhapsodises onwards, he arrives at a point where humans have no purpose and recede in the wake of 'the immensely more powerful unconscious race' (ch. 17). The competition between mankind and machine in the race for survival is a matter of perfecting the habit of a progressive accumulation of new ideas for improvement:

> Thus the feebler race, whose corporeal adjustments happened to be accompanied with a maniacal consciousness which imagined itself moving its mover, will have vanished, as all less adapted existences do before the fittest—*i.e.*, the existence composed of the most persistent groups of movements and the most capable of incorporating new groups in harmonious relation.

However, when tested against the hypothetically superior being—the automaton—Theophrastus' argument swings back upon itself in favour of human consciousness:

> Thus this planet may be filled with beings who will be blind and deaf as the inmost rock, yet will execute changes as delicate and complicated as those of human language and all the intricate web of what we call its effects, without sensitive impression, without sensitive impulse: there may be, let us say, mute orations, mute rhapsodies, mute discussions, and no consciousness there even to enjoy the silence.

The loss of pleasure in oration, rhapsody, discussion, and silence is mourned in the final phrase of Theophrastus' argument, inverting the essential superiority of beings who are not subject to 'the noises of our various follies as they soliloquise or converse in our brains' and acknowledging the messy, irrational beauty of the human psyche.

'Shadows of the Coming Race' concludes in ambiguity. Trost's grumbling response to Theophrastus' argument, 'Absurd!', may be shared by the reader—this sketch could easily be imagined as the blueprint for a work by Beckett, Camus, or Kafka, propelling *Impressions* at least partway, philosophically and aesthetically, into the next century of artistic expression and tone. Theophrastus recognises the premise of his reasoning as a product of his own 'screaming consciousness', admitting that his nightmare-vision of humanity's demise is inevitably born of germs that 'have found a sort of nidus among my melancholy fancies' (ch. 17). Weighing up the dense shifts, light touches, and playful reversals in this chapter, Theophrastus concludes the argument as follows: analogical reasoning is based on false premises, as premises belong to individual experience; and the habits of machines are and should remain passive to the touch of their inventors. That is, they should be assets created to reduce human suffering and increase the dissemination of knowledge by shouldering some of the mental and physical heavy-lifting, which is the proper expression of habit in inorganic material. Finally, Theophrastus poses the question: are our habits the essence of our character? Or is our level of consciousness of our habits (personal and communal), and our willingness or otherwise to expand, disrupt or break them when necessary, a more telling essence of identity? These questions go to the heart of the ambiguities that preoccupy George Eliot when it comes to the interplay of habit and character.

Conclusion

Despite the way *Impressions of Theophrastus Such* bristles and sulks at times, the work interrogates in multi-dimensional modes the knotty questions that George Eliot wrestled with throughout her life. *Impressions* examines and dissects the sinister side of sympathy, the fatuous and damaging behaviour that arises from uncontested mores, and the impossibility of a full and frank knowledge of the self. Yet, on balance, it is a work of hope. It animates the past and peers with curiosity at the future, and it believes that the quality and clarity of human consciousness can continue to improve with the active acquisition of habits of mind that cast aside the ego in the process of making judgements. Wayne Booth remarks that '[o]ne possible reaction to a fragmented society may be to retreat to a private world of values, but another might well be to build works of art that themselves help to mould a new consensus'.[41] George Eliot's final work of art embraces what is off-centre, eccentric, and ambiguous; it interrogates the habits of mind that form the basis of dogma and prejudice. Her creative risk in the form of the work is a conscious choice to spin away from the emotional resonance that defined her authorial voice in the preceding novels, into the wobbly outer-orbits that exemplify an antipodean way of thinking.

Notes

1 Claire Carlisle, *On Habit* (New York: Routledge, 2014), 7.
2 Theories of habit are explored extensively in: Spinoza, *Ethics* (1677); Hume, *An Enquiry Concerning Human Understanding* (1748); Hegel, *Philosophy of Mind* (1817); and Nietzsche, *The Gay Science* (1882).
3 Nietzsche, for example, in his amusing attack on his British counterparts:

These English psychologists—what do they really mean? We always find them voluntarily or involuntarily at the same task of pushing to the front the *partie honteuse* of our inner world, and looking for the efficient, governing, and decisive principle in that precise quarter where the intellectual self-respect of the race would be the most reluctant to find it (for example, in the *vis inertiæ* of habit, or in forgetfulness, or in a blind and fortuitous mechanism and association of ideas, or in some factor that is purely passive, reflex, molecular, or fundamentally stupid).

Friedrich Nietzsche, *A Genealogy of Morals,* ed. Alexander Tille, tr. William Haussmann (New York: Macmillan, 1907), 17.

4 Walter Pater, *Studies in the History of the Renaissance*, ed. Matthew Beaumont (Oxford: Oxford World's Classics, 2020), 119.

5 Pater, *Renaissance,* 120.

6 George Eliot, *Scenes of Clerical Life*, ed. Josie Billington and Thomas Noble (Oxford: Oxford World's Classics, 2015), 'The Sad Fortunes of the Reverend Amos Barton', ch. 5; 'Janet's Repentance', ch. 25; 'Mr Gilfil's Love Story', ch. 15.

7 George Eliot, *Adam Bede*, ed. Carol Martin (Oxford: Oxford World's Classics, 2008), ch. 50.

8 George Eliot, *The Lifted Veil; Brother Jacob*, ed. Helen Small (Oxford: Oxford World's Classics, 2009), ch. 1.

9 George Eliot, *Romola*, ed. Andrew Brown (Oxford: Oxford World's Classics, 1994), ch. 52.

10 George Eliot, *Middlemarch*, ed. David Carroll (Oxford: Oxford World's Classics, 2019), ch. 10. Further references to this edition appear parenthetically in text.

11 Carlisle, *On Habit*, 143.

12 Nicholas Dames, *The Physiology of the Novel: Reading, Neural Science, and the Form of Victorian Fiction* (Oxford: Oxford University Press, 2007), 150.

13 George Eliot, *Impressions of Theophrastus Such*, ed. Nancy Henry (Iowa: University of Iowa Press, 1994), frontispiece. Further references to this edition appear parenthetically in text.

14 Anonymous, 'Englishwomen in Recent Literature', *The Atlantic Monthly,* 44 (1879), 622. All further references will be made in text.

15 Robert Macfarlane, 'A Small Squealing Black Pig: George Eliot, Originality, and Plagiarism', *George Eliot-George Henry Lewes Studies,* 42/43 (2002), 26.

16 Rosemarie Bodenheimer, 'George Eliot's Last Stand: *Impressions of Theophrastus Such'*, *Victorian Literature and Culture,* 44 (2016), 607.

17 Richard Mallen, 'George Eliot and the Precious Mettle of Trust', *Victorian Studies,* 44 (2001), 64–5.

18 Henry, 'Introduction', xviii.

19 Helen Small, 'George Eliot and the Cosmopolitan Cynic', *Victorian Studies,* 55 (2012), 98.

20 S. Pearl Brilmyer, '"The Natural History of My Inward Self": Sensing Character in George Eliot's *Impressions of Theophrastus Such*', *PMLA,* 129 (2014), 36.

21 Small, 'Cosmopolitan'. 99.

22 Sarah Allison, *Reductive Reading: A Syntax of Victorian Moralizing* (Baltimore: John Hopkins University Press, 2018), 71.

23 *Essays of George Eliot*, ed. Thomas Pinney (London: Routledge and Kegan Paul, 1963), 213.

24 Bodenheimer, 'Last Stand', 619.

25 Brilmyer, 'Natural History', 42.

26 'It has not been sufficiently insisted on, that in the various branches of Social Science there is an advance from the general to the special, from the simple to the complex'. George Eliot, 'The Natural History of German Life' (1856), in *Essays of George Eliot*, ed. Thomas Pinney (New York: Columbia University Press, 1963), 289–90.

27 Allison, *Reductive Reading*, 62.

28 Theophrastus of Eresos uses similar definitive and generic constructions. In 'The Flatterer', for example, 'While his patron speaks, he bids the rest be silent. He sounds his praises in his hearing and after the patron's speech gives the cue for applause by "Bravo!"' Theophrastus, *Characters*, ed. James Diggle (Cambridge: Cambridge University Press, 2004), 8.

29 *Essays*, ed. Pinney, 443.

30 George Levine, 'George Eliot's Hypothesis of Reality', *Nineteenth-Century Fiction*, 35 (June 1980), 1. Theophrastus' own inward-looking in the opening chapter is consciously replaced with a philosophy of outward-looking: he strives for a 'non-human independence'—a vision unbiased by 'that inward squint which consists in a dissatisfied egoism or other want of mental balance' (*TS*, ch. 1). Brilmyer also comments on Theophrastus' wrestling with the distortions of the ego and stresses that both human and non-human animals suffer from this effect, with the saturation of allegorical names drawn from various species as evidence. See Brilmyer, 38.

31 *Essays*, ed. Pinney, 443–4.

32 *Essays*, ed. Pinney, 443–4.

33 Gillian Beer, *George Eliot and the Woman Question* (Brighton: Edward Everett Root, 2019), xix.

34 Beer, *George Eliot and the Woman Question*, xix.

35 Jennifer Judge, 'The Gendering of Habit in George Eliot's *Middlemarch*', *Victorian Review*, 39 (2013), 175.

36 Brilmyer, 'Natural History', 46.

37 Mallen, 'Precious Mettle', 63.

38 Small, 'Cosmopolitan', 99.

39 George Eliot, *Daniel Deronda*, ed. Graham Handley (Oxford: Oxford World's Classics, 1998), ch. 17.

40 *The George Eliot Letters*, 9 vols, ed. Gordon S. Haight (New Haven and London: Yale University Press, 1954–78), 5: 107.

41 Wayne Booth, *The Rhetoric of Fiction* (Chicago: University of Chicago Press, 1961), 393.

11 *Impressions of Theophrastus Such* and the Limitations of Depth

Matthew Sussman

Critics have long complained about the unsettling elements of Eliot's last published work, *Impressions of Theophrastus Such* (1879). It has a first-person narrator, but is neither a conventional novel nor a personal essay. It contains named characters, but they lack convincing interiority. It proclaims an ideal of humanitarian fellowship, but without Eliot's customary warmth. And it pays attention to the trivialities of everyday life, yet its technique is allegorical rather than realistic. Many have struggled with the appearance of contradiction, not only in the text itself but within the broader scope of Eliot's oeuvre. Is *Impressions* a novelistic experiment whose ethics and intentions are consonant with Eliot's other fictions? Or should the book be read as a species of the moralised essay and character sketch popularised in the seventeenth and eighteenth centuries, and thus a departure from novelistic norms?

Recent critics of *Impressions* favour the latter approach without fully repudiating the links to Eliot's novels. For example, James Buzard describes *Impressions* as 'a refusal to traffic in storytelling ... whose connection to Eliot's fictional practice might be found in its seeming exaggeration of a resistance to narrative not unknown to the great novels themselves'.[1] Sarah Allison calls it 'an experiment in a nineteenth-century version of neoclassical satire that grows out of the abstracting strain inherent to Eliot's realism'.[2] However, the perception of unexpected continuities does not extend to Eliot's handling of sympathy, which most critics regard as central to Eliot's art. As Buzard puts it, 'Eliot and Theophrastus recoil from the earlier novelistic argument that art must always be spreading our sympathy',[3] and Allison claims that 'the persona of Theophrastus Such is a kind of limit case of how one might make precise moral distinctions while escaping the imperative to sympathise with characters that structures Eliot's novels'.[4] Other scholars concur that *Impressions* is particularly devoid of kindness or fellow-feeling, with Fionualla Dillane calling it a 'calculated attack'[5] on Eliot's readers and Rosemarie Bodenheimer charging it with 'undisguised negativity', 'indignation', and 'disgust'.[6]

As Jonathan Farina argues, sympathy is intimately connected to the 'depth model' of character that permeates nineteenth-century fiction, and especially

DOI: 10.4324/9781003362821-12

Eliot's novels—a model that presumes that increasing our knowledge of a character's psychological interiority will enhance our understanding (and typically soften our judgements) of their outward behaviour.[7] This doctrine is roundly viewed as integral to Eliot's practice of moral realism, so its apparent absence in *Impressions* seems determinative of that text's literary and moral quality. However, Eliot does not eschew the depth model of character in *Impressions* so much as investigate sympathy by other means. By conjoining the essay and the sketch with other literary genres such as the confession and the anatomy, Eliot animates a conception of character that is more intellectualised than emotive and more socially determined than subjectively rich—a conception that is, therefore, superficial compared with the novel, but not when compared with *Impression*'s relevant generic comparands. If we are to get our impressions of *Impressions* right, we need a fuller, more historically situated sense of the text's literary and moral stakes.

Hence, in the first half of this chapter, I offer a general account of *Impressions* to clarify its generic lineage. I claim it is best understood as a confessional anatomy that reinterprets the contrast between psychological depth and surface, which is customary to the novel, as an ironic incongruity between an individual's self-perception and his or her assessment by others.[8] In the second part, I look more specifically at how the book's chapters explore the epistemology of comedy against the backdrop of nineteenth-century debates about wit, humour, and the purpose of laughter. In doing so, I show how this seemingly eccentric text straddles a recognisably Eliotic line between sympathetic humour and didactic ridicule, making it central, if not exactly to Eliot's career as a novelist, then certainly to the comic tradition in which she was working.

The Anatomy of Confession, or a Confession of Anatomy

Impressions announces at least part of its generic inheritance in its title. As many have noted, the text is inspired by the classical writings of Theophrastus, a disciple of Aristotle's, whose book of character types formalised ways of thinking about character that subsequently influenced the New Comedy of Terence and Menander.[9] Nancy Henry suggests that the surname 'Such' alludes specifically to the original Theophrastus' technique of introducing each sketch with a phrase translatable as 'such a type who',[10] with many of Eliot's essays describing a particular pattern of person or sensibility. The other explicit progenitor to Eliot's work is Jean de La Bruyère, whose *Les Caractères*, first published in 1688 and widely influential in Victorian culture, extended the Theophrastan model by illustrating character types through the activities of named individuals. In *Character and Person*, John Frow describes this 'slide from generality to personification—to the *naming* of the individual representing a type' as 'the crucial step taken beyond Theophrastus' that provided the basis for the character-based essays of Addison and Steele and, ultimately, 'the quasi-persons of the novel'.[11] On this view, Eliot's invocation of Theophrastus in the title of the work, and her quotation of La Bruyère at the start of chapter 10, imply a self-consciously anachronistic approach to character that focuses on its foundations in the stereotypes of short forms like the essay and sketch rather than the interiority of the modern novel, which privileges the illusion of characterological depth and uniqueness.[12]

At the same time, the text clearly contains features that are atypical of these earlier genres. As Dillane and Bodenheimer have noticed, Eliot investigates fluidity as well as predictability of character, and the first-person narrator draws attention to the sorts of 'novelistic' problems that occupy Eliot elsewhere, such as the dangers of egoism and the pitfalls of self-delusion. Stylistically, Eliot's work also departs from its predecessors, written with neither Theophrastus' lucid directness, nor La Bruyère's aphoristic cogency, but in an extravagantly learned and parabolic style that is far more reminiscent of Carlyle. Nor is it the case that Eliot's tone is consistently negative or ruefully judgemental, as has been said of Theophrastus and La Bruyère, both inclined to satirical sourness. On the contrary, the narrator is exquisitely conscious of his subjective motivations and shortcomings, confessing in the very first chapter that his desire to understand the characteristics of others stems from his own 'permanent longing for approbation, sympathy, and love'.[13] Rather than deliver judgements from on high, the narrator perceives that he 'cannot escape being compromised' (ch. 1), with a disposition that combines the shrewd observation of others with an ingratiating awareness of his own uncertainty and ignorance.

How to make sense of these seeming dissonances? Rather than suggest that Eliot sought a compromise between the novel and its antecedent forms, or that novelistic features persist, zombie-like, in an environment that is no longer hospitable to them, or even that the text deliberately flouts novelistic conventions so that their absence may be felt all the more sharply, it would be advantageous to give up the categorical relevance of the word 'novel' altogether. Of course, the usefulness of the term 'novel' is a long-standing critical problem, famously discussed by Northrop Frye in 1957's *Anatomy of Criticism*. There, Frye argues that 'the literary historian who identifies fiction with the novel is greatly embarrassed by the length of time that the world managed to get along without the novel',[14] and suggests that the term 'novel' should not cover all types of fiction but only one major form, the others being romance, confession, and anatomy. Although Frye concedes, like Bakhtin, that the novel tends to cannibalise surrounding genres, and that the four major types of prose fiction rarely appear in unalloyed purity, he insists that works normally regarded as hovering around the outer edges of the novel—books such as *The Pilgrim's Progress*, *Gulliver's Travels*, *The Wood Beyond the World*, and even Kierkegaard's *Either/Or*—appear less peripheral when placed in their proper generic habitats.

Frye argues that one form related to the novel but often confused with it is autobiography, since life-stories or memoirs are frequently governed by a fictionalising impulse to 'select only those events and experiences in the writer's life that go to build up an integrated pattern'.[15] Frye calls this form of autobiography 'confession', and links its origins in St. Augustine to its modern type in Rousseau, whom the narrator, throughout chapter 1, refers to in familiar terms ('Jean Jacques'). Although the chapter begins with the narrator saying, 'It is my habit to give an account to myself of the characters I meet with', the gaze immediately turns inward as he continues, 'can I give any true account of my own?' (ch. 1). In this way, the book begins by addressing itself to the epistemological difficulties not in attaining knowledge of others—the perceptual problem that characterises so many of Eliot's novels—but rather, as for Rousseau, in knowledge of the self. Accordingly, the external perspective is adamantly rejected, with the narrator insisting, 'Surely I ought to know myself better than these indifferent outsiders can know me' (ch. 1).

However, the narrator also recognises that the goal of self-knowledge is limited by the self's inevitable partiality and blindspots: 'Is it then possible to describe oneself at once faithfully and fully? In all autobiography there is, nay, ought to be, an incompleteness which may have the effect of falsity'. Because 'it is only by observing others' that the narrator can 'correct' his 'self-ignorance', he disavows autobiography as a complete or veracious form. 'I am not indeed writing an autobiography, or pretending to give an unreserved description of myself', he explains, 'but only offering some slight confessions in an apologetic light' (all ch. 1). As this statement indicates, the narrator belongs to a literary lineage that includes autobiography, confession, and even apologia, all of which are characterised by the dominance of the first-person point of view and the author's heightened self-reflexiveness. Yet what the narrator most seeks to apologise for or defend through his *Impressions* is not some idea or behaviour but rather his inability to convey the full truth about himself in either autobiographical or confessional form. This second-order scepticism is implied by the haziness of title word 'Impressions', and Eliot's original conceit of presenting herself as the editor of a ramshackle collection,[16] as if seeking to pre-empt the labour of the reader who must discern some coherent set of ideas of attitudes from the narrator's evident miscellany.[17] Whether this sort of speaker (whom most critics call 'Theophrastus', though he is never named) should even be described as a 'narrator' is debatable: while he provides a brief life history in the second chapter, and his voice dominates the whole, he doesn't narrate a story so much as provide a vehicle for reflections that lack an explicit plan or unifying set of topics. All of these features point to the other major prose form the book engages, namely anatomy, which leads it away from the subjective personalism of inward reflection and towards the more objective analysis of people and events that Eliot celebrates in her early essays, and which more assuredly encompasses character writing in the Theophrastan mode.

As Frye notes, the word 'anatomy' means 'dissection' or 'analysis' and is interchangeable with the genre of writing he calls 'Menippean satire'.[18] In

Frye's account, anatomy deals 'less with people as such than with mental attitudes', and in particular those 'diseases of the intellect'[19] that manifest as pomposity, pedantry, doctrinal extremism, and the like. Anatomy differs from the novel primarily in its approach to characterisation, which, Frye claims, is 'stylised rather than naturalistic, and presents people as mouthpieces of the ideas they represent'.[20] It is also ostentatiously intellectual, with the writer showing his 'exuberance ... by piling up an enormous mass of erudition about his theme or in overwhelming his pedantic targets with an avalanche of their own jargon'.[21] *Impressions* clearly approximates each point of this description, with the narrator focusing upon character types who tend not to realise the extent of their intellectual limitations, and doing so in a style that is sometimes forbiddingly erudite. The faults he dwells upon include plagiarism, diffidence, rigidity, over-confidence, and insincerity—all presented as deficiencies of intellectual suppleness, nuance, and flexibility. These problems lead to a gap between a person's self-perception and social performance, calling for the triangulating perspective of the Theophrastan observer as corrective (whether the narrator observes the characters or the reader observes the narrator[22]). In its more satirical forms, anatomy also foregrounds connections to the comedy of humours, another typological genre, and to the diagnostic and taxonomical impulses of nineteenth-century medicine, sociology, and natural science, in which Eliot was intensely interested and learned.

If the conceptual basis for the anatomising impulses of Eliot's social novels was laid in 'The Natural History of German Life' (1856), Carlyle's *Sartor Resartus* (1833–34), perhaps the greatest example of confessional anatomy in the nineteenth century,[23] provides the nearest point of comparison for *Impressions*. In an essay of 1855, Eliot praised Carlyle in superlative terms, stating 'there is hardly a superior or active mind of this generation that has not been modified by Carlyle's writings', and 'that many of the men who have the least agreement with his opinions are those to whom the reading of *Sartor Resartus* was an epoch in the history of their minds'.[24] Fionualla Dillane has sensitised critics to the long-standing influence of Eliot's periodical writing on her later writings, and it is certainly suggestive that *Sartor Resartus* also has a basis in periodical culture: first published in *Fraser's Magazine*, the work purports to be a biographical review of a German philosophical treatise, but widens into a far-reaching investigation of British intellectual and moral culture. Kerry McSweeney notes that Carlyle once considered as a title for the work, 'Thoughts on Clothes; or the Life and Opinions of Herr. D. Teufelsdröckh D.U.J', an allusion to Sterne's *The Life and Opinions of Tristram Shandy* (1760–67),[25] which, Frye observes, contains many 'features that belong to the anatomy', such as 'the digressing narrative, the catalogues, the stylising of character along "humor" lines ... and the constant ridicule of philosophers and pedantic critics'.[26] One may establish a persuasive genealogy, therefore, stretching from Sterne, to Carlyle, to Eliot, with each text using a first-person narrator to orchestrate a hybrid text that blends autobiographical confession with satirical and humoural analysis, treating each with a fluctuating (and sometimes dubious) gravitas that extends the concerns of the text well beyond its purported 'story' or topic (whether that 'story' refer to the character of the narrator or the characters he examines).

Eliot's equivocation over 'whether it will be better to say simply "By George Eliot" or "Edited by George Eliot"'[27] on the title page to *Impressions* may suggest an anxiety about hewing too closely to the Carlylean model. For, in *Sartor Resartus*, the voice of Carlyle's faux-editor assumes a stature almost equal to Teufelsdröckh's, an assertion of presence that Eliot, for reasons adumbrated by others, may have wished to avoid at this moment in her career.[28] She may also have wished to avoid excessive overlap with another comparatively neglected contribution to Victorian confessional anatomy, Matthew Arnold's *Friendship's Garland* (1871), a collection of essays whose full subtitle—*Being the Conversations, Letters and Opinions of the Late Arminius Baron Von Thunder-Ten-Tronckh, Collected and Edited with a Dedicatory Letter to Adolescens Leo, Esq., of the 'Daily Telegraph', by Matthew Arnold*—recalls both Sterne and especially Carlyle in its effort to collect the diverse views of a German metaphysician with an inarticulable surname.[29] Building on Carlyle's model, Arnold intensifies the tradition's self-reflexiveness by including himself as a protagonist in the genre, creating fictional letters that interpolate him as a character in the Baron's correspondence. However, the diffident and intellectually stiffened Arnold who appears in *Friendship's Garland* is clearly a self-parody or a mask, infusing the text with what Brian Nellist calls a 'serious playfulness'[30] as it ranges haphazardly over issues such as patriotism and public education.

When this history of influences is considered, then, it becomes evident that Eliot's *Impressions* is less an eccentric experiment in the future of the novel than a carefully considered contribution to a form of writing that had already been practised by two of the nineteenth-century's most significant moralists and stylists—three, if you include the Menippean satire of Thackeray's *Book of Snobs* (1848). In this context, the phrase 'serious playfulness' is especially suggestive, for the British tradition of confessional anatomy is a distinctly comedic genre, not funny in the modern sense of seeking to arouse laughter but comic in its analysis of human relations. In order to understand this literary sensibility, it is necessary to revisit the rich theory of wit and humour that emerged in the eighteenth and nineteenth centuries and exerted a powerful influence on Victorian culture, and in relation to which Eliot's *Impressions* is less a curious outlier than a decisive intervention.

'The Ridiculous Must Be Seen Where It Exists'

The most comprehensive account of Victorian comic theory may be found in Daniel Wickberg's now-classic study, *The Senses of Humour* (1998).[31] According to Wickberg, the idea of a 'sense of humour', or the capacity to laugh genially at ourselves and others, is a nineteenth-century invention whose origins may be traced to medieval physiology. According to the earlier science, one's humour, or bodily temperament, was equivalent to one's biological make-up, with an excess of black bile producing a melancholic temperament, blood manifesting as sanguinity, and the like. In the Jonsonian comedy of humours, exaggerated versions of these temperaments were set up for mockery or ridicule, in line with the Hobbesian conception of laughter as a 'sudden glory'[32] that registers the superiority of the mocking person in comparison to a deformed subject.[33] However, over time, a new sense of egalitarian personhood changed the way that 'humour' was understood: individuals may differ in striking ways, but they are morally equal and universally unique. As a result, 'the man with a sense of humour was the man capable of seeing the objective Jonsonian humor within himself',[34] and to have a 'sense of humor' meant to cultivate a 'quality of mind'[35] that was amused by our universal eccentricities. Wickberg observes that the nature of laughter changed as well: 'humor came to mean both a sympathetic laughing with others and a laughing at oneself',[36] expressed in a spirit of humble fellowship rather than judgemental derision.

As we have seen, the narrator of *Impressions* toggles between an external awareness of the faults of others and an inward sense of his own limitations, and in this way exemplifies the combination of objective and subjective perception that Wickberg argues is crucial for an effective sense of humour. For example, in 'Looking Inward', the narrator acknowledges, 'I must still come under the common fatality of mankind to share the liability to be absurd without knowing I am absurd', and notes that he became cognisant of this problem 'only by observing the self-ignorance of others' (ch. 1). Later on, he confesses:

> It is my way when I observe any instance of folly, any queer habit, any absurd illusion, straightway to look for something of the same type in myself, feeling sure that amid all differences there will be a certain correspondence.
>
> (ch. 13)

On this view, 'introspection' becomes a process of 'finding out one's own absurdities' (ch. 13), a dynamic that is risible, good-natured, and sympathetic:

> Thus if I laugh at you, O fellow-men … it is not that I feel myself aloof from you: the more intimately I seem to discern your weaknesses, the stronger to me is the proof that I share them.
>
> (ch. 1)

The narrator's preoccupation with sympathetic laughter, which is egalitarian and communal rather than superior and self-flattering, is so overt that many readers of *Impressions* simply overlook its prominence. Belying received ideas about the text's lack of unity, the end of the first chapter fulfils, in plain sight, the usual function of providing an overarching topic or argument for the text: 'That a gratified sense of superiority is at the root of barbarous laughter may be at least half the truth. But there is a loving laughter in which the only recognised superiority is that of the ideal self' (ch. 1).

Eliot's interest in the nature of comic laughter persists across the text and is further prepared by the biographical details offered in chapter 2. In reviewing his childhood, the narrator celebrates his 'impartiality' (ch. 2) to historical periods, noting that the temptation to assume one's temporal superiority is an illusion that ignores the persistence of folly through time. When the narrator writes, 'I gather, too, from the undeniable testimony of his disciple Theophrastus that there were bores, ill-bred persons, and detractors even in Athens, of species remarkably corresponding to the English' (ch. 2), he underscores the 'universal existence' (ch. 2), or omnipresence of particularity, to which the Victorian sense of humour was especially sensitive. Far from 'boasting about enlightenment', the narrator cherishes his father's legacy as a country parson because he was 'well acquainted with all ranks of his neighbours' and lacked the 'misfortune of high birth' that 'shuts a man out of from the large sympathetic knowledge of human experience which comes from contact with various classes on their own level' (all ch. 2). This cosmopolitan perspective—the narrator describes himself as 'a modern with some interest in advocating tolerance' who inhabits the 'Nation of London' rather than some narrow aristocratic milieu (ch. 2)—reflects what Wickberg calls 'the triumph of a subjectivist notion of humor as a mode of perception associated with benevolence, sympathy, tolerance, and democracy'.[37]

The next chapter, 'How We Encourage Research', offers an example of this sensibility in action by focusing on a critique of its opposite, presenting a case in which laughter is deployed for the purpose of cruelty and exclusion rather than sympathetic understanding. Merman is an amateur historian whose strength is intellectual curiosity and whose weakness is self-love. He enjoys his hobby of research as long as he maintains the ineffectuality of the dilettante, but once he criticises Grampus, an authority in the field, the professionals close ranks and seek to undercut the pretender. They do so primarily through ridicule, the witty form of character assassination (as well as truth-seeking, a function ironically abandoned here[38]) popular in the eighteenth century but which, as Stuart Tave argues, was later replaced by a friendlier ideal of good nature and amiable bonhomie.[39] In the hands of Grampus' confederates, clever phrases get weaponised as mocking terms of abuse, and the sequence of interactions becomes a veritable battlefield of discourse: Merman is ultimately defeated because 'the sharp epigrams with which the victim was lacerated, and the soaring fountains of acrid mud which were shot upward and poured over the fresh wounds, were found amusing in recital' (ch. 3). According to Tave, 'raillery was the aristocratic social mode of intelligence, carefully distinguished from the merely stupid backbiting or insulting effrontery of the witlings',[40] and the narrator parodies that elitism here by associating the 'laugh of the initiated' with the professionals' wish to see an aspiring non-member 'punished' (ch. 3). A similar, if inverted, dynamic may be observed in chapter 10, 'Debasing the Moral Currency', which deals with cases in which small-minded people assert their 'superiority' over greater exemplars by yanking them down through parody and burlesque. In making anything and everything the object of laughter, such figures degrade spiritual ideals, instilling the 'moral imbecility of an inward giggle at that which might have stimulated their high emulation or fed the fountains of compassion, trust, and constancy' (ch. 10). The solution is not to eschew laughter, even about serious topics, but to channel it appropriately towards appropriate ends. As the narrator quotes La Bruyère: 'le ridicule qui est quelque part, il faut l'y voir, l'en tirer avec grâce et d'une manière qui plaise and qui instruise',[41] which 'depends on a discrimination only compatible with the varied sensibilities which give sympathetic insight, and with the justice of perception which is another name for grave knowledge' (ch. 10).

Throughout *Impressions*, the narrator insists that he is neither 'indiscriminately' laughing nor 'deficient' in his 'sense of the ludicrous' (ch. 10). Instead, he claims that the comic observation of 'absurdities', when rightly conducted and universally applied, produces 'shocks of laughter and its irrepressible smiles' (ch. 10) that are wholesome and morally instructive. Still, many readers of *Impressions* register the presence of a satirical bitterness that lacks this generosity or warmth, particularly when the narrator targets unwitting or good-natured individuals. For example, in chapter 4, 'A Man Surprised at His Own Originality', the narrator dedicates considerable space to 'the egoistic claims' that are 'hidden under an apparent neutrality' of Lentelus, an 'unpretending' society man whose casual judgements suggest a whiff of superiority or smugness. Though Lentelus is blithely unconscious of his effect, the narrator resents the fact that Lentelus 'was a less remarkable man than he had seemed to imply' (ch. 4); hence, when the narrator gives thanks at the end of the chapter for 'the man who, having nothing to say, abstains from giving us wordy evidence of the fact', his tone feels more contemptuous than corrective. Conversely, chapter 5 quibbles with a 'too deferential man', Hinze, who is as profuse with his praise as Lentelus is withholding. Even though the narrator acknowledges that Hinze, like most people, is governed by the 'promptings of a wish to be agreeable' and remains 'unconscious of falsity', he nonetheless confesses to 'rage' when Hinze responds with 'reverent wonder' to the commonplace observations of a friend (all ch. 5). Similarly, chapter 7 deals with the paradoxical case of Spike, whose personal interests coincide with an enthusiasm for 'public benefit', and who is led by self-interest into progressive politics. In an oblique reference to Adam Smith's 'invisible hand', the narrator discounts whatever good works Spike might inspire because he lacks a disinterested intention. In each of these cases, the bar for virtue is set high enough that the narrator's criticisms start to sound like cavils, and the reader begins to wonder if the narrator lacks the sense of humour about universal foibles that he otherwise proffers as an antidote to misanthropy and cynicism.

There are further grounds for this suspicion. In an essay of 1876 called 'Humour', Eliot's sometime editor Leslie Stephen laments the fact that 'a fashion has sprung up of late years of regarding the sense of humour as one of the cardinal virtues'.[42] Stephen attributes the origin of this fashion to Carlyle, whose 'humour is so genuine and keen and his personality so vigorous that he has fairly bullied us into accepting this view of the immeasurable value of humour in the world';[43] so when it comes to defining humour, Stephen distances himself from the Carlylean model. In a well-known review of the writings of Jean-Paul Richter from 1827, Carlyle had argued that 'true humour springs not more from the head than from the heart; it is not contempt, its essence is love; it issues not in laughter, but in still smiles, which lie far deeper'.[44] With this review in mind, Abigail Bloom argues that Carlyle's use of humour to 'change the world' went 'beyond any of the theories of humor current in England',[45] but the claim is only partly true. As Robert Martin shows, Carlyle's conception of humour derives from an eighteenth-century opposition between dispassionate wit, associated with 'language and idea and intellect',[46] and sentimental humour, rooted in the sympathy and the heart.[47] Martin argues that this view dominated the early and mid-Victorian period—best exemplified in Thackeray's *Lectures on the English Humorists* (1853) and Dickens' novels—yet inspired distrust in a number of later critics such as Stephen, who were repulsed by its evolution into an overly indulgent and mawkish sentimentality. Hence, Stephen contrasts wit, which is 'purely intellectual',[48] with humour, which he calls a 'morbid secretion',[49] and suggests that modern humour lacks the 'manly … vigour'[50] of its eighteenth-century predecessors, who were comparatively 'savage' and 'reckless'.[51] Still, Stephen's main target is not humour itself—he grants that 'the true humorist dwells upon the contrasts of life … to teach us the most important of lessons'[52]—but an excessively cheerful form of humour that mollifies rather than instructs: 'A gentle optimism is the most popular of creeds, for we all want some excuse for turning away our eyes from certain facts'.[53]

It is likely that Eliot was familiar with Stephen's essay, which owes a debt to Eliot's own views about comic theory as presented in 'German Wit: Henrich Heine', a review essay of 1856, which, until *Impressions,* constituted her most sustained exploration of the subject. Her essay begins by quoting Goethe's statement that 'nothing … is more significant of men's character than what they find laughable'[54] and praises the 'high order of wit' that distinguishes the cultivated man from the 'jocularity' of the 'vulgar'.[55] The first pages of the essay seem to privilege wit, which Eliot associates with 'a ripe and strong mental development'.[56] 'Humor is of earlier growth' and 'has more affinity with the poetic tendencies', being rooted in 'situations and characteristics' rather than the 'ratiocinative intellect'.[57] Humour, in other words, is organic and sympathetic, and deals with 'incongruous elements in human nature and life', whereas wit is 'brief and sudden, and sharply defined like a crystal', and less susceptible to emotion or moralising.[58] As Louise Lee has noted, 'Critics have historically had a problem with Eliot and wit specifically—as opposed to the apparently more warmly inclusive humour—because it appears inimical to sympathy',[59] but others have shown how Eliot's comic sense is neither un-sympathetic nor anodyne. For example, Regina Barreca disputes Virginia Woolf's characterisation of Eliot's humour as 'broad' and 'homespun', arguing that the author 'manages to combine laughter and invective effectively'.[60] George Scott Christian shows how, in the Heine essay, Eliot does not privilege wit over humour (a view first popularised by Robert Martin[61]), but rather praises Heine precisely because he combines sympathetic humour with satirical 'scorching'.[62] And R.J. Jenkins, lamenting the general tendency to presume Eliot's seriousness, provides a long list of compliments from contemporaneous writers for her 'comedy' and 'humour', including R.H. Hutton's belief that in *Middlemarch* 'George Eliot laughs at the common modes of thought and feeling much more than with them'.[63] According to Jenkins, critics who emphasise Eliot's sympathetic humour on one hand, or sage-like wit on the other, overlook the extent to which she enjoys what she calls, in the Heine essay, 'barbaric humour', the rough satire or lively jeering that generates laughter for its own sake.[64]

Cleary, Eliot's comic sensibility is complicated, and this complexity is central to the project of *Impressions*. On one hand, the book argues for the dignity of eccentricity as the object of humorous tolerance, providing a more positive conception of egotism than Eliot is generally allowed. In 'Humour', Stephen argues that every 'humorist must also be an egotist' because 'the oddities of his own character give him utmost delight',[65] and Eliot's narrator generates a considerable amount of pleasure through critical introspections of this kind. In the final chapter, 'The Modern Hep! Hep! Hep!', he defends the egotism of an entire nation by citing J.S. Mill's belief that 'from the freedom of individual men to persist in idiosyncrasies the world may be enriched' (ch. 18). On the other hand, the book's account of egotism is distinctly double-edged, and several chapters (as in many of Eliot's works) reveal the dangers that occur when egotism is unaccustomed to correction. For example, in chapter 8, 'The Watch-Dog of Knowledge', we see another well-meaning person, Mordax, 'an admirable man, ardent in intellectual work, public-spirited, affectionate', whose inability to admit 'he has been in the wrong' is a major rather than minor failing. Like Touchwood in the preceding chapter, 'Only Temper', he becomes violent and tyrannical when his 'Conceited Ignorance' (ch. 8) is challenged.

In its cautionary portrayal of wounded vanity, *Impressions* invites comparison with George Meredith's *The Egoist,* which was also published in 1879 and with which there are many suggestive parallels. For example, in their first chapters, both texts imagine the world as a 'great book'[66] whose many pages condense into the forms of different yet recognisable characters, and both texts condemn the 'stupidity of a murmuring self-occupation' (*TS,* ch. 1).[67] But *The Egoist* represents what happens when anatomy evolves into the novel, with Meredith focusing on the personal relations of a few well-rounded characters. In contrast, *Impressions* shows what happens when character transforms into sophisticated caricature, with complex persons reduced to their most symptomatic parts. An even better comparison with Meredith would invoke *An Essay on Comedy, and the Uses of the Comic Spirit,* which Meredith published in 1877, and which does much to clarify the theoretical background and tone of Eliot's work. Although some critics have found this tone to be unpleasantly Swiftian, the narrator, as we have seen, is less a denunciatory judge than a self-conscious diagnostician who does not exempt himself from the book's portrayal of ignorance and self-deception: 'Dear blunderers, I am one of you. I wince at the fact, but I am not ignorant of it, that I too am laughable on unsuspected occasions' (ch. 1). The laughter underscored here is not the hard-hearted laughter of derision or mockery, but rather what Meredith calls the 'humanely malign'[68] laughter of the comic spirit, which addresses itself to 'the wits'[69] or 'men's intellects'[70] without necessarily chilling the kindness of the heart. According to Meredith,

> you may estimate your capacity for Comic perception by being able to detect the ridicule of them you love, without loving them less: and more by being able to see yourself somewhat ridiculous in dear eyes, and accepting the correction their image of you proposes.[71]

Eliot's narrator expresses a similar sentiment when he declares, 'in noting the weaknesses of my acquaintances I am conscious of my fellowship with them' (ch. 1). *Impressions,* then, is a comedy in the Meredithian mode, produced at a time when the nature of humour was a topic of lively theoretical discussion. But the sympathy that undergirds the narrator's feeling of fellowship does not arise from a novelistic familiarity with human beings in their deepest interiority but rather from the impersonal or typological view granted by what Meredith calls the 'general mind'.[72] As in a novel, generalities about human nature get instantiated by particular exemplars. But Eliot's book of 'well-founded ridicule' (ch. 1) mainly targets abstracted personifications of common sense (or non-sense), anatomising the egotism of confession, with both sympathy and spite, through the genre of confessional anatomy.

Notes

1 James Buzard, '*Impressions of Theophrastus Such:* "Not a Story"', in *A Companion to George Eliot,* ed. Amanda Anderson and Harry E. Shaw (Chichester: Wiley-Blackwell, 2013), 205.

2 Sarah Allison, *Reductive Reading: A Syntax of Victorian Moralizing* (Baltimore: Johns Hopkins University Press, 2018), 85.

3 Buzard, '*Impressions*', 209.

4 Allison, *Syntax*, 85.

5 Fionnuala Dillane, *Before George Eliot: Marian Evans and the Periodical Press* (Cambridge: Cambridge University Press, 2013), 169.

6 Rosemarie Bodenheimer, 'George Eliot's Last Stand: *Impressions of Theophrastus Such*', *Victorian Literature and Culture*, 44.3 (2016), 607.

7 Jonathan Farina, *Everyday Words and the Character of Prose in Nineteenth-Century Britain* (Cambridge: Cambridge University Press, 2017), 38. Farina's conception of character depth draws on Andrea K. Henderson, *Romantic Identities: Varieties of Subjectivity, 1774-1830* (Cambridge: Cambridge University Press, 1996). For a different conceptualisation of surface and depth with respect to *Impressions*, see S. Pearl Brilmyer, '"The Natural History of My Inward Self": Sensing Character in George Eliot's *Impressions of Theophrastus Such*', *PMLA*, 129.1 (2014), 35–51.

8 Scott Thompson explores a similar dynamic, though his contexts are more psycho-scientific than literary; see 'Subjective Realism and Diligent Imagination: G.H. Lewes' Theory of Psychology and George Eliot's *Impressions of Theophrastus Such*', *Victorian Review*, 44.2 (Fall 2018), 197–214.

9 For the fullest discussions, see Nancy Henry, 'Introduction', *Impressions of Theophrastus Such*, ed. Nancy Henry (Iowa: University of Iowa Press, 1994), xii–xx and Dillane, *Before George Eliot*, 171–2 and 179–82.

10 Henry, 'Introduction', xvii.

11 John Frow, *Character and Person* (Oxford: Oxford University Press, 2014), 110.

12 The relationship between person and type, or individual and species, is a major topic of nineteenth-century aesthetic and scientific thought. However, as Catherine Gallagher writes, 'Fictional characters may *refer* to people in the world by conforming to type, but they only *resemble* people in their *non*conformity'. See Catherine Gallagher, 'George Eliot: Immanent Victorian', *Representations*, 90.1 (Spring 2005), 66.

13 George Eliot, *Impressions of Theophrastus Such*, ed. Nancy Henry (Iowa: University of Iowa Press, 1994), ch. 1. All subsequent references to this edition will be made parenthetically in text.

14 Northrop Frye, *Anatomy of Criticism* (Princeton: Princeton University Press, 1957), 303.

15 Frye, *Anatomy*, 307.

16 Dillane, *Before George Eliot*, 171.

17 For Bodenheimer, '*Impressions* is a miscellany shaped by no overall plan, no idea of development,' though this desultory surface conceals 'themes' and 'typical concerns' that 'are often recognizable as distilled versions of characters and situations in George Eliot's novels' ('George Eliot's Last Stand', 608). Dillane offers the most robust (if narrowly conceived) defence of the text's implicit unity, reading it as an 'attack on the ways the periodical press in particular (and not just intellectual culture in general) cultivates types of intellectual discourses that are personality-focused, often commercially oriented, and that as a result, narrow and demean cultural life' (*Before George Eliot*, 169).

18 Frye, *Anatomy*, 311–2.

19 Frye, *Anatomy*, 309.

20 Frye, *Anatomy*, 309.

21 Frye, *Anatomy*, 311.

22 Scholars who emphasise the reader's role in examining the narrator as a character include Henry, 'Introduction', xx; Thompson, 'Subjective Realism', 205–6; and Bodenheimer, 'George Eliot's Last Stand', 607.

23 Frye claims that *Sartor Resartus* is a 'hybrid' form, joining confession with anatomy, and compares it to Kierkeegard's *Either/Or* (*Anatomy*, 312-3). He also notes that the 'later novels' of George Eliot are 'influenced by the anatomy' (313), though it is doubtful that he was familiar with *Impressions* (which is certainly not a 'novel') at his time of writing.

24 George Eliot, *Selected Essays, Poems, and Other Writings*, ed. A.S. Byatt (London: Penguin, 1990), 344.

25 Kerry McSweeny, 'Introduction', *Sartor Resartus*, by Thomas Carlyle, ed. Kerry McSweeney (Oxford: Oxford University Press, 1991), xiv.

26 Frye, *Anatomy*, 312.

27 George Eliot, Letter to John Blackwood (22 March 1989), in *The Letters of George Eliot*, 9 vols, ed. Gordon S. Haight (New Haven and London: Yale University Press, 1954–78), 7: 119.

28 For Eliot's personal and professional history in relation to the 'character' (or mask) of the narrator, see Dillane, *Before George Eliot*, ch. 5; Henry, 'Introduction', vii-xv; and Bodenheimer, 'George Eliot's Last Stand', 607–12.

29 The placename of the title—Thunder-ten-Tronckh—also recalls Voltaire's *Candide*, whose eponymous hero hails from the same location.

30 Brian Nellist, 'Disconcerting the Reader: *Friendship's Garland* and the True Voices of "Mr. Arnold"', *Essays and Studies*, 41 (1988), 30.

31 Daniel Wickberg, *The Senses of Humour: Self and Laughter in Modern America* (Ithaca: Cornell University Press, 1998). *Pace* its subtitle, Wickberg's book is primarily concerned with the intellectual history of the idea of the sense of humour as it evolved in eighteenth- and nineteenth-century Britain.

32 Thomas Hobbes, *Leviathan* (1651), quoted in Wickberg, *Senses of Humour*, 48.

33 For a fuller account of the 'superiority' theory of laughter, see Wickberg, *Senses of Humour*, 46–57. For other useful accounts of Victorian comic theory and its antecedents, see Stuart Tave, *The Amiable Humorist: A Study in the Comic Theory and Criticism of the Eighteenth and Early Nineteenth Centuries* (Chicago: University of Chicago Press, 1960) and Robert Bernard Martin, *The Triumph of Wit: A Study of Victorian Comic Theory* (Oxford: Clarendon Press, 1974).

34 Wickberg, *Senses of Humour*, 101.

35 Wickberg, *Senses of Humour*, 25.

36 Wickberg, *Senses of Humour*, 67.

37 Wickberg, *Senses of Humour*, 196.

38 On ridicule as a 'test of truth', see Wickberg, *Senses of Humour*, 72.

39 On ridicule and raillery, see Tave, *Amiable Humorist*, 16–39.

40 Tave, *Amiable Humorist*, 16.

41 In Henry's translation: 'the ridiculous must be seen where it exists, and some of it pointed out with a grace and in a manner which pleases and instructs' (see 177, ch. 10, n. 2).

42 Leslie Stephen, 'Humour', *Cornhill Magazine*, 33.195 (March 1876), 318.

43 Stephen, 'Humour', 319.

44 Thomas Carlyle, *The Works of Thomas Carlyle*, ed. Henry Duff Traill (New York: AMS, 1980), vol. 26, 17.

45 Abigail Burnham Bloom, 'Transcendence through Incongruity: The Background of Humor in Carlyle's *Sartor Resartus*', in *The Victorian Comic Spirit*, ed. Jennifer A. Wagner-Law (London: Routledge, 2017), 153.

46 Martin, *Triumph of Wit*, ix.

47 Martin, *Triumph of Wit*, 2.

48 Stephen, 'Humour', 319.

49 Stephen, 'Humour', 320.

50 Stephen, 'Humour', 326.

51 Stephen, 'Humour', 326.

52 Stephen, 'Humour', 323.

53 Stephen, 'Humour', 325.

54 George Eliot, 'German Wit: Henrich Heine,' in *Selected Essays*, ed. Byatt, 69.

55 Eliot, 'German Wit', 69.

56 Eliot, 'German Wit', 69.

57 Eliot, 'German Wit', 70.

58 Eliot, 'German Wit', 70.

59 Louise Lee, 'George Eliot's Jokes,' in *Victorian Comedy and Laughter: Conviviality, Jokes, and Dissent*, ed. Louise Lee (London: Palgrave Macmillan, 2020), 168.

60 Regina Barreca, *Untamed and Unabashed: Essays on Women and Humor in British Literature* (Detroit: Wayne State University Press, 1994), 82–3.

61 See Martin, *Triumph of Wit*, 82–5.

62 George Scott Christian, 'Comic George Eliot', *The George Eliot Review*, 34 (2003), 24.

63 Quoted in R.J. Jenkins, 'Laughing with George Eliot', *The George Eliot Review*, 37 (2006), 43.

64 Jenkins, 'Laughing', 41.

65 Stephen, 'Humour', 320.

66 See *TS*, ch. 1, and George Meredith, *The Egoist,* ed. George Woodcock (London: Penguin, 1987), 35.

67 Compare to Meredith's, 'The Egoist surely inspires pity. He who would desire to clothe himself at everybody's expense, and is of that desire condemned to strip himself stark naked … might be taken for the actual person' (*The Egoist*, 36).

68 George Meredith, *An Essay on Comedy, and the Uses of the Comic Spirit* (London: A. Constable, 1903), 90.

69 Meredith, *Essay*, 70.

70 Meredith, *Essay*, 90.

71 Meredith, *Essay*, 83.

72 Meredith, *Essay*, 90.

Works Cited

Works by George Eliot

Eliot, George. *Adam Bede*, ed. Carol Martin (1859; Oxford: Oxford World's Classics, 2008).

[Eliot, George]. 'The Art of the Ancients', *The Leader*, 6 (March 1855), 257–8.

Eliot, George. *The Complete Shorter Poetry of George Eliot*, ed. Antonie Gerard van der Broek, 2 vols (London: Pickering and Chatto, 2005).

Eliot, George. *Daniel Deronda*, ed. Graham Handley (1876; Oxford: Oxford World's Classics, 2014).

Eliot George. *Felix Holt, the Radical*, ed. Fred C. Thomson (1866; Oxford: Oxford World's Classics, 1988).

Eliot, George. *The George Eliot Letters*, 9 vols, ed. Gordon S. Haight (New Haven and London: Yale University Press, 1954–78).

Eliot, George. *Essays of George Eliot*, ed. Thomas Pinney (London and New York: Routledge and Kegan Paul, 1963).

[Eliot, George]. 'Heine's Poems', *The Leader*, 6 (September 1855), 843–4.

[Eliot, George]. 'History, Biography, Voyages and Travels', *Westminster Review*, 67 (January 1857), 288–306.

Eliot, George. *Impressions of Theophrastus Such*, ed. Nancy Henry (1879; Iowa: University of Iowa Press, 1994).

Eliot, George. *The Journals of George Eliot*, ed. Margaret Harris and Judith Johnston (Cambridge: Cambridge University Press, 1998).

Eliot, George. *The Lifted Veil; Brother Jacob*, ed. Helen Small (Oxford: Oxford University Press, 2009).

[Eliot, George]. 'Liszt, Wagner, and Weimar', *Fraser's Magazine* (July 1855), 48–62.

[Eliot, George]. 'Margaret Fuller's Letters from Italy', *The Leader*, 7 (17 May 1856), 475.

Eliot, George. *Middlemarch: A Study of Provincial Life*, ed. David R. Carroll (1872; Oxford: Oxford World's Classics, 1998/2019).

Eliot, George. *The Mill on the Floss*, ed. Gordon S. Haight and Juliette Atkinson (1860; Oxford: Oxford World's Classics, 2015).

Eliot, George. *Romola*, ed. Andrew Brown (1863; Oxford: Oxford University Press, 1994).

Eliot, George. *Scenes of Clerical Life*, ed. Josie Billington and Thomas Noble (1858; Oxford: Oxford World's Classics, 2015).

Eliot, George. *Selected Critical Writings*, ed. Rosemary Ashton (Oxford: Oxford University Press, 2000).

Eliot, George. *Selected Essays, Poems and Other Writings*, ed. A.S. Byatt and Nicholas Warren (Harmondsworth: Penguin, 1991).

[Eliot, George]. 'Sight-seeing in Germany and the Tyrol', *The Saturday Review* (6 September 1856), 424–5.

Eliot, George. *The Spanish Gypsy*, ed. Antonie Gerard van der Broek (1868; London: Pickering and Chatto, 2008).

[Eliot, George]. 'Three Months in Weimar', *Fraser's Magazine* (June 1855), 699–706.

Other sources

Albrecht, Thomas. 'Sympathy and Telepathy: The Problem of Ethics in George Eliot's "The Lifted Veil"', *English Literary History*, 73.2 (2006), 437–63.

[Allardyce, Alexander]. 'George Eliot', *Blackwood's Magazine* (February 1881), 255–68.

Allison, Mark. 'Utopian Socialism, Women's Emancipation and the Origins of *Middlemarch*', *English Literary History*, 78.3 (Fall 2011), 715–39.

Allison, Sarah. *Reductive Reading: A Syntax of Victorian Moralizing* (Baltimore: Johns Hopkins University Press, 2018).

Anderson, Amanda. *The Powers of Distance: Cosmopolitanism and the Cultivation of Detachment* (Princeton: Princeton University Press, 2001).

Anderson, Amanda and Harry E. Shaw. 'Introduction', in *A Companion to George Eliot*, ed. Amanda Anderson and Harry E. Shaw (Chichester: Wiley-Blackwell, 2013), 1–18.

Anderson, George K. *The Legend of the Wandering Jew* (Providence: Brown University Press, 1970).

Anger, Suzy. 'George Eliot and Philosophy', in *The Cambridge Companion to George Eliot*, ed. George Levine and Nancy Henry (Cambridge: Cambridge University Press, 2019), 215–35.

Anon, ed. *Essays on Reform* (London: Macmillan, 1867).

Anon. 'The *Bulletin* Favours—', *Sydney Bulletin* (17 November 1894), 2.

Anon. 'Englishwomen in Recent Literature', *The Atlantic Monthly*, 44 (1879), 611–22.

Anon. 'George Eliot', *Saturday Review*, 69 (15 February 1890), 2040–5.

Anon. 'The Improved Character of the Government', *Tait's Edinburgh Magazine*, n.s. 1.7 (August 1834), 433–8.

Anon. '*National Life and Character*', *Saturday Review*, 75 (1894), 209–10.

Anon. 'Review of *Marcella*', *Edinburgh Review* (July 1894), 108–30.

Anon. 'Three Small Books by Great Writers', *Fraser's Magazine*, 115 (July 1879), 103–24.

Appadurai, Arjun. *Modernity at Large: Cultural Dimensions of Globalization* (Minneapolis: University of Minnesota Press, 1996).

Armstrong, Heather V. *Character and Ethical Development in Three Novels of George Eliot:* Middlemarch, Romola, Daniel Deronda (Lewiston: Edwin Mellen Press, 2001).

Armstrong, Isobel and Carolyn Burdett. 'Introduction', *19: Interdisciplinary Studies in the Long Nineteenth Century*, 29 (2020), 1–2.

Arnett, James. 'Daniel Deronda, Professor of Spinoza', *Victorian Literature and Culture*, 44.4 (2016), 833–54.

Arnold, Jean, Lila Marz Harper, and Thomas Pinney. 'Introduction', in *George Eliot: Interdisciplinary Essays*, ed. Jean Arnold and Lila Marz Harper (London: Palgrave, 2019), 1–15.

Ashton, Rosemary. *G.H. Lewes: An Unconventional Victorian* (London: Pimlico, 2000).

Ashton, Rosemary. *George Eliot. A Life* (London: Penguin, 1996).

Ashton, Rosemary. 'How George Eliot Came to Write Fiction', *The George Eliot Review*, 40 (2009), 7–13.

Astley, John. *Nuneaton Diary: Memorandum Book of Occurrences 1810–1845*, 9 vols, Nuneaton Library and Information Centre, MS.

Atkinson, Juliette. 'Critical Responses: 1970-Present', in *George Eliot in Context*, ed. Margaret Harris (Cambridge: Cambridge University Press, 2013), 83–91.

Baker, William. *George Eliot and Judaism* (Salzburg: Universität Salzburg, 1975).

Baker, William. 'A New George Eliot Manuscript', in *George Eliot: Centenary Essays and an Unpublished Fragment*, ed. Anne Smith (London: Vision, 1980), 9–20.

Bamford, Samuel. *Passages in the Life of a Radical, and Early Days*, 2 vols, ed. Henry Dunckley (London: T. Fisher Unwin, 1893).

Bandyopadhyay, Bibhutibhushan. *Pather Panchali: Song of the Road*, tr. T.W. Clark and T. Mukherji (London: George Allen and Unwin, 1968).

Barreca, Regina. *Untamed and Unabashed: Essays on Women and Humor in British Literature* (Detroit: Wayne State University Press, 1994).

Beer, Gillian. *Darwin's Plots: Evolutionary Narrative in Darwin, George Eliot and Nineteenth-Century Fiction*, 3rd edn (1983; 2000; Cambridge: Cambridge University Press, 2009).

Beer, Gillian. *George Eliot* (Sussex: Harvester, 1986).

Beer, Gillian. *George Eliot and the Woman Question* (1986; Brighton: Edward Everett Root, 2019).

Berry, Mark. *Treacherous Bonds and Laughing Fire: Politics and Religion in Wagner's Ring* (London: Ashgate, 2016).

Bhabha, Homi. 'Of Mimicry and Man: The Ambivalence of Colonial Discourse', in *The Location of Culture*, ed. Homi K. Bhabha (London and New York: Routledge, 1994), 85–92.

Birrell, Augustine. 'The Bona-Fide Traveller', *Speaker* (26 April 1890), 452–3.

Bloom, Abigail Burnham. 'Transcendence through Incongruity: The Background of Humor in Carlyle's *Sartor Resartus*', in *The Victorian Comic Spirit*, ed. Jennifer A. Wagner-Law (London: Routledge, 2017), 153–72.

Bloom, Harold. *Novelists and Novels: A Collection of Critical Essays* (New York: Checkmark Books, 2007).

Bloom, Harold. *The Western Canon: The Books and School of the Ages* (New York: Riverhead Books, 1994).

Blumberg, Ilana M. 'Sacrificial Value: Beyond the Cash Nexus in George Eliot's *Romola*', in *Economic Women: Essays on Desire and Dispossession in Nineteenth-Century British Culture*, ed. Lana L. Dalley and Jill Rappoport (Columbus: Ohio State University Press, 2013), 60–74.

Bodenheimer, Rosemarie. 'George Eliot's Last Stand: *Impressions of Theophrastus Such*', *Victorian Literature and Culture*, 44 (2016), 607–21.

Bodenheimer, Rosemarie. *The Real Life of Mary Ann Evans: George Eliot, Her Letters and Fiction* (Ithaca: Cornell University Press, 1994).

Boehmer, Elleke. *Colonial and Postcolonial Literature: Migrant Metaphors*, 2nd edn (Oxford: Oxford University Press, 2005).

Booth, Wayne. *The Rhetoric of Fiction* (Chicago: University of Chicago Press, 1961).

Bose, Amalendu. 'Saratchandra: His Novelistic Technique', *Indian Literature*, 19 (1976), 69–81.

Brantlinger, Patrick. *Dark Vanishings: Discourse on the Extinction of Primitive Races, 1800-1930* (Ithaca: Cornell University Press, 2003).

Brilmyer, S. Pearl. '"The Natural History of My Inward Self": Sensing Character in George Eliot's *Impressions of Theophrastus Such*', *PMLA*, 129.1 (2014), 35–51.

Browning, Oscar. 'The Art of George Eliot', *Fortnightly Review*, 43 (1888), 538–53.

Bryce, James. *The Relations of the Advanced and the Backward Races of Mankind* (Oxford: Clarendon Press, 1903).

Bullen, J.B. 'George Eliot's *Romola* as a Positivist Allegory', *The Review of English Studies*, 26 (1975), 425–35.

Bullen, J.B. *The Myth of the Renaissance in Nineteenth-Century Writing* (Oxford: Oxford University Press, 1994).

Buzard, James. '*Impressions of Theophrastus Such*: "*Not* a Story"', in *A Companion to George Eliot*, ed. Amanda Anderson and Harry E. Shaw (Chichester: Wiley-Blackwell, 2013), 204–15.

Carlisle, Claire. *On Habit* (New York: Routledge, 2014).

Carlyle, Thomas. *The Works of Thomas Carlyle*, vol. 26, ed. Henry Duff Traill (New York: AMS, 1980).

Carroll, Alicia. *Dark Smiles: Race and Desire in George Eliot* (Ohio: Ohio State University Press, 2003).

Carroll, David, ed. *George Eliot: The Critical Heritage* (London: Routledge and Kegan Paul, 1971).

Cavendish, Henry. *Sir Henry Cavendish's Debates of the House of Commons*, 2 vols, ed. J. Wright (London: Longmans and Co., 1841-2).

Chattopadhyay, Saratchandra. *Narir Mulya (The Worth of Women)* (Kolkata: Bak-Sahitya Press, 1918).

Chaudhuri, Narayan. 'Social Changes as Reflected in Bengali Literature', *Indian Literature*, 14 (1971), 41–52.

Chew Bose, Durga. 'Constant Compass: Uma Das Gupta in *Pather Panchali*', in *The Criterion Collection* (Features, 8 May 2017) www.criterion.com/current/posts/4535-constant-compass-uma-das-gupta-in-pather-panchali, accessed 3 April 2020.

Christian, George Scott. 'Comic George Eliot', *The George Eliot Review*, 34 (2003), 21–6.

Churcher, Millicent. 'Can Empathy Be a Moral Resource? A Smithean Reply to Jesse Prinz', *Dialogue*, 55 (2016), 429–47.

Cobbett, William. *Cobbett's Parliamentary History of England*, vol. 17, ed. J. Wright (London: T.C. Hansard, 1813).

Coleman, Dermot. *George Eliot and Money: Economics, Ethics and Literature* (Cambridge: Cambridge University Press, 2014).

Colón, Susan E. *The Professional Ideal in the Victorian Novel: The Works of Disraeli, Trollope, Gaskell, and Eliot* (New York: Palgrave Macmillan, 2007).

Cottom, Daniel. *Social Figures: George Eliot, Social History and Literary Representation* (Minneapolis: University of Minnesota Press, 1987).

Cross, J.W. *George Eliot's Life, as Related in her Letters and Journals*, 3 vols (Edinburgh: William Blackwood, 1884).

Dames, Nicholas. *The Physiology of the Novel: Reading, Neural Science and the Form of Victorian Fiction* (Oxford: Oxford University Press, 2007).

David, Deirdre. '"Getting out of the Eel Jar": George Eliot's Literary Appreciation', in *Creditable Warriors, 1830-1876*, ed. Michael Cotsell (London: Ashfield, 1990), 257–72.

Davis, Philip. *The Transferred Life of George Eliot* (Oxford: Oxford University Press, 2017).

Deneau, Daniel P. 'Imagery in *The Scenes of Clerical Life*', *Victorian Newsletter*, 28 (1965), 18–22.

[Dick Lauder, Thomas]. 'The Edinburgh Gathering', *Tait's Edinburgh Magazine*, n.s. 1.9 (October 1834), 633–6.

Dillane, Fionualla. *Before George Eliot: Marian Evans and the Periodical Press* (Cambridge: Cambridge University Press, 2013).

Disraeli, Benjamin. *Tancred, or The New Crusade*, Bradenham edn (1847; London: Peter Davies, 1927).

Dolin, Tim. *George Eliot* (Oxford: Oxford University Press, 2005).

Duncan, Ian. 'The Provincial or Regional Novel', in *A Companion to the Victorian Novel*, ed. Patrick Brantlinger and William B. Thesing (Cambridge: Cambridge University Press, 2003), 318–35.

Eagles, John. *The Bristol Riots: Their Causes, Progress, and Consequences* (Bristol: Gutch and Martin, 1832).

Eagleton, Terry. *Criticism and Ideology: A Study in Marxist Literary Theory* (London: Verso, 1978).

Easley, Alexis. *First-Person Anonymous: Women Writers and Victorian Print Media, 1830-1870* (Burlington: Ashgate, 2004).

Easley, Alexis. 'Poet as Headliner: George Eliot and "Macmillan's Magazine"', *George Eliot- George Henry Lewes Studies*, 60/61 (September 2011), 107–25.

Ermarth, Elizabeth. 'George Eliot's Conception of Sympathy', *Nineteenth-Century Fiction*, 40 (1985), 23–42.

Farina, Jonathan. *Everyday Words and the Character of Prose in Nineteenth-Century Britain* (Cambridge: Cambridge University Press, 2017).

Fessenbecker, Patrick. *Reading Ideas in Victorian Literature: Literary Content as Artistic Experience* (Edinburgh: Edinburgh University Press, 2020).

Fessenbecker, Patrick. 'Sympathy, Vocation, and Moral Deliberation in George Eliot', *English Literary History*, 85.2 (2018), 501–32.

Feuerbach, Ludwig. *The Essence of Christianity*. tr. Marian Evans [George Eliot] (New York: Harper, 1957).

Feuerbach, Ludwig. *Principles of the Philosophy of the Future*, tr. M. Vogel (Indianapolis: Hackett, 1986).

Fleishman, Avrom. *George Eliot's Intellectual Life* (Cambridge: Cambridge University Press, 2010).

Fleischman, Avrom. 'George Eliot's Reading: A Chronological List', *George Eliot- George Henry Lewes Studies*, 54/55 (2008), 1–106.

Flint, Kate. 'Blood, Bodies, and "The Lifted Veil"', *Nineteenth-Century Literature*, 51.4 (1997), 455–73.

Frazer, Sophie. 'George Eliot and Spinoza: Toward a Theory of the Affects', *George Eliot-George Henry Lewes Studies*, 70.2 (2018), 128–42.

Freeman, Barbara Claire. *The Feminine Sublime: Gender and Excess in Women's Fiction* (Berkeley: University of California Press, 1995).

Frow, John. *Character and Person* (Oxford: Oxford University Press, 2014).

Frow, John. 'On Midlevel Concepts', *New Literary History*, 41 (2010), 237–52.

Frye, Northrop. *Anatomy of Criticism* (Princeton: Princeton University Press, 1957).

Gallagher, Catherine. 'George Eliot: Immanent Victorian', *Representations*, 90.1 (Spring 2005), 61–74.

Galton, Francis. *Hereditary Genius: An Inquiry into Its Laws and Consequences* (London: Macmillan, 1869).

Galton, Francis. *Memories of My Life* (London: Methuen, 1908).

Gatens, Moira. 'George Eliot's "Incarnation of the Divine" in *Romola* and Benedict Spinoza's "Blessedness": A Double Reading', *George Eliot-George Henry Lewes Studies*, 52/53 (2007), 76–92.

Gatens, Moira. 'Philosophy', in *George Eliot in Context*, ed. Margaret Harris (Cambridge: Cambridge University Press, 2013), 214–21.

Ghosh, S.L. 'An Introduction to Modern Bengali Fiction', *Indian Literature*, 12 (1969), 73–86.

Gilbert, Sandra M. and Susan Gubar. *The Madwoman in the Attic: The Woman Writer and the Nineteenth-Century Literary Imagination*, 2nd edn (New Haven: Yale University Press, 2000).

Giles, Paul. *American Literature and the Antipodean Imaginary: Imperialism, Transnationalism, Surrealism* (Oxford: Oxford University Press, 2014).

Goethe, Johann Wolfgang von. *Italian Journey [1786–1788]*, tr. W.H. Auden and Elizabeth Mayer (London: Penguin, 1970).

Goodlad, Lauren. 'Moral Character', in *Historicism and the Human Sciences in Victorian Britain*, ed. Mark Bevir (Cambridge: Cambridge University Press, 2017), 128–53.

Goodlad, Lauren. *The Victorian Geopolitical Aesthetic: Realism, Sovereignty, and Transnational Experience* (Oxford: Oxford University Press, 2015).

Gray, B.M. 'Pseudoscience and George Eliot's "The Lifted Veil"', *Nineteenth-Century Fiction*, 36.4 (1982), 407–23.

Gray, Beryl. *George Eliot and Music* (New York: Palgrave Macmillan, 1989).

Greiner, Rae. 'Sympathy Time: Adam Smith, George Eliot, and the Realist Novel', *Narrative*, 17.3 (2009), 291–311.

Greiner, Rae. *Sympathetic Realism in Nineteenth-Century British Fiction* (Baltimore: Johns Hopkins University Press, 2012).

Griffin, Cristina Richieri. 'George Eliot's Feuerbach: Senses, Sympathy, Omniscience and Secularism', *English Literary History*, 84.2 (2017), 475–502.

Griffith, George. 'The Face as Legible Text: Gazing at the Portraits of George Eliot', *Victorian Review*, 27.2 (2001), 20–41.

Guha, Ramachandra and Joan Martinez-Alier. *Varieties of Environmentalism: Essays North and South* (London: Earthscan, 1997).

Hack, Daniel. 'Transatlantic Eliot: African American Connections', in *A Companion to George Eliot*, ed. Amanda Anderson and Harry E. Shaw (Chichester: Wiley-Blackwell, 2013), 262–75.

Haight, Gordon S. *George Eliot: A Biography* (Oxford: Oxford University Press, 1968).

Haight, Gordon S. 'George Eliot's Originals and Contemporaries', in *Essays in Victorian Literary History and Biography*, ed. Hugh Witemeyer (Basingstoke: Macmillan, 1992), 68–77.

Haight, Gordon S., ed. *The George Eliot Letters*, 9 vols (New Haven and London: Yale University Press, 1954–78).

Haldar, Gopal. 'Tradition of Saratchandra in Bengali Novel', *Indian Literature*, 19 (1976), 61–8.

Hancock, Stephen. *The Romantic Sublime and Middle-Class Subjectivity in the Victorian Novel* (New York: Routledge, 2005).

Hannigan, D.F. 'Prospective Transformation of the Novel', *Westminster Review* (July 1893), 256–60.

Harris, Margaret. 'George Eliot's Reputation', in *The Cambridge Companion to George Eliot*, 2nd edn, ed. George Levine and Nancy Henry (Cambridge: Cambridge University Press, 2019), 236–58.

Hardy, Barbara. *George Eliot: A Critic's Biography* (London: Continuum, 2006).

Harvey, W.J. *The Art of George Eliot* (London: Chatto and Windus, 1961).

Helsinger, Elizabeth K. *Rural Scenes and National Representation: Britain, 1815-1850* (Princeton: Princeton University Press, 1997).

Henry, Nancy. *George Eliot and the British Empire* (Cambridge: Cambridge University Press, 2002).

Henry, Nancy. *The Cambridge Introduction to George Eliot* (Cambridge: Cambridge University Press, 2008).

Henry, Nancy. 'Introduction', in *Impressions of Theophrastus Such*, ed. Nancy Henry (Iowa: University of Iowa Press, 1994), vii–xxxvii.

Henry, Nancy and George Levine. 'Introduction: George Eliot and the Art of Realism', in *The Cambridge Companion to George Eliot*, 2nd edn, ed. Nancy Henry and George Levine (Cambridge: Cambridge University Press, 2019), 1–18.

Hensley, Nathan. *Forms of Empire: the Poetics of Victorian Sovereignty* (Oxford: Oxford University Press, 2016).

Hertz, Neil. *George Eliot's Pulse* (Stanford: Stanford University Press, 2003).

Hewitt, Martin. 'Radicalism and the Victorian Working Class', *The Historical Journal*, 34.4 (1991), 872–92.

Hoffman, Meechal. '"Her Soul Cried Out for Some Explanation": Knowledge and Acknowledgement in George Eliot's *Romola*', *George Eliot-George Henry Lewes Studies*, 68 (2016), 43–59.

Hueffer, Francis. *Half a Century of Musical Life in England 1837–1887: Essays Towards a History* (London: Chapman and Hall, 1889).

Huggins, Cynthia. '*Adam Bede*: Author, Narrator and Narrative', *The George Eliot Review*, 23 (1992), 35–9.

Irwin, Jane, ed. *George Eliot's Daniel Deronda Notebooks* (Cambridge: Cambridge University Press, 1996).

James, Henry. 'Review of John Walter Cross, *George Eliot's Life* (1885)', in *The Atlantic Monthly* (May 1885), 668–78, reprinted in *George Eliot: The Critical Heritage*, ed. David Carroll (London: Routledge and Kegan Paul, 1971), 490–504.

Jameson, Fredric. *The Antinomies of Realism* (London and New York: Verso, 2013).

Jenkins, R.J. 'Laughing with George Eliot', *The George Eliot Review*, 37 (2006), 36–45.

Jewusiak, Jacob. 'Large-Scale Sympathy and Simultaneity in George Eliot's *Romola*', *Studies in English Literature*, 54 (2014), 853–74.

[Johnstone, Christian]. 'Political Register', *Tait's Edinburgh Magazine*, n.s. 1.11 (December 1834), 779–80.

[Johnstone, Christian]. 'Scenes in Edinburgh' (The 'Pry Bureau') series, in *Tait's Edinburgh Magazine*: 'What is Going On. No. 1.—Scenes in Edinburgh', n.s. 1.6 (July 1834), 419–30; 'What is Going On. No. II. —Scenes in Edinburgh', n.s. 1.7 (August 1834), 491–7; 'Scenes in Edinburgh.—No. III. I The Pry Bureau. II.—The Fiddlers' Gallery, at the Grey Dinner', n.s. 1.9 (October 1834), 637–46; 'Scenes in Edinburgh.—No. IV. The Pry Bureau', n.s. 2.1 (February 1835), 129–37; 'The Pry Bureau.—No. V. Branch Establishment, Birmingham', n.s. 2.2 (March 1835), 195–202.

Judge, Jennifer. 'The Gendering of Habit in George Eliot's *Middlemarch*', *Victorian Review*, 39 (2013), 158–81.

Jumeau, Alain. 'Scenes of Clerical Life: George Eliot's Own Version of Conversion', *The George Eliot Review*, 40 (2009), 15–24.

[Kebbel, T.E.]. 'Village Life of George Eliot', *Fraser's Magazine* (February 1881), 263–76.

Kellner, Douglas. *Media Culture: Cultural Studies, Identity, and Politics in the Contemporary Moment* (New York: Routledge, 2020).

King, Amy M. 'George Eliot and Science', in *The Cambridge Companion to George Eliot*, ed. George Levine and Nancy Henry (Cambridge: Cambridge University Press, 2019), 175–94.

Knopf, David. *British Orientalism and the Bengal Renaissance: The Dynamics of Indian Modernization 1773-1835* (Berkeley: University of California Press, 1969).

Knoepflmacher, U.C. *George Eliot's Early Novels: The Limits of Realism* (Berkeley and Los Angeles: University of California Press, 1968).

Knox, Robert. *The Races of Men: A Fragment* (London: H. Renshaw, 1850).

Kucich, John. 'The Organic Appeal in *Felix Holt*: Social Problem Fiction, Paternalism and the Welfare State', *Victorian Studies*, 59.4 (2017), 609–35.

Kuehn, Julia. 'Realism's Connections: George Eliot's and Fanny Lewald's Poetics', *George Eliot-George Henry Lewes Studies*, 68 (2016), 91–115.

Kurnick, David. 'Unspeakable George Eliot', *Victorian Literature and Culture*, 38 (2010), 489–509.

Lake, Marilyn and Henry Reynolds. *Drawing the Global Colour Line: White Men's Countries and the International Challenge of Racial Equality* (Cambridge: Cambridge University Press, 2008).

LaPorte, Charles. 'George Eliot, the Poetess as Prophet', *Victorian Literature and Culture*, 31 (2003), 159–79.

Leavis, F.R. *The Great Tradition: George Eliot, Henry James, Joseph Conrad* (New York: Stewart, 1950).

Lee, Louise. 'George Eliot's Jokes', in *Victorian Comedy and Laughter: Conviviality, Jokes, and Dissent*, ed. Louise Lee (London: Palgrave Macmillan, 2020), 141–85.

Lerner, Lawrence. *The Truthtellers: Jane Austen, George Eliot, D.H. Lawrence* (London: Chatto and Windus, 1967).

Levine, Caroline. *The Serious Pleasures of Suspense: Victorian Realism and Narrative Doubt* (Charlottesville: University of Virginia Press, 2003).

Levine, Caroline. 'Surprising Realism', in *A Companion to George Eliot*, ed. Amanda Anderson and Harry E. Shaw (Chichester: Wiley-Blackwell, 2013), 62–75.

Levine, George. 'George Eliot's Hypothesis of Reality', *Nineteenth-Century Fiction*, 30 (1980), 1–28.

Levine, George. 'Introduction: George Eliot and the Art of Realism', in *The Cambridge Companion to George Eliot*, ed. George Levine (Cambridge: Cambridge University Press, 2001), 1–19.

[Lewes, George Henry]. 'African Life', *Westminster Review* (January 1858), 1–16.

Lewes, George Henry. 'The Romantic School of Music', *The Leader* (October 28, 1854), 1027–8.

Lewes, George Henry. *On Actors and the Art of Acting* (London: Smith, Elder, and Co., 1875).

Livesey, Ruth. 'On Writing Portable Place: George Eliot's Mobile Midlands', *Mobilities*, 12.4 (2017), 559–71.

Lovesey, Oliver. *Postcolonial George Eliot* (Basingstoke: Palgrave Macmillan, 2017).

Lowe, Robert. *Speeches and Letters on Reform; with a Preface*, 2nd edn (London: Robert John Bush, 1867).

Macfarlane, Robert. 'A Small Squealing Black Pig: George Eliot, Originality, and Plagiarism', *George Eliot-George Henry Lewes Studies*, 42/43 (2002), 1–29.

Macintyre, Stuart. *A Colonial Liberalism: The Lost World of Three Victorian Visionaries* (South Melbourne: Oxford University Press, 1991).

Mansell, Darrell. 'Ruskin and George Eliot's "Realism"', *Criticism*, 7 (Summer 1965), 203–16.

Magee, Bryan. *Aspects of Wagner* (London: Panther, 1972).

Mallen, Richard. 'George Eliot and the Precious Mettle of Trust', *Victorian Studies*, 44 (2001), 41–75.

Markovits, Stefanie. 'George Eliot's Problem with Action', *Studies in English Literature*, 41.4 (Autumn 2001), 785–803.

Martin, Robert Bernard. *The Triumph of Wit: A Study of Victorian Comic Theory* (Oxford: Clarendon Press, 1974).

Massumi, Brian. *Parables for the Virtual: Movement, Affect, Sensation* (Durham: Duke University Press, 2002).

McAuley, Kyle. 'George Eliot's Estuarial Form', *Victorian Literature and Culture*, 48 (2020), 187–217.

McCaw, Neil. 'Beyond "A Water and Toast Sympathy": George Eliot and the Silence of Ireland', *George Eliot-George Henry Lewes Studies*, 38/39 (2000), 3–17.

McCormack, Kathleen. *George Eliot in Society: Travels Abroad and Sundays at the Priory* (Ohio: Ohio State University Press, 2013).

McCormack, Kathleen. *George Eliot's English Travels: Composite Characters and Coded Communication* (New York and London: Routledge, 2005).

McQueen, Humphrey. *A New Britannia: An Argument Concerning the Social Origins of Australian Radicalism and Nationalism*, 4th edn (St Lucia: University of Queensland Press, 2004).

McSweeny, Kerry. 'Introduction', in *Sartor Resartus*, by Thomas Carlyle, ed. Kerry McSweeney (Oxford: Oxford University Press, 1991), vii–xxxiii.

Menke, Richard. *Telegraphic Realism: Victorian Fiction and Other Information Systems* (Stanford: Stanford University Press, 2008).

Meredith, George. *The Egoist*, ed. George Woodcock (London: Penguin, 1987).

Meredith, George. *An Essay on Comedy, and the Uses of the Comic Spirit* (Westminster: A. Constable, 1903).

Miller, Elizabeth Carolyn. *Extraction Ecologies and the Literature of the Long Exhaustion* (Princeton: Princeton University Press, 2021).

Morley, John. 'Life of George Eliot' [1885]. Reprinted in John Morley, *Critical Miscellanies*, 3 (London: Macmillan, 1909), 95–132.

Morrison, Robert. 'William Blackwood and the Dynamics of Success', in *Print Culture and the Blackwood Tradition, 1805–1930*, ed. David Finkelstein (Toronto: University of Toronto Press, 2006), 21–48.

Mossmann, Mark. "Violence, Temptation and Narrative in George Eliot's 'Janet's Repentance'", *Journal of the Short Story in English*, 35 (Autumn 2000), 9–20.

Moyal, Ann. *Clear across Australia: A History of Telecommunications* (Melbourne: Nelson, 1984).

Mukherjee, Meenakshi. 'An Analysis of *Pather Panchali*', *Journal of Arts and Ideas*, 3 (1983), 19–33.

Mukherjee, Meenakshi. 'The House and the Road: Two Modes of Autobiographical Fiction', *Journal of Caribbean Literatures*, 5 (2008), 61–74.

Mukherjee, Pablo. 'Victorian Empire', in *The Cambridge History of Victorian Literature*, ed. Kate Flint (Cambridge: Cambridge University Press, 2012), 641–61.

Naess, Arne Shrewy. *Ecology, Community, Lifestyle: Outline of an Ecosophy* (Cambridge: Cambridge University Press, 1989).

Nellist, Brian. 'Disconcerting the Reader: *Friendship's Garland* and the True Voices of "Mr. Arnold"', *Essays and Studies*, 41 (1988), 30–44.

Nestor, Pauline. *George Eliot* (Basingstoke: Palgrave, 2002).

Newton, K.M. *George Eliot: Romantic Humanist: A Study of the Philosophical Structure of Her Novels* (London: Macmillan, 1981).

Newton, K.M. 'The Role of the Narrator in George Eliot's Novels', *The Journal of Narrative Theory*, 3 (1973), 97–107.

Nicholl, Catherine. Scenes of Clerical Life: *George Eliot's Apprenticeship*, PhD dissertation (University of Minnesota, 1971).

Nichols, Shaun and Stephen Stich. *Mindreading: An Integrated Account of Pretence, Self-Awareness, and Understanding Other Minds* (Oxford: Oxford University Press, 2003).

Nietzsche, Friedrich. *A Genealogy of Morals*, ed. Alexander Tille, tr. William Haussmann (New York: Macmillan, 1907).

Nightingale, Florence. 'A Note of Interrogation', *Fraser's Magazine*, n.s. 7.41 (May 1873), 567–77.

Nippel, W. 'Reading the Riot Act: The Discourse of Law-Enforcement in 18th Century England', *History and Anthropology*, 1.2 (1985), 399–426.

Nixon, Rob. 'Environmentalism and Postcolonialism', in *Postcolonial Studies and Beyond*, ed. Ania Loomba and Suvir Kaul (Durham: Duke University Press, 2005), 233–51.

Nixon, Rob. *Slow Violence and the Environmentalism of the Poor* (Cambridge: Harvard University Press, 2011).

Noble, Thomas A. *George Eliot's Scenes of Clerical Life* (New Haven: Yale University Press, 1965).

Otis, Laura. *Networking: Communicating with Bodies and Machines in the Nineteenth Century* (Ann Arbor: University of Michigan Press, 2001).

Parham, John. 'Editorial: Victorian Ecology', *Green Letters: Studies in Ecocriticism*, 14 (2011), 5–9.

Parham, John. 'Was There a Victorian Ecology?', in *The Environmental Tradition in English Literature*, ed. John Parham (Aldershot: Ashgate, 2002), 156–71.

Paris, Bernard J. *Experiments in Life: George Eliot's Quest for Values* (Detroit: Wayne State University Press, 1965).

Pascal, Roy. *The Dual Voice: Free Indirect Speech and its Functioning in the Nineteenth-Century European Novel* (Manchester: Manchester University Press, 1977).

Pater, Walter. *Studies in the History of the Renaissance*, ed. Matthew Beaumont (Oxford: Oxford World's Classics, 2020).

Paxton, Nancy L. *George Eliot and Herbert Spencer: Feminism, Evolutionism, and the Reconstruction of Gender* (Princeton: Princeton University Press, 1991).

Pearson, Charles H. 'Democracy in Victoria', *Fortnightly Review*, 25 (1879), 688–717.

Pearson, Charles H. *National Life and Character: A Forecast* (London: Macmillan, 1894).

Pearson, Charles H. 'On the Working of Australian Institutions', in *Essays on Reform*, ed. Anon. (London: Robert John Bush, 1867), 191–216.

Perkins, Pam. *Women Writers and the Edinburgh Enlightenment* (Amsterdam: Rodopi, 2010).

Petersen, Kirsten Holst and Anna Rutherford, eds. *A Double Colonization: Colonial and Post-colonial Women's Writing* (Mundelstrup and Oxford: Dangaroo Press, 1986).

Peterson, Virgil A. '*Romola*: A Victorian Quest for Values', *Philological Papers*, 16 (1967), 49–62.

Plotz, John. *Semi-Detached: The Aesthetics of Virtual Experience Since Dickens* (Princeton: Princeton University Press, 2018).

Plotz, John. 'The Semi-Detached Victorian Novel', *Victorian Studies*, 53 (2011), 405–16.

Poland, Matthew. '*Middlemarch* in Melbourne', *George Eliot-George Henry Lewes Studies*, 73.2 (2021), 131–41.

Prabhakar, Vishnu. *Great Vagabond: Biography and Immortal Works of Sarat Chandra Chatterjee*, tr. Jai Ratan (New Delhi: B.R. Publishing, 1990).

Pratt-Smith, Stella. 'Inside-Out: Texture and Belief in George Eliot's "Bubble-World"', *George Eliot-George Henry Lewes Studies*, 60/61 (2011), 62–76.

Prinz, Jesse. 'Is Empathy Necessary for Morality?' in *Empathy: Philosophical and Psychological Perspectives*, ed. Amy Coplan and Peter Goldie (Oxford: Oxford University Press, 2011), 211–29.

Quinault, R. 'The Warwickshire County Magistracy and Public Order, c.1830-1870', in *Popular Protests and Public Order: Six Studies in British History 1790-1920*, ed. R. Quinault and J. Stevenson (London: George Allen and Unwin, 1974).

Raines, Melissa Anne. 'Knowing Too Much: the Burden of Omniscience in "The Lifted Veil"', *The George Eliot Review*, 43 (2012), 39–46.

Raines, Melissa Anne. *George Eliot's Grammar of Being* (London: Anthem, 2011).

Raines, Melissa Anne. '"The Stream of Human Thought and Deed" in "Mr Gilfil's Love-Story"', *The George Eliot Review*, 40 (2009), 37–42.

Rather, L.J. *Reading Wagner: A Study in the History of Ideas* (Baton Rouge: Louisiana State University, 1990).

Ray, Satyajit. 'Notes on Filming Bibhuti Bhusan', in *Satyajit Ray on Cinema*, ed. Sandip Ray, Satyajit Ray, Dhritiman Chatterji, Arup K. De, Deepak Mukherjee, Debasis Mukhopadhyay, and Shyam Benegal (New York: Columbia University Press, 2011), 9–12.

Reibel, David A. 'Hidden Parallels in George Eliot's *Daniel Deronda*: Julius Klesmer, Richard Wagner, Franz Liszt', *George Eliot-George Henry Lewes Studies*, 64/65 (2013), 16–52.

Reilly, Ariana. 'Always Sympathize! Surface Reading, Affect, and George Eliot's *Romola*', *Victorian Studies*, 55 (2013), 629–46.

Rignall, John. *George Eliot, European Novelist* (Farnham: Ashgate, 2011).

Rignall, John. 'George Eliot and the Idea of Travel', *Yearbook of English Studies*, 36 (2006), 139–52.

Rignall, John, ed. *George Eliot and Europe* (Aldershot: Scolar, 1997).

Robbins, Bruce. 'The Cosmopolitan Eliot', in *A Companion to George Eliot*, ed. Amanda Anderson and Harry E. Shaw (Chichester: Wiley-Blackwell, 2013), 400–12.

Rodensky, Lisa. *The Crime in Mind: Criminal Responsibility and the Victorian Novel* (New York: Oxford University Press, 2003).

Röder-Bolton, Gerlinde. *George Eliot in Germany, 1854–55: 'Cherished Memories'* (Aldershot: Ashgate, 2006).

Rose, Paul Lawrence. *Wagner: Race and Revolution* (London: Faber and Faber, 1992).

Ross, Alex. *Wagnerism: Art and Politics in the Shadow of Music* (London: Farrar, Strauss, and Giroux, 2020).

Rudy, Jason R. 'Settled: *Dorrit* Down Under', *Nineteenth-Century Literature*, 75.2 (2020), 184–206.

Sarker, Subhash Chandra. 'Sarat Chandra Chatterjee: The Great Humanist', *Indian Literature*, 20 (1977), 49–77.

Schramm, Jan-Melissa. *Testimony and Advocacy in Victorian Law, Literature, and Theology* (Cambridge: Cambridge University Press, 2000).

Semmel, Bernard. *George Eliot and the Politics of National Inheritance* (Oxford: Oxford University Press, 1994).

Sessa, Anne Dzamba. *Richard Wagner and the English* (Rutherford: Fairleigh Dickinson University Press, 1979).

Shelley, Percy Bysshe. *Shelley's Poetry and Prose*, ed. Neil Fraistat and Donald Reiman (New York: Norton, 2010).

Shinbrot, Victoria. '"The Risks That Lie Within": Beauty, Boredom, and the Sublime in *Daniel Deronda*', *Pacific Coast Philology*, 55 (2020), 68–82.

Shuttleworth Sally. *George Eliot and Nineteenth-Century Science: The Make-Believe of a Beginning* (Cambridge: Cambridge University Press, 1984).

Sil, Narasingha Prasad. *The Life of Sharatchandra Chattopadhyay: Drifter and Dreamer* (Madison, NJ and British Columbia: Fairleigh Dickinson University Press, 2012).

Skelton, Geoffrey. 'George Eliot and Cosima Wagner: A Newly Discovered Letter from George Henry Lewes', *George Eliot Fellowship Review*, 13 (1982), 27–30.

Small, Helen. 'George Eliot and the Cosmopolitan Cynic', *Victorian Studies*, 55.1 (2012), 85–105.

da Sousa Correa, Delia. 'George Eliot and the Germanic "Musical Magus"', in *George Eliot and Europe*, ed. John Rignall (Aldershot: Scolar, 1997), 98–112.

da Sousa Correa, Delia. *George Eliot, Music and Victorian Culture* (Basingstoke: Palgrave Macmillan, 2003).

Spinoza, Benedict. *Spinoza's Ethics: Translated by George Eliot*, ed. Clare Carlisle (Princeton: Princeton University Pres, 2019).

Spinoza, Benedict. *Ethics*, in *The Collected Works of Spinoza*, vol. 1, ed. and tr. Edwin Curley (Princeton: Princeton University Press, 1985).

Spinoza, Benedict. *The Political Treatise*, in *The Collected Works of Spinoza*, vol. 2, ed. and tr. Edwin Curley (Princeton: Princeton University Press, 2016).

Stahr, Adolf. *Ein Jahr In Italien* (Oldenburg: Schulze, n.y).

Stebbing, W., ed. *Charles Henry Pearson, Fellow of Oriel and Education Minister in Victoria* (London: Longmans, Green, and Co., 1900).

Steedman, Carolyn. 'Going to *Middlemarch*: History and the Novel', *Michigan Quarterly Review*, 40.3 (Summer 2001), 531–52.

Steiner, George. 'A Preface to Middlemarch', *Nineteenth Century Fiction*, 9 (1955), 262–79.

[Stephen, Leslie]. 'George Eliot', *Cornhill Magazine* (February 1881), 152–68.

Stephen, Leslie. 'Humour', *Cornhill Magazine* (March 1876), 318–26.

Stevenson, J. 'Social Control and the Prevention of Riots in England, 1789-1829', in *Social Control in Nineteenth-Century Britain*, ed. A.P. Donajgrodski (London: Croom Helm, 1979), 27–50.

Stević, Aleksandar. 'Convenient Cosmopolitanism: *Daniel Deronda*, Nationalism, and the Critics', *Victorian Literature and Culture*, 45 (2017), 593–614.

Stewart, David. *Romantic Magazines and Metropolitan Literary Culture* (Basingstoke: Palgrave Macmillan, 2011).

Strauss, David Friedrich. *The Life of Jesus Critically Examined*, ed. Peter C. Hodgson, tr. Marian Evans [George Eliot] (1846; Philadelphia: Fortress Press, 1972).

Sullivan, William J. 'Piero di Cosimo and the Higher Primitivism in *Romola*', *Nineteenth-Century Fiction*, 26 (1972), 390–405.

Sussman, Charlotte. *Consuming Anxieties: Consumer Protest, Gender, and British Slavery, 1713-1833* (Stanford: Stanford University Press, 2000).

Takaki, Ronald. *Strangers from a Different Shore: A History of Asian Americans* (Boston/New York: Little Brown and Co., 1998).

Tave, Stuart. *The Amiable Humorist: A Study in the Comic Theory and Criticism of the Eighteenth and Early Nineteenth Centuries* (Chicago: University of Chicago Press, 1960).

Tegan, Mary Beth. 'Strange Sympathies: George Eliot and the Literary Science of Sensation', *Women's Writing*, 20 (2013), 168–85.

Theophrastus. *Characters*, ed. James Diggle (Cambridge: Cambridge University Press, 2004).

Thomas, Claire. 'From the Sublime to the Picturesque: Dorothea's Husbands, Embodied in Rome', *George Eliot-George Henry Lewes Studies*, 71 (2019), 1–17.

Thompson, Scott. 'Subjective Realism and Diligent Imagination: G.H. Lewes's Theory of Psychology and George Eliot's *Impressions of Theophrastus Such*', *Victorian Review*, 44.2 (2018), 197–214.

Townsend, Patty and Lillian Russell. *George Eliot: Her Early Home*, arr. Emily Swinnerton (London: Raphael Tuck, 1891).

Tregenza, John. *Professor of Democracy: The Life of Charles Henry Pearson, 1830-1894, Oxford Don and Australian Radical* (Carlton: Melbourne University Press, 1968).

Wagner, Cosima. *Cosima Wagner's Diaries*, 2 vols, ed. Martin Gregor-Dellin and Dietrich Mack, tr. Geoffrey Skelton (New York and London: Harcourt Brace Jovanovich, 1978).

Wagner, Richard. *Art and Politics*, tr. W. Ashton Ellis (Lincoln: University of Nebraska Press, 1995).

Wagner, Richard. *Gesammelte Schriften und Dichtungen*, 10 vols (Leipzig: E. W. Fritzsch, 1897-98).

Wagner, Richard. *Stories and Essays*, ed. Charles Osborne (London: Peter Owen, 1973).

Wagner, Richard. *Wagner on Music and Drama: A Selection from Richard Wagner's Prose Works*, ed. Albert Goodman and Evert Sprinchorn; tr. H. [*sic*] Ashton Ellis (London: Gollancz, 1970).

Walker, David. *Anxious Nation: Australia and the Rise of Asia, 1850-1939* (St Lucia: University of Queensland Press, 1999).

Weber, Cara. '"The Continuity of Married Companionship": Marriage, Sympathy, and the Self in *Middlemarch*', *Nineteenth-Century Literature*, 66 (2012), 494–530.

Wickberg, Daniel. *The Senses of Humour: Self and Laughter in Modern America* (Ithaca: Cornell University Press, 1998).

Wilkes, Joanne. 'Confronting the 1840s: Christian Johnstone in Criticism and Fiction', in *British Women's Writing from Brontë to Bloomsbury, Volume I: 1840s and 1850s*, ed. Adrienne E. Gavin and Carolyn W. de la L. Oulton (Cham, Switzerland: Palgrave Macmillan, 2018), 67–80.

Williams, Raymond. *Marxism and Literature* (Oxford: Oxford University Press, 1977).

Williams, Wendy S. *George Eliot, Poetess* (Farnham: Ashgate, 2014).

Witemeyer, Hugh. *George Eliot and the Visual Arts* (New Haven: Yale University Press, 1979).

Woloch, Alex. *The One vs. The Many: Minor Characters and the Space of the Protagonist in the Novel*, (Princeton: Princeton University Press, 2003).

Woolf, Virginia. 'George Eliot' (1919), in *A Century of George Eliot Criticism*, ed. Gordon S. Haight (Boston: Houghton Mifflin, 1965), 183–9.

Wordsworth, William. *The Prelude: 1799, 1805, 1850*, ed. Jonathan Wordsworth, M.H. Abrams, and Stephen Gill (New York: W.W. Norton, 1979).

Youngkin, Molly. '"Narrative Readings of the Images She Sees": Principles of Nineteenth-Century Narrative Painting in George Eliot's Fiction', *George Eliot-George Henry Lewes Studies*, 67 (2015), 1–29.

Yovel, Yirmiyahu. *Spinoza and Other Heretics: The Adventures of Immanence* (Princeton: Princeton University Press, 1989).

Index